*The Recovery of Doctrine
in the Contemporary Church*

The Recovery of Doctrine
in the Contemporary Church

An Essay in Philosophical Ecclesiology

Richard Heyduck

Baylor University Press
Waco, Texas

Copyright © 2002 by
Baylor University Press
Waco, Texas 76798
All Rights Reserved

Library of Congress Cataloging-in-Publication Data

Heyduck, Richard.
  The recovery of doctrine in the contemporary church : an essay in philosophical ecclesiology / Richard Heyduck.
    p. cm.
  Includes bibliographical references and index.
  ISBN 978-1-60258-344-3
  1. Theology, Doctrinal. 2. Speech acts (Linguistics)--Religious aspects--Christianity. 3. Church. I. Title.
 BT22 .H49 2002
 230--dc21
                            2001005002

Printed in the United States of America on acid-free paper.

Contents

Preface vii

Chapter One
The Modern Marginalization of Doctrine 1

Chapter Two
Doctrine as a Complex Speech Act of the Church 51

Chapter Three
The Church as Agent of Doctrine 107

Chapter Four
The Historical Questions Relating to Doctrine 139

Chapter Five
Putting It All Together 183

Bibliography 223

Index 237

Preface

ONE OF THE OFT-EXPRESSED FEARS CHRISTIANS HAVE OF POSTMODERNITY is relativism. Postmodernity, it is said, rejects the notion of absolute truth and destroys the foundations of knowledge. Given this perspective, one might expect a book that seeks to renew the place of doctrine in the church to be an extended argument *against* postmodernity. After all, conservatives and traditionalists in mainline churches see doctrinal relativism, indifferentism and chaos on all levels of the church. In my own denomination, United Methodism, this is expressed in a variety of ways. "Don't worry about what you see in other places—just pay your apportionments." "Be big enough to allow people to differ from you. You don't have a corner on the truth." "Doctrine divides, service unites." "All religions are really the same, aren't they?" All these are expressions of a kind of relativism. It is natural for one who sees these attitudes as unhealthy to stand against postmodernity, the accused progenitor.

In this book, I present a case for seeing postmodernity as an ally of doctrinal renewal. Instead of effecting the demise of doctrine, certain varieties of postmodernism provide resources for its renewal and recovery. The other side of this claim is that instead of providing the sure foundation for doctrine, with its proven methodologies, emphasis on clear and distinct ideas and commitment to rationality, modernity rather than postmodernity is to be seen as the origin of relativism and doctrinal indifference.

Of course, modernity did not begin by espousing relativism. With the religious conflicts growing out of the Reformation, thinkers sought to find a way to compel agreement, not through force of arms but through force of argument. The philosophy that developed in this period sought to find truths that all rational people would accept. These truths were few, but through the proper method, they could be built upon, resulting in justification for all knowledge claims. In recent years this approach to philosophy has become known as foundationalism.

At our best, we humans like to ask "Why?" For a while, foundationalism seemed to provide the best framework for answering "why" questions. Examine any knowledge claim. Is it indubitable? If yes, then it must be foundational. If no, analyze it. On what other claims is it based? Are *these* claims indubitable? If not, continue the process until the claim under consideration is connected to indubitable foundations.

It did not take long for foundationalism to begin cracking. Two kinds of challenges came first: claims that what was considered indubitable (the foundation) were not truly indubitable and contentions that the links connecting the foundation to the structure above did not succeed in connecting. A third kind of challenge resulted from the application of the first two: What about claims that did not fit the foundationalist approach?

In the church when we speak of doctrine we do not explicitly defer to foundationalism. When we hear appeals to inerrant scripture, infallible tradition or the assured results of biblical criticism, we can be assured that foundationalism is nearby. Consider the inerrancy of scripture for a moment. Why do we need an inerrant scripture? The usual answer is that we need a source for our true beliefs. We can depend on scripture. We will find no errors in it, only truth. It is not long, however, until the first two challenges to foundationalism appear. First, the questions about the foundation itself: How do we know scripture is inerrant? Scripture is inerrant because all scripture is God-breathed. How do we know all scripture is God-breathed? Well, II Timothy 3:16 says that it is. How do we know that the author of II Timothy meant the same thing by "scripture" that we do (especially when it seems natural to take him to be speaking of the Old Testament—not the Bible as we know it). How do we know this claim is true (without circular reasoning)? Where does this questioning stop? Where do we find something that *compels* us to accept biblical inerrancy? We do not.

But let us say we did find suitable indubitable foundations for inerrancy. At this point the second kind of challenge appears. Depending on the direction we are going, we might ask either "Given an inerrant bible, how do we produce our doctrines?" or, "How are our doctrines developed from the inerrant bible?" Either way we are asking about the methodology of linking doctrinal claims (our knowledge superstructure) to the inerrant foundation. Without exploring this question with any depth, the fact that a variety of groups that espouse an inerrant bible turn out to have very different—and even contradictory—doctrines make the epistemological strategy of inerrancy dubious. It is essential at this point to see that scriptural inerrancy has functioned more as an epistemological theory—a way of playing the modern knowledge game—than as a theological theory.

The third kind of challenge comes into view when once we have arrived at the knowledge that scripture is inerrant we also realize that inerrancy is something most fittingly attributed to propositions. Our problem is that the bible is not just a list of propositions. Consider the poetic sections of scripture. Here we are faced with texts that do not easily reduce to propositions. It is at this point that we see most clearly that the problem is not with scripture but in our *use* of scripture.

Given all these problems with the knowledge structure upon which doctrine is built, we might come up with a number of responses. First we can just say that the problem is illusory, the result of unbelief. Second, we might say that we simply need to work harder on securing the foundation and clarifying the method of building upon it. Thirdly, we might say that because foundationalism is fatally flawed there is no such thing as knowledge (in our case *doctrinal* knowledge), only opinion. This final option looks a lot like doctrinal relativism or indifferentism. But notice its origin: this kind of relativism results from the acceptance of the modern conviction that true knowledge is knowledge that is properly built upon indubitable foundations. If foundationalism fails, then what we are left with, on such a view, is no knowledge at all. Some versions of postmodernism take exactly this stance. Since real knowledge (foundationally certified knowledge) is an illusion, all pretensions to such are merely power plays. Given its acceptance of the rules laid down by modernity, however, this kind of postmodernity is better understood as a *reductio ad absurdum* of modernity itself.

The good news is that we need not take modernity as our starting point. Although I have used the inerrancy of scripture as an example, scripture is not the problem. It is possible to have a high view of the authority of scripture without succumbing to the thrills of epistemology. Competing versions of postmodernity reject the notion that epistemology (the theory of what knowledge is and how it works) is the proper starting point. My book begins with the observation that church doctrine has problems. How we characterize these problems, what remedy we suggest, and what health state we desire all depend on our characterization of what doctrine is.

If, with modernity, we see doctrine primarily as a claim to knowledge, we will see a need to reestablish the proper foundations. This can be the approach either of conservatives (who tend to turn to scripture or tradition) or of liberals (who tend to turn to science—the natural sciences and the scientific study of religion).

My contention is that while the problem of the marginalization of doctrine in the modern church has roots in the modern centrality of knowledge, the solution lies not in a better theory of knowledge (which is simply continuing to play by modern rules) but in better ecclesiology. Ultimately the question "What is doctrine?" is not about knowledge, but about the church.

Others have recognized that doctrine has been marginalized in the modern church. George Lindbeck is perhaps the most prominent. Given the importance of his approach, dialogue with his regulative theory of doctrine—based upon a cultural linguistic theory of religion—forms a major part of my first two chapters. Using Lindbeck and modernity as foils, I develop an alternative view that Christianity is best understood not as a system of knowledge or as a culture, but as an ongoing drama. Doctrine is that which tells the church how to live the drama. Doctrine shows us the plot, the setting and the *dramatis personae*. Given this model, the problem to be overcome by a reappropriation of doctrine is not ignorance, but disobedience. If this is so, the commonly expressed notion that the church needs to focus on carrying out its mission and let doctrinal questions wait until later is profoundly misguided. Doctrine and mission are intimately related.

Although the main ideas in this book came about before I was aware of Henry Blackaby's devotional work, it seems possible to read this book as philosophical background to his *Experiencing God* workbook. The key reality is not what we know about God but that God is active in the world today (the main character in the play) and that God invites us to join in the mission (become actors in the play).

Chapter one explores what it means to say that doctrine has been marginalized in the church and suggests ways this marginalization is a result of certain modern convictions. I recognize that the modern convictions I highlight—the centrality of epistemology, individualism, and dehistoricization—did not come from nowhere, but were themselves outgrowths of earlier features of western culture. In identifying modernity as the seedbed of doctrinal marginalization, I am claiming that whatever the doctrinal failures of earlier eras, it was in this period that significant segments of the church came to see doctrine itself as dispensable, or perhaps worthy of outright rejection.

Given its commitments to foundationalism, individualism, and dehistoricization, modernity was limited in the ways it could conceive religion in general and Christianity in particular. Once these commitments are set aside, new models of what Christianity is can be developed, and with them, new ways to conceive the nature of doctrine. In the second chapter I borrow from the work of Ludwig Wittgenstein, J. L Austin, and Charles Taylor to suggest that doctrine is a speech act of the church. Within this framework doctrine functions to lead the church in its life in God's Kingdom.

But what can it mean to attribute a speech act to a community as a whole? Chapter three delves into the nature of the church, inquiring particularly into the relationship between church and culture. There are three reasons for this. First, Lindbeck has suggested that religion is a cultural linguistic phenomenon and that doctrine is the grammar of that culture. In other words, doctrine functions to make the saying of something possible, not for the actual making of religious utterances. Second, Stanley Hauerwas has made the claim that the church *is* a culture. While I am sympathetic to this point of view, I think the claim must be balanced by the reality that Christianity has become indigenous in a number of vastly different cultures. Finally, by considering doctrine to be a speech act of the *church*, we confront the individualism of modernity head on.

I have mentioned dehistoricization a couple of times already but have not defined it. By dehistoricization I mean the tendency to value the general, the universal, and the timeless over the particular, the local and the contingent. Scripture is to a great degree narratival in form. The creeds of the church are narratival in form. Through an emphasis on what could be accepted by any rational person anywhere, the contingent, i.e., historical, elements of Christianity were seen as expendable. Chapter four explores ways postmodern philosophy allows us to recover the historical dimension of Christianity.

What are the consequences of my model for the church? This is the question of chapter five. After illustrating what a speech act model of doctrine might look like, I step back and consider the big picture. How is life in the church affected when we come to understand Christianity as an ongoing participation with God in history? Such a shift has profound consequences for our understanding of the Christian life and of evangelism in particular. To put it very briefly, evangelism is no longer simply inviting people to believe in Jesus, have their sins forgiven and receive eternal life. Instead, these elements of salvation are included in the larger invitation of becoming willing participants in what God is doing in history.

The questions with which this book deals became important to me in my days as an undergraduate. Over the years many have encouraged me and helped shape my thought. I wish to thank Norman Spellman, John Score, Farley Snell, Weldon Crowley, Steve Seamands, David Bundy, Darrell Whiteman, Jim McClendon, Jim Bradley, Mel Robeck, and Miroslav Volf for the time they spent teaching me and listening to me. Though I have never met him, I have found the work of Tom Wright especially encouraging. Special thanks go to Nancey Murphy and Billy Abraham who urged me to publish this manuscript.

I could not have done this work without support from the church. I owe a huge debt of gratitude to Cedar Bayou United Methodist, Fountain Valley First United Methodist, Hooks First United Methodist, and Westbury United Methodist. If I were from a different ecclesial tradition this book and its arguments would take a very different form. I believe the basic premises about the nature of the church, the faith and of doctrine will fit with most Christian traditions. I leave it to participants in these other traditions to adapt the work to their own settings.

Finally, I could not have done this without the support of my family. My parents and Christi's parents have supported me the whole way. Emily, Paul, and Hannah have had to learn too early in life what a life of scholarship is all about—fortunately they still honor me as their father. Most of all I thank my wife, Christi. She has supported me even at the hardest times and has tolerated my incessant study, thinking, and writing.

I pray that this book will be a blessing to many.

Chapter One

The Modern Marginalization of Doctrine

> Much of what we thought was standard and minimal, a kind of point of departure, is no longer quite that. There is hardly anything but the sight of theologians talking past one another. Now, in the name of theology, we can espouse worldliness; by theologizing, we can aver that God is dead; via theology, we can declare that scripture is mythology; and through erstwhile theological reflection, we can find symbols everywhere and little to be symbolized ... an air of tolerance settles over the entire array, almost as if it makes slight difference what is believed.
> —Paul Holmer, *The Grammar of Faith*[1]

THE DOCTRINAL CRISIS

THAT AMERICAN MAINLINE CHURCHES ARE FACING A CRISIS IS A commonplace. Annual membership losses are the norm. Each year the average age of the membership of these churches gets older, as they fail to win or keep the younger generations (often including their own children and grandchildren). The crisis is more than a demographic issue. Many within these denominations see the primary cause as doctrinal. I know the United Methodist Church best, so my examples will be drawn from that community. William Abraham's recent book *Waking from Doctrinal Amnesia* is a helpful point of departure. His thesis is that to a large degree the United Methodist Church has "systematically forgotten the place of Christian doctrine in their life and service to God. As a result they have not been able to appreciate the predicament thrown up by their own internal squabbles."[2] Abraham speaks of "forgetting" instead of marginalizing, but the concept of marginalization easily fits with the picture he presents. There is no consistent or coherent understanding of the role of doctrine, resulting in its subsequent devaluation and marginalization. United Methodists have forgotten their doctrine—yet life goes on. Abraham's position is that United Methodists have not only forgotten their own doctrine, but have also come to believe wrongly that substantial doctrine is not even needed. We continue to speak of ourselves as *United* Methodists, yet it is not doctrine that unites us. In fact, it is commonly held that a focus on doctrine is divisive since there is no common viewpoint from which to assess doctrinal disputes. United Methodists have a reputation for being able to believe anything that suits their fancy,[3] while finding their unity elsewhere.

There are other voices saying similar things. From a quite different theological perspective Schubert Ogden echoes Abraham's observation that within the United Methodist Church doctrinal indifferentism has become the norm.

> For a long time now, I have had the distinct impression that the body of Christians who boast of a Discipline are among the most undisciplined persons in Christendom, especially when it comes to matters of doctrine. It is notorious that, at every level in the church, from the local congregation to the General Conference, it is possible to disseminate the widest range of doctrines, both theological and ethical, regardless of the extent of their contrariety to the doctrinal standards we have officially acknowledged.[4]

Abraham and Ogden are from different ends of the theological spectrum: one leans toward process thought while the other is in the tradition of orthodox Wesleyanism. Yet, both see the same reality in the church.

The marginalization of doctrine is not something present only in the seminaries and pulpits, but is found at all levels of church life. As one who grew up in the United Methodist Church, Rodney Clapp reflects on his training in the faith: "I distinctly remember Sunday School curriculum that taught us Christians are people who are polite to the postman," leading him to conclude that, "If there is no more to it than that, Christianity is just archaic language and mystified formalities that get in the way."[5] If Clapp's experience is as common as it appears, we can suggest a connection between the marginalization of doctrine and the decline in numbers. As the clarity and distinctness of Christian identity have eroded within mainline denominations, fewer and fewer people have found any reason to remain in the church.

Marginalization, amnesia, theological indifferentism, incoherence—taken together they are symptoms of a serious doctrinal disease within the church. One can see doctrinal failure in other areas as well. Consider George Lindbeck's claim that, "Doctrines . . . do not behave the way they should, given our customary suppositions about the kinds of things they are."[6] Broadly speaking, Lindbeck is referring to the difficulty traditional theories of doctrine have with accounting for the phenomenon of doctrinal change and doctrinal constancy, with specific reference to the doctrinal reconciliation sought in the ecumenical movement.[7] How are ecclesial communities to understand the doctrinal reconciliation they seek? Since their differences are rooted in historically established doctrinal positions, is such reconciliation even possible? Perhaps the only way to describe the action is as capitulation. The questions I deal with here focus more on how constancy and change work within, not between, ecclesial communities. Capitulation, when it happens, is capitulation to forces outside the church, not to the claims of other ecclesial communities.

Though we see division between ecclesial communities, the greater difficulty, I believe, is fragmentation *within* them. Traditional doctrinal positions within communities are questioned, denied, reinterpreted, or simply ignored. Doctrine not only fails to bring unity to different communities, but it serves less and less to provide unity within the bounds of a community. The failings highlighted by Abraham and Ogden are instances of this internal fragmentation. Is there a way to understand how doctrine functions that will help us both understand what has happened and find strategies for renewal? Answering this question is my aim. My underlying assumption is that doctrine correctly received and practiced is essential to the health and well-being of the church.

There is a dialectical relationship between church and doctrine. Not only does the one not exist apart from the other, but doctrine is produced in the life of actual Christian community, while simultaneously serving as a constitutive element of that very community. Given this connection, it is not surprising to see the erosion of Christian communities and doctrine at the same time. Liberal and conservative theologies have had good reasons—intelligible in the light of modern philosophy—to marginalize the life of the church, but this practice has undermined Christianity rather than helped it.

MODERNITY AND THE MARGINALIZATION OF DOCTRINE

It is possible that the marginalization of doctrine within the church is merely coincidentally related to modernity. I believe there are reasons, however, to believe that this is no coincidence. Though my focus will be on the impact of modern philosophy, I see at least two other factors that lie behind the marginalization of doctrine in the modern church. First, there are political reasons. Because of the violent transitions in control of the church in England in the sixteenth century, a certain level of tolerance and even intentional doctrinal ambiguity arose. The Articles of Religion shaped the church, but there was an aversion to developing an official interpretation of these Articles. Donald Thorsen has discussed how this bears on John Wesley.[8] It is possible that as an offshoot of the Church of England, Methodism has picked up some of the tendency of the Mother church.[9] Though this may be a factor, I doubt that it has much relevance for explaining the status of doctrine within the United Methodist Church. Most of the formative influence on early American Methodism came from American culture itself. We can find within the philosophy of the last three centuries many characteristics that fit such a transition and make it more intelligible.

As strange as it might seem, there are likely to be theological reasons behind the marginalization also. I will only deal with one of these here— the effect of Constantinianism on the understanding of the church. I see a need to do further work in the future that would develop the links between Christianity and culture in the west. This would necessarily involve a thorough examination of the ways in which modernity itself is a child (whether legitimate or not) of the Christian tradition in Western Europe. Though the seeds of the doctrinal marginalization we see in modernity may have originated in earlier eras, the kind of marginalization I describe in the modern church only came to fruition in the modern era. Before we look more closely at the reasons for the marginalization, however, we must make an initial inquiry regarding what it might mean to say that doctrine has been marginalized.

The Marginalization of Doctrinal Substance

The problem with doctrine in the church is often perceived as having at least two dimensions, broadly characterizable by two questions: Which doctrines should we hold? (the substantive dimension); What is doctrine? (the conceptual dimension). In some situations, due to particular conceptualities of doctrine, this latter question has led to the further question, "Why have doctrine?" If we look no further than the divide between theological liberals and conservatives, we can see vast disagreement on substantive issues. The doctrinal positions of liberals are such as to lead conservatives to characterize liberalism sometimes as a different religion.[10] Liberals, on the other hand, have accused the conservatives of both holding on to outdated cultural husks (and missing the true kernel of the Gospel), and identifying too closely with American culture. Either side would claim that individual doctrines have been misconceived and misrepresented. Though the difference between liberals and conservatives is often framed on the substantive level, I believe Lindbeck is correct in identifying the real divide as conceptual.

Ecclesial communities have broad internal disagreement regarding the function of doctrine. Is doctrine merely part of the heritage of the denomination? Is it still to be literally understood and juridically enforced? Is faithfulness or originality the main thing to be sought in doctrinal theology? Faithfulness to what or to whom? To the canons of historical criticism? To the American way of life? To "our" heritage?

Within the United Methodist Church debates have centered on the question of what doctrine the church has—the substantive dimension.[11] The church has been very tentative and unclear on exactly what its doctrine is, often acting as if it still has its doctrine to find. There is the long observed problem of an erosion of doctrine in the church. It is tempting to put the blame on the liberals for this. Thirty years ago when Alasdair MacIntyre observed that theologians were "giving atheists less and less in which to disbelieve," he had people like Rudolf Bultmann, Paul Tillich, Bishop John Robinson, and Paul Van Buren in mind.[12] At least some participants in the liberal tradition seem willing to admit (though in some cases *claim* would be a better word) such a description of their objectives. Clapp mentions Episcopalian Bishop John Shelby Spong in his discussion of the minimalization of doctrine. Spong identifies liberals as those who are brave enough to interact with the world. These liberals may be "honest, but for the most part they have no real message."[13] We must resist, however, the temptation to blame the liberals. There are too many indications that marginalization, though perhaps more pronounced and advanced where liberal theology prevails, is just as much a reality in conservative or evangelical churches.

Kurt Anders Richardson speaks of the same phenomenon on a different level, offering factors behind the minimalism that include both liberals and conservatives:

> Modern theology has been typified by doctrinal minimalism. For Protestants the roots of this go back to interconfessional conflict and the encounter with modern

science. Evangelicals were minimalist in the interest of spiritual awakening and common cause with all like-minded. Liberals, however, were minimalist in the interest of a public theology that could embrace as many nominal Christians as possible—indeed, perhaps the whole society.[14]

Moving beyond academic theology, we can see factors within the evangelical wing of the church as a whole that influence doctrinal marginalization. In light of the evangelical church's preoccupation with the "therapeutic" and the "practical" Clapp asks,

> Is *redemption* really any less practical or down-to-earth than *self-esteem*? The difference is not that psychological grammar is inherently more practical, more 'real,' more concrete than theological grammar. The difference is that there is a community ready to concretize and put into practice psychological grammar, while the church has accepted the marginalization of its language; it has concretized and practiced theological grammar less and less.[15]

Both ends of the theological spectrum are heavily invested in importing the broad cultural emphasis on the therapeutic. As the church centers on making people feel good—or having healthy relationships—in terms of popular psychology, the focus is less on specifically Christian objectives; or else these activities are matched up with theological concepts. Just as "mission" so often became "social work" in the past century, "salvation" has become "emotional wholeness" and "self-acceptance" in recent years.

The Misconceptualization of Doctrine

Modernity has led simultaneously to a misconceptualization of doctrine as a whole and of the nature and purpose of the church (the particular doctrine of ecclesiology). The controversy between liberal and conservative theology on these matters has been so vehement because both have developed in the womb of modern philosophy. If we can overcome the influence of modern philosophy—and certain options in postmodern philosophy offer such prospects—we can perhaps overcome the divide between liberals and conservatives as well.[16] Such a hope is central to Nancey Murphy's work in *Beyond Liberalism and Fundamentalism*. I am not as optimistic, however, about overcoming the divide between liberals and conservatives. Though both traditions originated in the matrix of particularly modern philosophical positions, they have developed substantive theological differences that have come to be definitive in each tradition. There seem to be adequate resources within postmodern philosophy to allow these substantive differences to continue on the same trajectories. There is no simple way to forget the history of the movements. A shift to a postmodern philosophical framework would enable them to see more clearly what it is that divides them and allow for some convergence.

Why has modernity played this role? Modernity has played this role simply because it has become the dominant framework in which Western Christians have lived in the past couple of centuries. Christianity has always been influenced by its host culture,[17] and only in recent years have tools been developed that help it identify this influence. A blessing of cultural pluralism is that we can see that our culture's way of doing something is not the only way. We can attempt the strategy of dismissing all other options as "primitive" or "misguided," but such a strategy only works for so long. Within Christianity, the tremendous rise in nonwestern forms of the faith has catalyzed much work in this area. One of our challenges is that the more educated we are the more we become enculturated into the culture of modernity. Our understanding of what it means to be an educated person has been indistinguishable from that of the broader culture—being educated means having degrees from accredited institutions of higher learning. Those institutions have been built on the foundations of modernity. Because of the common commitment to modernity, denominational colleges and universities have been, except for occasional and usually sparsely attended chapel services, essentially the same as their secular counterparts. In this environment, it is not surprising that many formerly religious schools have dropped their religious affiliation.[18] We have trouble questioning the cultural conviction that science has all the answers anyone could ever need or that the best way to understand ourselves is as autonomous moral agents. That happiness is the highest goal in life seems obvious, however much we may differ on how this is to be achieved. Charles Taylor notes:

> Cartesian dualism is immediately understandable to undergraduates on day one. The idea that the only two viable alternatives might be Hobbes or Descartes is espoused by many, and is a perfectly comprehensible thesis even to those who passionately reject it. They feel its power, and the need to refute it. Such was not the situation in the 1640s.[19]

Modernity is what is obvious to us. Our culture provides us with the plausibility structures that make daily living intelligible. The common sense (which can be taken as an abbreviation of *"community* sense") United Methodists and other modern Christians hold is the common sense of modernity, not the common sense of Christianity. We are too deeply enculturated for anything else to be the case.[20] George Lindbeck notes that what we take to be real is primarily socially constructed. "What seems credible or incredible to contemporary theologians is likely to be more the product of their milieu and intellectual conditioning than of their science, philosophy or theological reasoning."[21] John Milbank takes Lindbeck's assessment even farther:

> The pathos of modern theology is a false humility. For theology, this must be a fatal disease, because once theology surrenders its claim to be a metadiscourse, it cannot any longer articulate the word of the creator God, but is bound to turn into the oracular voice of some finite idol, such as historical scholarship, humanist psychology, or transcendental philosophy.[22]

I am not claiming that modern culture is monolithic—if it were we would not be hearing the complaints of a loss of common sense in America. Although American culture is fragmenting, its dominant strands remain deeply indebted to modernity—and it is these various strains that often continue to be the primary culture for Christians. If modern culture is this powerful, we ought to consider its influence on Christianity.

Christian Accommodation to Modernity

There is an even more important reason to consider the influence of modernity. There are reasons to believe this influence has been less than benign. Alasdair MacIntyre highlights the key difficulty: "The moral presuppositions of liberal modernity, whether in its theory or in its social institutions, are inescapably hostile to Christianity and ... all attempts to adapt Christianity to liberal modernity are bound to fail."[23] Christianity has an internal drive to communicate with people in every culture it encounters. Though a claim to the contrary has often been made, there is no one culture that has a natural fit with Christianity. The adaptation to culture is necessary in both directions—Christianity seeks to become indigenous in the culture at the same time it seeks to be a change agent in that culture, but all too easily adaptation becomes accommodation. In Christianity's relations with modernity, the latter has too often become the leading partner. According to Stanley Hauerwas, ever since the Enlightenment, theology has aimed above all else to "make the gospel credible to the modern world."[24] The way this is done is by paring down what one takes to be essentially Christian. As what moderns consider credible is narrowed, Christian doctrine finds itself pared as well. Why? Once doctrine came to be understood in a particular way, it often became dispensable. This is an instance of modernity having an effect on doctrinal substance.

Examples of this accommodationism are not hard to find: It takes two forms. The first is a studied attempt to avoid conflict with that paragon of modern knowledge, science. Science has not only been preeminently successful in the modern era, but it also serves as the model of foundationalist rationality. For an example, we need look no further than Friedrich Schleiermacher. He seeks a theology that in no way conflicts with science (and can thus itself be truly scientific).[25] He says,

> Unless the Reformation from which our church first emerged endeavors to establish an eternal covenant between the living Christian faith and completely free, independent scientific inquiry, so that faith does not hinder science and science does not exclude faith, it fails to meet adequately the needs of our time and we need another one, no matter what it takes to establish it. . . . Precisely this position . . . represents my *Glaubenslehre* . . . I thought I should show as best I could that every dogma that truly represents an element of our Christian consciousness can be so formulated that it remains free from entanglements with science.[26]

Some of the doctrines affected by his strategy include creation,[27] miracles,[28] Christology,[29] and scripture.[30] Such a strategy is not limited to those in the liberal tradition, though they are the more likely to claim such a motivation explicitly. In conservative circles, we see a different application that is more likely to be used to explain scriptural texts. Where the liberal might simply describe the crossing of the *yam suph* as a myth, the conservative apologist will describe it as a "miracle of timing." The people arrived at the sea at just the moment a strong wind was blowing and so were able to cross the sea. In the effort to compete before the bar of rationality, apologetic theology thinks it necessary to show that God could have used "completely natural" means to accomplish the event.

Methodist theologian Albert Knudson is representative of those who see in science something to be unquestioningly accepted alongside Christianity. Methodist theological training in the early part of the twentieth century was concentrated at Drew, Garrett, and Boston, with the latter in a position of prominence. In his position as professor and later as dean at Boston, Knudson directly and indirectly influenced Methodist pastors and leaders for a generation. William John McCutcheon points out that Boston University's influence was so great that by midcentury a majority of Methodist institutions of higher learning had Boston alumni as presidents. One example of this influence can be seen in the role Knudson's critique played in Methodism's containing the influence of Barth and neoorthodoxy. Because of Knudson's central role in teaching a generation of Methodist thinkers and in shaping the ethos of Methodist theology, he will be one of my exemplars throughout as I seek to understand and delineate the effect of modernity on the place of doctrine.[31]

Knudson felt compelled to resolve conflicts between common sense and science on the one side, and the traditional Christian worldview on the other.[32] To find his way out of the dilemma Knudson suggests that Christianity simply is not in the same business as science or "common sense."

> The Christian religion in its essence has no cosmology. It is not necessarily bound up with the biblical cosmology any more than it is with the Aristotelian or Ptolemaic. It is consistent with any purely scientific cosmology.[33]

If theology is to be acceptable in this age it must "square itself" with science.[34] Modern sensibility is the leading partner in the relationship with theology. Knudson was convinced this change could be made without altering the substance (or better, the "essence") of Christianity at all.

The second aspect of accommodationism was more troublesome. Rather than the negative project of avoiding offense, it is the positive goal of making the gospel intelligible (and logical) on modern terms. MacIntyre observes this in the intellectual movements of the late nineteenth century:

> The theologians of the late nineteenth century ... could not but be responsive to the recurrent attempts within every major Christian denomination to reshape and to diminish central Christian doctrine in a way that made it acceptable to post-Enlightenment culture....[35]

The power of enculturation within modernity shows itself again. In this atmosphere Knudson insisted that the "great theological task of the present is to reinterpret Christian doctrine in the light of the personalistic type of thought."[36] Elsewhere he explicitly identified "the personalistic type of thought" as

> a modernist movement ... [that] stands intimately related to the latest and most significant developments of modern speculative thought. It is charged throughout with the spirit of modernity, and as such cannot but be out of harmony with certain aspects of traditional Christianity.[37]

Being modern or being acceptable to modern people is what counts. This apologetic impetus led Knudson to deemphasize or reinterpret many key doctrines. Committed to a modern conception of "person," the personalist approach to the doctrine of Trinity found "three persons in one being" too polytheistic. A modalistic Trinity was therefore to be preferred. Eschatology for Knudson became secularized into social progress, another key commitment of moderns (at least early twentieth-century Americans).[38]

Knudson was not able to differentiate between modern culture and Christianity. His conception of the doctrines of conversion and the church were clearly affected. On conversion he claims that

> In New Testament times most of the Christians had been either Jews or pagans, and for them the acceptance of Christianity involved a radical change that was properly described as conversion or regeneration or a new creation. But with us the situation is different. Children are now born and reared in Christian homes, and of them no such radical change is as a rule to be expected. 'Conversion' in their case is not necessary. Christian nurture properly takes its place.[39]

The universal expectation of conversion that existed while the church held to a version of the Augustinian doctrine of original sin had been drastically changed by Knudson's psychologized version of the doctrine of sin. This kind of conversion his theology expected was primarily ethical rather than religious. The need for such a conversion is not based on sin, but

> is grounded in the law that governs the development of our common human nature. We begin on the natural pleasure seeking plane; and later it becomes our task to moralize our native impulses and to rise to a spiritual or altruistic plane of conduct. To fulfill this task is extremely difficult for every one, and out of the moral struggle involved in it there arises a felt need of a power not of ourselves that makes for righteousness. When this power invades our lives and becomes dominant in us, conversion has taken place.[40]

With redemption seen as education, it is not surprising to see conversion understood in similar terms. Of course, this view is not simply the result of modernity. It is a powerful synthesis of a distinctly modern humanistic optimism with a conviction that the broad culture can be (and in the case of early twentieth-century America, actually *is*) Christian. The Christendom thesis was near the end of its credibility in this era,[41] but American Protestantism, and Methodism in particular, had been so successful in the nineteenth century that many felt there was still plenty of supporting evidence for it.

Knudson's theology is highly individualistic. The person (or self) understood from a radically individualist point of view is the center of his metaphysical thinking, and little attention is given to the corporate dimension.[42] Although his discussions of various doctrines are always accompanied by an overview of their historical and traditional development, overall church tradition seems to be valued little. He is sociologically astute enough, however, not to build on the common distinction between religion and *organized* religion. Religion is necessarily social, he admits, but this facet of religion receives little attention in his work.[43] Subsidiary doctrines receive even less attention. In *The Doctrine of Redemption*, after the historical treatment, baptism is addressed in two paragraphs, one on the baptism of infants, one on its proper mode.[44] The church, for Knudson, serves as an agent of the Kingdom of God, but the Kingdom is reinterpreted in ethical terms as "The Christian Social Ideal."[45]

Modernity has influenced Methodist theology and doctrine—and rightly so, according to Knudson. He was immersed in modernity and was therefore as aware of it as we are of the air we breathe. Today modernity is falling apart around us. We see that its convictions and commitments are just that: they are not truly rational conclusions available to all rightly thinking people everywhere.[46] So far, we have seen some characteristics of modernity, but in what follows I consider these in greater detail.

WHAT IS MODERNITY?

The definitions of modernity are almost as numerous as the definers. Thus far, we have seen modernity to be characterized by a tendency toward scientism as well as toward individualism. These will be discussed in more detail below. The beginning of modernity has been variously dated in terms of politics, social developments, science, art, and architecture. The forces I see at work date roughly from the early seventeenth century and find their clearest initial statement in the writings of Descartes. Most of the elements present in his thought were not original to him. His originality lies in his forceful synthesis and development of ideas, many present in Western culture since Antiquity.[47]

A Picture of the Modern

A good place to start is with the synopsis of modern and postmodern theologies suggested by Nancey Murphy and James McClendon. We can better understand modernity now that we see some places to stand beyond it. They develop a picture of the space inhabited by each, enabling us to identify the characteristics that set modern theology apart. My interest at this point is not in modern theology *per se*, but in the philosophical background that has constrained it. Murphy and McClendon suggest that modern thought inhabits space defined by three fundamental convictions. The first is the epistemological. All real knowledge is to be justifiable by direct relation to indubitable first principles. Foundationalism has reigned in theology just as it has in most other disciplines. The second key conviction is about the nature of language. Language was either referential or it was expressive. Most considered science to be the paradigm of referential use, and liberals and conservatives differed on whether the model of science was relevant to theological knowledge. Liberals rejected the position that reference worked in theology the same way as in science, claiming instead that religious language was expressive. The third conviction is that the best way to approach systems is through reductionism. Complex wholes are best understood when broken down into their constituent parts (atoms) and then reassembled. This reductionism found expression in the focus on methodologies and in sociopolitical thought, resulting in individualism in the latter and mechanistic science in the former.[48]

The Characteristics of Modernity

For my purposes, the focus will be on epistemology, individualism and a third factor not mentioned by Murphy and McClendon, dehistoricization. The first two features are closely intertwined[49] and spawn a number of other convictions within modern thought, which in turn have influenced the place of doctrine within the church. For Descartes, a quest for certainty leads to a foundationally secured structure of knowledge, waiting to be discovered by the individual. Though the content of the foundation and some of the methodology of building upon it have changed, Descartes' model has continued to prove central to modern philosophy. In the section that follows, I will consider the relevant emphases of modernity, identifying ways in which each has influenced modern (and especially modern Methodist) theology.

Many voices claim the modern infatuation with epistemology has been unhealthy for theology. William Abraham for one identifies epistemology as the biggest challenge facing mainline Protestantism.[50] James McClendon and James Smith see foundationalist epistemology determined to push theology to pare down its convictions, a correlate to the marginalization of doctrine in the church as a whole.[51] Foundationalism does this as proposed doctrines are examined to determine their rationality. As they fail the test of being rationally founded, they either are reinterpreted so they can be deemed rational or are discarded as "nonessential." Such doctrines may be accepted on faith, but such an option is really only open to those who choose to be less than fully rational.[52] Ellen Charry sees modern theology in a dangerous position. Having committed so strongly to modern epistemology, theology finds itself on dangerous ground as that very epistemology is inverted in some prevailing forms of postmodernism.[53] Liberals and conservatives alike assume the centrality of epistemology. Charry observes,

> The difference between them is not that conservatives cling to pre-Enlightenment epistemology while liberals embrace modern epistemology. Both have embraced modern epistemology, which requires assent to propositions that are coherent and intelligible. The difference between them is that liberals apply the criteria of credibility and intelligibility more stringently than conservatives usually do.[54]

Modern epistemology provided for ways to secure knowledge. In some forms of postmodernity it is not simply some claims to knowledge that are disputed, but the whole project of knowledge itself. To some, a form of Nietzscheanism, with its reduction of knowledge claims to assertions of will, seems the only viable option.[55]

The centrality of epistemology can also be seen in Albert Knudson's work. In a claim based directly on Descartes' *Cogito*, Knudson says that biblical authority is a problem for the modern Christian. "Modern thought is autonomous . . . it recognizes no supernatural standards of truth, no external authority superior to the human mind. It finds in experience, reason, and utility the sole sources of truth. . . . The ultimate test of truth must be found within the mind itself."[56] In roughly the same era that William James was writing about the *varieties* of religious experience, Knudson was writing about the *validity* of religious experience. Religious experience was rationally acceptable because of the *a priori* structure in the human mind. Knudson's Kantianism claimed an *a priori* not only to guarantee theoretical and moral knowledge, but also, following Ernst Troeltsch, religious knowledge as well. Faith is not so much grounded on the *a priori*, but turns out to be the *a priori* itself seen from a different perspective.

> As a matter of fact, the antithesis between the two terms is not necessarily so sharp as all this. In the notion of an a priori there is involved the idea of something super-individual and so transcendent. On the other hand, the feeling of absolute dependence does not necessarily mean passive submission. It may mean and does mean active self-

surrender—in other words, faith. Faith is thus an essential constituent of the religious a priori. It is faith that makes possible religious experience. It is not religious experience that gives rise to faith but the reverse. Faith is the a priori, the formal principle, that alone makes religious experience possible.[57]

By merging the Kantian *a priori* and his own religious *a priori* together—and calling the result "faith," Knudson is effectively changing the object of faith from God to one's own mental faculties.

Modern epistemology often takes the form of procedural rationality, identifying the proper method to be employed to arrive at real knowledge.[58] Charles Taylor compares the substantive rationality of premodernity with the procedural rationality of modernity. Before Descartes, a platonic worldview that found reason existing in the order of the world itself dominated. In the platonic world, one was considered rational if one aligned oneself with reality. In modernity, rationality was achieved by disengaging from the world and following the right procedures, usually those modeled on the natural sciences. Reason shifted from being on the outside—in the world—to being on the inside—in the mind of the thinker.[59]

A form of procedural rationality has found its way into mainstream theology. Books and articles on theological method have proliferated in the past couple of centuries. It has often been assumed that once one has identified the correct method—and there *is* a correct method—one could proceed with the rest of the work. The quest for correct method has proved frustrating, however, as theologians have been unable to find either an indubitable foundation on which to build, or a method of resolving disputes about the method of building thereupon. Doctrine has been marginalized in the church sometimes simply for the reason that the church has spent too much time discussing the appropriate method with which to proceed and has never gotten to doctrine proper.[60] Of course, sometimes the avoidance of substantive issues was exactly what was desired.[61]

The United Methodist Church was born in 1968 in the merger of the Methodist Church and the Evangelical United Brethren. By 1972 General Conference had approved a theological statement that did not establish any substantive doctrines as the core of the new denomination, but rather a variant of procedural rationality: the so-called Wesleyan Quadrilateral. One was supposed to start with doctrines that were helpful in making the Quadrilateral work smoothly. This intentional minimalism emphasized the doctrine of normative doctrinal pluralism. The gospel of Wesley and the early Methodists, it says, "was rooted in the biblical message of God's gracious response to man's deep need, in his self-giving love revealed in Jesus Christ" and as such "their interest in dogma was minimal."[62] Immediately after this the statement gives its first quote from Wesley's tract, *The Character of a Methodist*: "As to all opinions *which do not strike at the root of Christianity*, we think and let think."[63]

Curiously, from this quotation the statement infers that Wesley was "fully committed to the principles of religious toleration and doctrinal pluralism."[64] Wesley *was* well known for his tolerance. He *was* quite willing to reckon members of almost any denomination or church as Christian. The Methodist Societies *were not* doctrinally based.[65] Yet doctrinal pluralism is a modern concept: even if it meant something to Wesley, it meant something different than it does to us in the latter part of the twentieth century. Even if Wesley was "fully committed" to a doctrinal pluralism, it seems far-fetched to put such a pluralism at the very center of his thought. Yet this is exactly what the 1972 Statement seeks to do. The next phrase of the statement says that in spite of this commitment to pluralism, Wesley was "equally confident that there is a 'marrow' of Christian doctrine that can be identified and that must be conserved." (p. 41) Where is this "marrow" to be found? It "stands revealed in Scripture, illumined by tradition, vivified in personal experience, and confirmed by reason." (p. 41). This is the first occurrence in the text of what has come to be known as the Wesleyan Quadrilateral, a phrase coined by theologian Albert Outler, one of the principal architects of the 1972 Statement.[66]

Doctrinal pluralism would be hard to understand as normative within the United Methodist tradition considering that its Articles of Religion apparently align the denomination with traditional Christian doctrine. The 1972 Statement accomplished this by putting forth the Quadrilateral as definitive of proper method in doctrine and theology. It says,

> Since 'our present existing and established standards of doctrine' cited in the first two Restrictive Rules of the Constitution of The United Methodist Church are not to be construed literally and juridically, then by what methods can our doctrinal reflection and construction be most fruitful and fulfilling? The answer comes in terms of our free enquiry within the boundaries defined by four main sources and guidelines for Christian theology: Scripture, tradition, experience, reason. These four are interdependent; none can be defined unambiguously. They allow for, indeed positively encourage, variety in United Methodist theologizing. Jointly, they have provided a broad and stable

context for reflection and formulation.... There is a primacy that goes with Scripture.... In practice, however, theological reflection may find its point of departure in tradition, 'experience,' or rational analysis. What matters most is that all four guidelines be brought to bear upon every doctrinal consideration.[67]

What is most important is not one's adherence to or understanding of any particular set of doctrines. What matters is one's proper adherence to an extremely flexible theological method.

The 1972 Statement proved to be a point of contention for a number of years.[68] General Conference established a study commission that brought forward and adopted a new statement in 1988. The 1988 Statement is much clearer for a number of reasons. First, it makes a distinction between theology and doctrine. Doctrine "assists us in the discernment of Christian truth in ever changing contexts," while theology involves "the testing, renewal, elaboration, and application of our doctrinal perspective in carrying out our calling 'to spread scriptural holiness over these lands.'" Doctrine constitutes our core beliefs, those things that are constants for the church, while theology uses these doctrines as the times change so that mission might be effective.[69]

Second, while the 1988 Statement does recognize what it calls "diversity," it does not speak of doctrinal pluralism as normative, unlike the 1972 Statement. Where the 1972 Statement spoke of Wesley's commitment to "religious toleration and doctrinal pluralism," the 1988 Statement takes its paragraph over exactly, except for changing "doctrinal pluralism" to "theological diversity."[70] This change in perspective is also evident in the placement of the paragraph: instead of prefacing the discussion of the core of Christian doctrine, it is placed at the end, effectively moving pluralism from the foundation of United Methodist theologizing to a secondary principle.

The 1988 statement recognizes the trend represented in the 1972 statement as dating from the early twentieth century. It speaks of

> the waning force of doctrinal discipline and the decreasing influence of the Wesleyan theological heritage among American Methodists, along with minor but significant changes in the wording of the *Book of Discipline* regarding doctrinal statements, led to a dilution in force of the Articles of Religion as the Church's constitutional standards of doctrine.[71]

Finally, the 1988 Statement does not speak of the "Wesleyan Quadrilateral" though it does speak of the same four "sources" and "guidelines." The move is clearly away from the procedural rationality evidenced in the 1972 Statement. By and large, however, United Methodists still think in terms of the 1972 Statement and though it is no longer part of the *Discipline*, the procedural rationality that statement exemplifies still prevails on many levels of the church.

Individualism is a necessary component of modern epistemology. The autonomous individual pursues rationality by use of the correct methods and stands in need of no one. Within religion this is characterized by a position that individual experience and conscience are the arbiters of doctrine. For this to work, doctrine must be redefined as "beliefs." In an era of autonomous freedom, doctrine cannot be that which is communally normative since, as Lindbeck notes, "The modern period is antipathetic to the very notion of communal norms."[72] Individualism has not only caused the minimalization of doctrine (in an attempt to appeal to rational autonomous individuals) but also an ultimately fatal reconceptualization of doctrine itself.[73] Individualism is so ingrained in moderns that we have even come to believe it is a thoroughly Christian position.[74] As I will discuss in detail in chapter three, individualism has enfeebled the doctrine of the church in mainline Protestantism, leaving us with no understanding of the church except that of "voluntary association," a collection of like-*minded* individuals pursuing some democratically decided upon goals.

The other side of individualism has been the rejection of tradition (a rejection named by Hans-Georg Gadamer, the "prejudice against prejudice").[75] Modern philosophy on the whole has rejected tradition as nonrational and overly authoritarian. Such a rejection presupposes, of course, the centrality of epistemology that reduces tradition to a body of inherited information, leaving moderns blind to their own immersion in (and subservience to) a tradition.[76]

The rejection of tradition was a declaration by the modern that he or she stood alone, outside the confines of any particular community. Allegiance was to be offered to reason and its dictates alone.[77] Once religion was reduced to a set of beliefs or common pattern of morality, tradition was seen as something inimical to true religion. The morality of the Christian was what was morally obvious to anyone who thought about it properly; the beliefs were equally accessible and capable of evaluation by anyone, regardless of where he or she was located. Those immersed in religion could not but be tied to tradition, so the shift was made to seeing the outsider as having a privileged position in understanding religion, since he or she is not blinded by commitment.[78] Knudson illustrates how this stance relates to the modern practice of comparative religion. Speaking from a chosen position outside the Christian tradition, he asserts, "There is no fundamental cleavage between Christianity and other religions. They all consciously or unconsciously appeal for their validation to the common religious reason. The difference between them is a difference of degree."[79] Because religion is primarily a phenomenon of rational individuals, commitment to a particular tradition or community has no real role to play. Following one of his liberal forbears (Schleiermacher) Knudson finds greater authority in personal experience than in the church tradition. Knudson says, "Theological empiricism relieves the believer of the burden of accepting traditional doctrines that stand in no living relation to the Christian consciousness of today."[80] I.e., tradition that does not measure up to current experience is expendable.

Foundationalist epistemology marginalizes the particular and local in favor of the general and universal. It assumes that attention to particular situations and differences can only lead to error and distortion. Foundationalist knowledge must be founded on indubitable structures—not merely indubitable to you and me and our neighbors, but indubitable to any conceivable rational person, i.e., any person who properly thinks out the matter. In this drive toward the universal and the nonperspectival, history was found to be too messy, too varied, too undependable, and most of all, too contingent. Through hard work and proper application of the right methods, one *might* come up with the facts about what happened. But how could such an event be understood? What might it *mean*? Surely it was impossible to draw universal conclusions (and all *rational* conclusions were universal) from historical events. Therefore, if we assume foundationalism, history gets us nowhere in our quest to be rational. Once we take the fateful step of tying the essence of religion to reason, we have effectively severed any link between religion and history.[81]

The clearest exposition of rationalistic dehistoricization is that of G. E. Lessing, an articulation I will consider in chapter four. At this point I only wish to claim that foundationalist epistemology and its partner, individualism, have combined to marginalize the place of history in modern approaches to religion, and that this marginalization of history has had both a substantive and a methodological effect on Christian doctrine. Robert Osborn claims that,

> We may observe that Christian theology did something to itself; it doubly distorted its own vision. It reduced the Christological to the anthropological, and the eschatological to the ontological. In a false triumphalism it turned the

> universal promises of Christ into the present and universal reality of being. Where true Christianity proclaims the promised eschatological coming of Jesus Christ and his universal reign, religious Christianity discovers that universal reign in the ever present ontological depth of existence. Whereas true Christian 'religion' is the response of the Christian to the grace of God manifest in the events of the so-called *Heilsgeschichte*, the response also made possible and actual in that grace, religious Christianity in abstraction from Jesus Christ and the story of which he is a part, becomes the response to the divine depth of being.[82]

Thus it was not only doctrine that was dehistoricized, but consequently the whole understanding of what Christianity was about. After history became marginal, it seemed only natural for the Christian to understand his or her "religious" life as one compartment among many, decontextualized from the rest of the existence.

Charles Taylor paints an interesting picture of the process by which this happened. It is not merely a story of philosophy directly removing history from theology, but rather an indirect influence that worked by changing theological positions and emphases in the seventeenth and eighteenth centuries. This influence led gradually to a position like Lessing's, which came to dominate so much modern thought.

Early modern philosophy admired nothing as much as the success of Newtonian mechanics. Beginning in the seventeenth century and finding fuller expression in the eighteenth, theologians who lived in an intellectual milieu shaped by Newton sought ways to understand the spiritual world in Newtonian terms as well. The result was an emphasis on the *order* of creation. Within this order, if we do our part, God is constrained to do his part.[83] The chief doctrine in such a setting becomes providence.[84] Taylor comments, "The design of an order for the good of instrumentally rational creatures leaves God no choice, as it were, but to establish laws which he will leave to operate without interference." God's goodness leads to a position where miracles are seen as an unwarranted (and ungodly) intrusion into such a blessed order. This order also

> marginalizes history. The 'historical' nature of Judaism, Christianity, [and] Islam . . . is intrinsically connected with their recognition of the extra dimension [beyond natural mechanistic order]. . . . Once the notion of order becomes paramount, it makes no more sense to give them a crucial status in religious life. It becomes an embarrassment to religion that it should be bound to belief in particular events which divide one group from another and are in any case

open to cavil. The great truths of religion are all universal. Reason extracts these from the general course of things.[85]

Peter Harrison draws a similar picture:

> In much the same way that the world became the object of scientific inquiry in the 16th and 17th centuries through a process of desacralization, so too, religious practices . . . were demystified by the imposition of natural laws. As the physical world ceased to be a theatre in which the drama of creation was constantly re-directed by divine interventions, human expressions of religious faith came increasingly to be seen as outcomes of natural processes rather than the work of God or of Satan and his legions.[86]

History is intimately tied to a view of humans (and God) as agents. Modernity, in contrast, is committed to an anthropology that sees humans primarily as knowers (trapped in the boxes of their bodies). Modern philosophy creates (and is partly created by) modern science. As intellectuals practice theology, philosophy, and science in close conjunction, they reinterpret doctrines in ways that fit with the developing scientific worldview. This mechanistic worldview of Newtonian science is the natural companion of the philosophical world populated with rational, autonomous individuals. Such individuals are who they are completely through self-definition, not through participation in some larger order, whether church or nature. Attention to communal and historical location cloud and distort judgment. Historical events may illustrate general truths, but that is all.[87]

But can Christianity maintain its identity once history has been marginalized? It takes no great powers of analysis to see that the primary form in Scripture is history-like narrative.[88] A glance at the historic creeds of the church can discern their narrative structure. They purport not merely to state who Jesus is and how he is to be understood in relation to God, but also and centrally to assert that certain events transpired and that God was the chief agent in these events that were done for our salvation. Thus historical events certainly *appear* to be central to Christian identity. What would Christianity be without them? Is it perhaps an option to consider the narrative *form* separable from the *content* of that narrative?[89]

Langdon Gilkey investigates this question from the perspective of neo-orthodox biblical theology. This theological tradition clearly wanted to retain classical Christian identity, and clearly emphasized the narrative *form* of scripture. Yet, Gilkey asserts, its modern philosophical commitments left the status of the *content* of those narratives in question.

> ...As modern men perusing the Scripture, we have rejected as invalid all the innumerable cases of God's acting and speaking; but as neo-orthodox men looking for a word from the Bible, we have induced from all these cases the theological generalization that God is he who acts and speaks. This general truth about God we then assert while denying all the particular cases on the basis of which the generalization was first made.[90]

What remains once we have determined that no individual action can be attributed to God while at the same time we continue to speak as if such actions were real? The change in position does not mean that we need to change our liturgies and our Sunday school lessons. What is Christian talk about God-events really about? This is not the approach of liberals—who are often willing simply to admit that things did not happen as the Bible says and that such historical events are really unimportant to the Christian faith.[91] Rather, Gilkey is speaking of those who *affirm* the centrality of history in Christian identity.

Dehistoricization, whether it occurs in a liberal, neo-orthodox, or conservative form, affects the status of doctrine within the church by paring down its content and reducing it to timeless generalizations.[92] It does this additionally by bringing wholesale change (or elimination) to a key doctrine of the church: eschatology. Conservative dehistoricization leads to an individualization of eschatology into emphasis on heaven and hell and a focus on the return of Christ at the end of the age. The current era is uniformly characterized by sin and the absence of God. Liberals, like Knudson, humanize eschatology into social progress.[93] Yet Christianity without eschatology is incoherent.[94]

Dehistoricization, more than any other result of modernity, has resulted in the marginalization of doctrine. Not only has it marginalized particular doctrines, but it has also limited the options for the conceptualization of doctrine as well. In the next section of this chapter I will use George Lindbeck's discussion of the conceptualization of doctrine as a foil in dealing with this aspect of the problem of marginalization. His *The Nature of Doctrine* has provoked a massive response from a wide variety of perspectives. Though many may find his position unsatisfactory (and inaccurate in its detail), his analysis of doctrine demands attention. I find Lindbeck especially helpful because of his attention to the underlying philosophical issues, especially the influences of modernity. Lindbeck brings certain postmodern philosophical movements into the picture, most importantly in the philosophy of language. The bulk of his treatment is of the various conceptualizations of the nature and function of doctrine.[95]

Lindbeck and *The Nature of Doctrine*

Lindbeck's main goal in discussing doctrine is to develop an understanding of doctrine that makes better sense of the problems of doctrinal change and faithfulness. How can Christians be faithful to the doctrine of their church while at the same time seeking doctrinal reconciliation with other ecclesial communities? The main context in which he has encountered these questions is ecumenism, and this dimension of the problem is present throughout the book. He finds none of the currently available conceptualizations of doctrine to be ecumenically helpful.

Modernity has not only affected the place of doctrine in the church, but has also influenced the relations between ecclesial communities. The influence of modernity has not so much led to new denominations,[96] as it has created divisions internal to the churches. As we will see, Lindbeck's account, focused as it is on external relations, does not give enough attention to the incoherence *within* churches that results from the interaction with modernity.[97]

Many have criticized Lindbeck's accounts as overly simplistic caricatures of highly nuanced positions.[98] His schema, though definitely highly idealized, is nonetheless useful. As we examine each theory we can recognize that though no one may hold the ideal position, each represents a particular expression of modernity, especially in the area of epistemology. Lindbeck does not frame each position as a response to specifically modern developments, tending (wrongly, I believe) to a narrative that sees propositionalism as premodern, experiential expressivism as modern, and his own cultural linguistic approach as postmodern.[99] It is all too easy to read Lindbeck as equating "liberal," "modern," and "experiential expressive." Though there are clear overlaps between these categories, the lack of clear distinction will cripple an attempt to develop a postliberal theology. I will argue later that both propositionalism and experiential expressivism (as depicted by Lindbeck) represent responses—opposite ones, albeit—to modernity. As responses to modernity, they have a number of presuppositions in common as will be shown below.

Three Basic Accounts of the Nature of Doctrine

Doctrine operates in the realm of religion and each conception of religion implies a particular conception of doctrine. How one conceptualizes religion is inseparable from how one conceptualizes doctrine. Once one has come to a conclusion on the nature of religion, one is inclined to have a particular view of the role of doctrine. I find it easiest to approach Lindbeck's typology by considering the controlling image associated with each approach. Modernity plays a key role in shaping the controlling image for religion in two ways. Particular movements within (and in competition with) modernity lend each model its controlling image. In the end, I will suggest a different controlling image, an image excluded by the ethos of modernity (since history is central to my proposed new image), and not even considered by Lindbeck, who in this respect, seems committed to a liberal (though not experiential expressive) position.

Science is the realm of real knowledge. The rise of modern science paralleled the development of modern epistemology, the cornerstone of modern thought. In line with these developments, propositionalism's controlling image is religion as a science. It is true that a theory of doctrine must account for the fact that at least in their traditional form doctrines *look* like propositions. The first theory of doctrine identified by Lindbeck, Propositionalism, makes the easy transition from seeing that doctrines are propositional in *form* to claiming they are propositional in *function*, along the lines of scientific propositions. The purpose of science is to give us true knowledge about the world. Religious doctrines do the same thing, especially in relation to things connected to the divine. Religion is a partner of science in the quest to give the individual a systematic view of reality. As such, doctrinal statements, like scientific statements, accurately and truthfully refer to objective reality.[100]

Linked as it is to a particular stance toward knowledge, the viability of religion at any given time is closely tied to the vicissitudes of the reigning epistemological theories. As foundationalist models of science flourished, theologians looked to foundationalism as a promising model for understanding their own realm. With the ongoing demise of foundationalism, the field of religious studies seems to have not yet latched on to any replacement theory, leaving them in a state of general pessimism with regard to knowledge claims in religion. Reasoning thus is simple. Real knowledge is foundationalistic. Foundationalism does not work: Therefore, there is no real knowledge. I deny the first premise, not the second.

Modern philosophy's conception of religion has been epistemologically centered. As approaches to the possibility and nature of religious knowledge have changed, the theory of what religion is about has also changed. The driving factor has not been a consideration of religion itself, but rather, the assumption that religion requires a certain kind of theistic stance. This theoretical stance has then been analyzed and critiqued from an epistemological perspective. Sometimes the results were "friendly" toward religion: religion can have knowledge of God after all, though always under carefully delimited conditions. Sometimes the results are less "friendly": Our cognitive faculties and the nature of reality conspire to keep us from knowing anything about God. This in turn leads to two further possibilities. One can retain the notion that religion has to do with knowledge and simply admit that religion is in itself incoherent in the face of this epistemological pessimism. Another option, the more common one in fact, is to shift from knowledge as the essence of religion, to the search for something else to serve as foundational. After Hume's skeptical conclusions were published, Kant was compelled to rule out the possibility of a theoretical knowledge of God. In the first *Critique* Kant divides the world into phenomena and noumena. Phenomena are the things that we know through the categories built into the human mind. Through proper application of these categories knowledge is certain. Behind the phenomena are the noumena, the things in themselves which are unknowable. So, contrary to Hume, we need not be skeptical about the world around us. Because there is no room for freedom in the world of the phenomenal, Kant located it in the realm of the noumenal. Since God could not be known, being noumenal, Kant claimed that humans related to God solely through morality. This led him to identify religion with the realm of the moral, a place where it could be truly an expression of freedom. Though knowledge is no longer central in Kant's view of religion, it is evident that his position is nonetheless rooted in particular epistemological developments.

When religion is seen as like a science (or, stronger yet, *as* a science), doctrines are understood as propositions that accurately and truthfully refer to objective reality, just like the propositions of science. Also like the propositions of science, doctrines are expected to fit together into a deductive structure (modeled on the axioms and proofs of geometry). A propositionalist can be either optimistic or pessimistic. An optimistic propositionalist would say that the knowledge represented in Christian doctrine is surely knowable, resulting in doctrinal maximalism. In other words, the canons of epistemology are such that we have warrants to consider all Christian doctrine as real knowledge. A pessimistic propositionalist, on the other hand, would adhere to a more skeptical epistemology and find that many Christian doctrines simply do not measure up as true knowledge. Since only those doctrines that do measure up can be counted as proper doctrines, the result is a doctrinal minimalism.

Once we identify propositionalism in terms of its controlling image instead of in terms of modern epistemology, an interesting option arises. As the epistemology associated with science shifts toward a postmodern one, perhaps there will be a postmodern type of propositionalism as well. If this is possible, it might help explain why so many premodern positions are identified as instances of propositionalism, even though they are not determined by modern epistemology. If we can have a postmodern propositionalism that truly overcomes the problems associated with modern epistemology, we are still left, however, with the controlling image of religion as a science. Whether scientism will be seriously affected in the shift from a modern to a postmodern world remains to be seen. Perhaps science will have a different kind of prestige and will no longer command the obeisance that is today so common from other disciplines and areas of life. My claim is not that a postmodern propositionalism is impossible or bad, but rather that the controlling image upon which the model is based is not only harmful to the church, but also too easily ignorant of key substantive positions in the Christian tradition and an impediment to the practice of doctrine.

Within the propositionalist model the chief function of language is reference. Though language may indeed do many other things, reference is the most important. Since doctrine is expressed in language, doctrine's main job is to refer to objective reality. It is easy to see the connection with modern epistemology here. Because of this model, the key doctrine for propositionalists has been Revelation. The first step in such a theology is religious epistemology: how do we know God? How do we obtain information from him? Numerous theories of inspiration have arisen in this period, specifying how the Bible has come to us as the Word of God and is thus qualified to serve as the foundation for our doctrines and beliefs.[101]

Lindbeck terms the second understanding of religion Experiential Expressivism. He is less explicit about the controlling image of experiential expressivism, probably because the movement itself was in a sense negatively defined. Where cognitivism had (usually) unreflectedly seen itself as akin to science, experiential expressivism began in a denial of this very model. According to this scheme, religion is more like an aesthetic experience. We might say that the controlling image here has been art, especially as theorized by Schleiermacher's romantic contemporaries.[102] Religion is about feeling and expression and comes from within the individual, not from without. As in art, freedom, creativity, and autonomy are highly valued.

From the experiential expressive perspective doctrines are understood to function as "noninformative and nondiscursive symbols of inner feelings, attitudes, or existential orientations."[103] They express inner human experiences. As experience changes, the expressions (doctrines) may change, though it is possible for expression to remain the same while the experience changes. In other words, there is no direct and determinate connection between experience and expression.

This model again evidences the centrality of epistemology, though from the negative side. It is a combination of Kant's position (that objective knowledge of God is impossible) with a commitment to continue to talk about God as real.[104] In the shift to experiential expressivism science (and foundationally established knowledge) lost none of the esteem in which it had been held. It simply became unbelievable that religion could be understood as science. If religion was to be kept—and this was the desire expressed in Schleiermacher's *Speeches*, it must be reconceptualized. This understanding has penetrated all levels of the church and has been the dominant understanding of religion in the mainline churches for at least a century.[105]

While propositionalism adheres to a primarily referential theory of language, experiential expressivism goes a step further, developing a more complex theory. Language as reference may work fine in the area of science, but religious language has no external referent, being instead the expression of the inner depths of human consciousness. At times it looks like this is merely a moving of the point of reference from the outside to the inside, but thinkers in this tradition have wanted to maintain that religion is not merely (though it may be primarily) an individual phenomenon.

The key doctrine for those within this model is anthropology. Schleiermacher argues in the *Speeches* that even the "cultured despisers" of religion would find something in themselves indicative of the divine, if only they looked carefully. Religion is a universal human phenomenon. Various thinkers locate this basicness in different places, but find that such a universality is present in them all.

With Lindbeck's third model we see a potential break with modernity. While both propositionalism and experiential expressivism are conceptualized in the categories of modern epistemology, the shift of controlling image from science or art to culture/language breaks the tie to individualism (directly) and epistemology (indirectly). Cultures and languages are social institutions—they simply are inconceivable as individualist phenomena. When religion is understood in terms of science, one "becomes religious" by attaining a certain kind of knowledge. When religion is conceived along experiential expressivist lines, religion is inherent in being human (for liberal experiential expressivists) or based on having certain types of experience (for pietistic experiential expressivists). Once we see religion as more like a culture, one becomes religious as one is enculturated into the religious community. Acknowledgment of certain facts may be a small part of religion, but is not at all determinative. Religious experience is important also, but is a product of "being religious"—of being enculturated into a religious community—not the source of it.

Religions are best understood as "comprehensive interpretive schemes, usually embodied in myths or narratives and heavily ritualized, which structure human experience and understanding of self and world."[106] Lindbeck claims further that

> ... a religion can be viewed as a kind of cultural and/or linguistic framework or medium that shapes the entirety of life and thought. It functions somewhat like a Kantian *a priori*, although in this case the *a priori* is a set of acquired skills that could be different. It is not primarily an array of beliefs about the true and the good ... [contrary to the cognitive propositional view], or a symbolism expressive of basic attitudes, feelings, or sentiments [contrary to the experiential expressivism]. ... Like a culture or language, it is a communal phenomenon that shapes the subjectivities of individuals rather than being primarily a manifestation of those subjectivities. It comprises a vocabulary of discursive and nondiscursive symbols together with a distinct logic or grammar in terms of which this vocabulary can be meaningfully deployed.[107]

The Kantian *a priori* was developed to ensure the objectivity of experience. By combining the *a priori* with a Cartesian turn to the self in his so-called "Copernican Revolution," Kant let his whole case ride on the dependability of his argument defending the universality of the categories. The *a priori* was a universal interpretive framework that enabled us to live confidently in a stable world. The categories are necessarily the way they are and through being the same for all people at all times, guarantee objectivity. Later scholars in the Kantian tradition, Troeltsch on the continent, and personalists like Knudson in America, were to develop the notion of a specifically religious *a priori*. Rejecting the apparent Kantian reduction of religion to morality, they sought a way to maintain the objectivity of religion while at the same time retaining modern philosophy (which for them entailed an acceptance of Kant's objectivism over Hume's skepticism). Though Lindbeck seems aware of this use of the *a priori* in religion, I do not believe this is the genealogy of the use we find in his work. Unlike Kant, the *a priori* "could be different." There is no reason to assume that it is the same for all people at all places and times. Rather, it seems that his appropriation is by way of the anthropological and sociological tradition mediated through Clifford Geertz, and before him, Emile Durkheim. Such an *a priori* is socially mediated, not genetically or physically mediated. The question remains, however, whether such a position is a remnant of modern epistemology. In spite of taking this approach, Lindbeck does not deny the propositionalist's claim that what ecclesial communities put forth as doctrines *look* like propositions. They are not about objective reality, however, but rather are second-order utterances used to regulate the first-order ones.

The background of Lindbeck's conception is found in three dimensions: the philosophical (Ludwig Wittgenstein, J. L. Austin, and Peter Winch), the social scientific (Karl Marx, Emile Durkheim, Peter Berger, and Clifford Geertz),[108] and the theological (the traditional notion of the *regula fidei*, Martin Luther, and Karl Barth).[109] His appeal to Christian tradition in this regard is subordinated to his philosophy of language, but because that philosophy is community or tradition based (he would say "language" based), he is not merely making an apologetic move, but actually putting his theory into practice. Since his position is nonfoundational it would be a mistake to try to identify one of these streams of influence as playing the role of foundation to the model.

Turning to the substance of his position, we see that to understand religion truly, we must pay heed to its communal nature. Just as Wittgenstein would say that there is no such thing as a private language, Lindbeck would claim that there is no such thing as a private religion. In this Lindbeck makes a clear break from the modern tradition in which individualism has played such a dominant role. Individualism has prevailed whether the model is cognitive (concerned with the contents of the individual believer's mind) or experiential (concerned with the individual's experience). By attending to the centrality of community in religion, ecclesiology regains its place in theology. The individualism underlying propositionalism and experiential expressivism tended to marginalize the church, making it primarily a voluntary association, either for those with common beliefs or those with a common experience.

Where propositionalism sees religious language as primarily referential and experiential expressivism highlights the expressive dimension, Lindbeck focuses on language as a human tool. Meaning is not determined by correspondence to an object or by authentic connection with the speaker's inner intention, but by use. We discover what doctrines *mean*, by attending to what they *do*. In chapter two I will in much greater detail examine doctrine from the perspective of language. I will argue that Lindbeck's use of postmodern theories of language is, in the end, incomplete. His model would have been much better if he had paid greater attention to those theories and dealt with them in a more thorough manner.

Since epistemology is no longer the foundation of religion, the key doctrine need not be revelation (religious epistemology) nor anthropology (a justification of inherent human religiousness). In my reading of Lindbeck the key doctrine becomes that of the church. Neither of the peculiarly modern theories of religion or doctrine had any great use for ecclesiology. Once religion is seen as communal in its very essence, and doctrine is seen as the grammar regulating that community, the church becomes central. Doctrines do not reside in the mind of the individual but are the authoritative teachings of the church. In Lindbeck we see that Cyprian's dictum, "Nulla sallus extra ecclesiam," gains new meaning. It is no longer to be understood in terms of Roman (or any other) exclusivism, but is simply a truism given the nature of religion, and hence of salvation. In this model the hard division between the theoretical and practical is done away with. Indoctrination is not the forcing of illogical and irrational beliefs on gullible minds; it is, rather, the necessary enculturation of Christians into a way of life.[110]

The Nature of Doctrine and Doctrine's Ills

Lindbeck's schematic understanding of the various conceptualizations of doctrine clarifies the problem of the marginalization of doctrine. Propositionalism and experiential expressivism are the most readily available conceptualizations of doctrine offered by modernity. If we operate in a universe in which these are the only options, marginalization seems like a needed strategy. Unfortunately, most debate has been on the level of substance, while the deepest differences were in the area of conceptuality. There is another dimension, however, that both modern options fail to recognize because of their common commitment to individualism. This third dimension is performance.

As James W. McClendon observes, doctrine is primarily an *action* of the church.[111] Both faulty conceptualization and the exclusion of key doctrines impair performance, while accurate conceptualization and the inclusion of all necessary doctrine in no way guarantee proper performance. In the case of modernity, the initial redefinition of the church in individualist terms causes blindness to this whole dimension. Lindbeck recognizes the issue of performance, but does not treat it explicitly enough.[112] The failure is not simply that the church has done some bad thinking, but that the church has done some poor living—when judged by its own standards. It has not succeeded in maintaining its identity (a chief role of doctrine) vis-à-vis the cultures in which it has found itself.

Propositionalists who find doctrine to be marginalized define this marginalization in substantive terms. Necessary doctrines have been neglected, corrupted, or expunged. Doctrines have been warped or distorted by leaving out important points or adding extraneous ones. Experiential expressivists, on the other hand, may look to the conceptual dimension. My guess is that they would say that supposed marginalization of doctrine is a nonproblem caused by a misconception of doctrine. Lindbeck observes:

> For the experiential-expressive symbolists . . . religiously significant meanings can vary while doctrines remain the same, and conversely doctrines can alter without change of meaning. . . . The general principle is that insofar as doctrines function as nondiscursive symbols, they are polyvalent in import and therefore subject to changes of meaning or even a total loss of meaningfulness. . . . They are not crucial for religious agreement or disagreement, because these are constituted by harmony or conflict in underlying feelings, attitudes, existential orientations, or practices, rather than by what happens on the level of symbolic . . . objectifications.[113]

Experiential expressivists would say propositionalists only see the problem because they wrongly think Christians need to believe particular things, typically things simply not credible in the modern age. In contrast to both, those who see religion as being similar to a culture or a language would see the marginalization of doctrine in the failure of doctrines to shape the community. Such a failure can take a wide variety of forms.

One of Lindbeck's aims, as we have seen, is to have a theory that would make coherent the doctrinal reconciliation sought in ecumenical efforts. The conservative propositionalist[114] could argue that what we actually see in the ecumenical movement is a prior capitulation on the status of doctrine. So-called reconciliation is really apostasy. Those who are able to reconcile without admitting any past error have simply accepted the premise that doctrine does not refer to anything, so any doctrine can be reconciled with any other. Liberal propositionalists would probably describe what happened as an exclusion of doctrinal chaff. Both positions fail once we see the actual functioning of the ecumenical movement. Those who are pursuing reconciliation do not see the currently dividing issues as being of no substance. Their strategy does not betray the conviction imputed to them by such propositionalists, i.e., that doctrines do not refer at all.

Lindbeck makes a very important set of distinctions: between explicit and implicit doctrine and between operative and official doctrine.

> Church doctrines are communally authoritative teachings regarding beliefs and practices that are considered essential to the identity or welfare of the group in question. They may be formally stated or informally operative, but in any case they indicate what constitutes faithful adherence to a community. To disagree with Methodist, Quaker, or Roman Catholic doctrine indicates that one is not a 'good' Methodist, Quaker or Roman Catholic. Someone who opposes pacifism, for example, will not be regarded as fully what a member of the Society of Friends should be. If this conclusion is not drawn, it is evident that the belief has ceased to be communally formative, and it is therefore no longer an operational doctrine though it may continue to be a formal or official one.[115]

The doctrines that define a community and its life may be either explicit or implicit. Even ecclesial communities that claim "no doctrine but the bible" have doctrines, though they may not be explicit. Lindbeck rightly observes that "a religious body cannot exist as a recognizably distinctive collectivity unless it has some beliefs and/or practices by which it can be identified."[116]

Notice that with its inclusion of the notion of the church as community, the concept of operational doctrine only makes sense in a cultural linguistic framework. The reality of official yet nonoperative doctrine, however, seems most descriptive of mainline liberalism. In American Methodism, for example, while the church's official doctrine has been constant since 1808, the most operational (explicit) doctrines in United Methodism today are variants of normative pluralism and the Wesleyan Quadrilateral. Since these doctrines, especially the first, tend to work against communal identity, what plays that role in

Methodism today? My guess is that it is our polity. United Methodists are not so much people who hold such and such theological views, but rather people who have a connectional ministry, pay apportionments, and structure their work by procedures in the *Book of Discipline*. The current fractures in the church, however, seem to indicate that polity alone is not a sufficient basis for denominational identity.

Lindbeck and Modernity

Lindbeck clearly positions himself as postliberal. But is he really post*liberal*? He rejects the foundational perspective of Schleiermacher and the tradition associated with him, but does liberalism begin with Schleiermacher? At the very least we can say that he is post-experiential expressivist. He is postmodern in his decentering of epistemology, in his rejection of individualism, and in his philosophy of language. But what about the modern turn from history? How does Lindbeck deal with this feature of modernity?

The answer is ambiguous. On the one hand, Lindbeck emphasizes the role of narrative in religion.[117] In this he follows fellow Yale theologian Hans Frei who convincingly demonstrates that modernity has marginalized the narrative reading of Scripture.[118] Propositionalists, however much they affirm the historicity of Scripture, tend to reduce the narrative to propositions. Experiential expressivists reduce narrative to a record of religious experiences. Both tend to see narrative as merely illustrative of general truths. Lindbeck appears to avoid this.

On the other hand, his handling of narrative seems to fit just fine with modern dehistoricization, depicting it more like a universal category (as in Ronald Thiemann's discussion). To see this let us consider a lengthy passage:

> It is possible to specify the primary function of the canonical narrative.... It is 'to render a character..., offer an identity description of an agent,' namely God. It does this not by telling what God is in and of himself, but by accounts of the interaction of his deeds and purposes with those of creatures.... These accounts reach their climax in what the Gospels say of the risen, ascended, and ever-present Jesus Christ whose identity as the divine-human agent is unsubstitutably enacted in the stories of Jesus of Nazareth. The climax, however, is logically inseparable from what precedes it. The Jesus of the Gospels is the Son of the God of Abraham, Isaac, and Jacob in the same strong sense that the Hamlet of Shakespeare's play is the Prince of Denmark. In both cases, the title with its reference to the wider context irreplaceably rather than contingently identifies the bearer of the name.[119]

So the biblical narrative tells us who Jesus is in the same way "Hamlet" tells us who Hamlet is. Has anyone met Hamlet? Did Shakespeare know Hamlet? Did any of the writers of the New Testament know Jesus? Did anyone know Jesus? Does it make any difference? Lindbeck goes on to indicate that the "intratextual" theology that results from such an approach to biblical narrative can be quite varied, allowing for widely divergent characterizations of "the divine agent at work in the biblical stories."[120] He goes on, however, to say that in the light of "modern science and historical studies" we can "make a distinction . . . between realistic narrative and historical or scientific descriptions."[121] The Bible

> can therefore be taken seriously in the first respect as a delineator of the character of divine and human agents, even when its history or science is challenged. As parables such as that of the prodigal son remind us, the rendering of God's character is not in every instance logically dependent on the facticity of the story.[122]

But where does this get us? Are we now as postmoderns (or postliberals) to have any different approach to history than moderns? Surely not all narrative can be reduced to parable. Parable only works when it is in the larger context of nonparable. Though "the rendering of God's character is not in every instance logically dependent on the facticity of the story," does it ever so depend? The community of people who have built their lives around Hamlet has a very different history (and relation with Hamlet) from the people who have built their lives around Jesus. This is at least in part because what Jesus did is taken as constitutive of our lives today in a way impossible for followers of Hamlet. If we were Danes and Hamlet had been an actual Prince of Denmark, the case might be different. But Hamlet is a fictional character.

Another indication that history (and finally, even narrative) is not very important in Lindbeck's model is the place it finds in his discussion of the nature of truth in religious language and the problem of reference. He speaks of truth in three dimensions: intrasystematic (coherence), ontological (correspondence), and categorial. The place of narrative in all this is not clear. When he turns to the problem of the referentiality of language he chooses a very unhelpful example: "This car is red."[123] Most ordinary uses of this sentence are completely unproblematic. It is when sentences like this are considered apart from any context that they become questionable. Lindbeck claims context is what makes a sentence function referentially. This would be an excellent place to discuss narrative context, but he does not.

As I said above, Lindbeck's position is ambiguous. These passages can be taken in a sense that allows for a recovery of history. But does he get beyond the neo-orthodox position identified by Gilkey? Lindbeck appears to believe that at least some of the events narrated in Scripture actually happened. There are, however, other indications that ahistorical tendencies remain in his position. The most obvious is his controlling image for religion—a culture or language. Languages do not have narratives—they are used to tell stories. Grammar is a rather ahistorical category, functioning best as description of current features.[124]

Another ahistorical feature is his choice of examples and use of language regarding them. The general, the universal, and the timeless seem to be emphasized over the particular, the local, and the temporal. Consider his discussion of religious language. The claim he investigates is "Jesus is Lord."[125] With his emphasis on the performative dimension of this speech act, he takes it in abstraction from the history of Jesus.[126] When the first Christians said, "Jesus is Lord," they were speaking existentially: they were claiming Jesus as *their* Lord. But the New Testament usage also connects to the Old Testament narrative where κύριος meant not merely *master*, but *Yahweh*. This is particularly true of Paul's speech about the Lordship of Jesus in Philippians 2:5ff., which is an echo of Isaiah 45:23, a passage focusing on *Yahweh* as κύριος. Lindbeck deals with the issue of the resurrection of Jesus, a topic one would think conducive to inclusion of historical issues. His focus, however, remains on the level of the conceptual, shifting too easily from talk about *the* resurrection to talk about *resurrection*. He says later, amid "shifts in Christological affirmations and in the corresponding experiences of Jesus Christ, the story of passion and resurrection and the basic rules for its use remain the same." Where are the definite articles? Is he talking about *the* passion and *the* resurrection? These do not come to us as mere concepts. Within the biblical narrative they are heartily described: the passion was a real suffering that led to a real death. The resurrection was an event that led to an empty tomb and a risen Jesus who fellowshipped with his disciples.[127]

Finally, Lindbeck's decision to start with a theory of religion seems to be akin to the modern gambit toward universalism. If Peter Harrison[128] and Robert Osborn are indeed correct to see the category "religion" as an outgrowth of a distinctly modern approach *within Christendom*, does not the category lose its usefulness in assisting the effort of overcoming modern influence? Does it really help us to start off with the assumption that Christianity is a species of this genus? Clearly there are phenomena called religions that are nonhistorical.

History has no real significance for them. In the modern urge toward abstraction and generalization it is all too easy to reduce a "religion" to the lowest common denominator—like a system having to do with what is "more important than everything else in the universe."[129] This maintains the modern habit of beginning with an outsider's view, an action I do not believe consistent with Lindbeck's overall program. It is likely that Lindbeck's position has this ahistorical tendency because of his reliance on Wittgenstein's philosophy. In spite of his powerful arguments against so many modern positions, Wittgenstein too often remained aloof from the particular, especially with regard to religion. In his "Lectures on Religious Belief,"[130] he speaks about the believer's belief in a future judgment and how that belief functions in the believer's life. Christians, however, do not merely confess belief in a future judgment, but that "Jesus will come again to judge the living and the dead." This latter language is very particular and places the believer's (current) belief about the future into the context of the narrative of Jesus, and through being confessed using the creed, it is also contextualized into the life of the church as a whole.

Summary Thus Far

Modernity has seen—and been a chief cause of—the marginalization of doctrine in American mainline churches. The twin roots of this problem are the modern centering on epistemology and individualism. Out of these two basic commitments have flowed subsidiary commitments that have been detrimental to the role of doctrine within the church. These additional influences include an emphasis on procedural rationality, a rejection of tradition, an atomistic reductionism, and most significantly for Christianity, a tendency toward dehistoricization. All of these are interrelated, and it is likely that any attempt to overcome the marginalization of doctrine caused by modernity will have to counteract all of these features.

This marginalization of doctrine takes place in three dimensions: substance, conceptuality, and performance. We examined George Lindbeck's proposal that Christianity (as a religion) is best understood as a culture or a language, in opposition to the two chief rivals birthed in modernity: propositionalism that sees religion (and thus Christianity) as a science, and experiential expressivism that sees religion as an aesthetic enterprise. Both of these latter options are birthed in the context of modern thought. Lindbeck's strategy of approaching the problem through the conceptual dimension is exactly right. Some may argue that propositionalism is more faithful than its competitor is since it retains more of the substance of traditional Christian doctrine. To argue this assumes the correctness of the model, which naturally asserts: "The best understanding of doctrine is the one that retains the maximal number of beliefs."

Propositionalism fails for at least two reasons in this regard. First, the argument assumes that propositionalism is always conservative. It is just as possible to understand religion as propositions and see these propositions as completely misguided or wrong, hence leading to a doctrinal minimalization. Secondly, and more profoundly, propositionalism assumes that quantity of doctrine is the only issue, which when combined with the modern tendency to dichotomize belief and action, leads to a neglect of doctrinal performance. Has maintaining a maximal amount of beliefs made any difference in church life? On the contrary, the very individualism of the model has marginalized the church itself. Following propositionalism, we find ourselves in a predicament similar to the fellow who wanted to swim (and knew how to swim quite well), but found there was no water in the pool.

Within experiential expressivism, it is difficult to conceptualize the marginalization of doctrine. Since religion flows out of human experience, and that human experience is universal in at least some dimensions,[131] doctrine has less importance to begin with, or at least that importance is less explicit. If Lindbeck is right, and religion is more like a culture or a language, and that in such a context doctrine functions to form and shape the community, there is no doctrine-less religion. In the case of some versions of liberalism, my suspicion is that an ecclesiology that is essentially Constantinian has had a part in forming the "grammar" of their communities. Thus, instead of having doctrine that reflects the particularities of their own Christian tradition, their distinctive doctrines are shaped to minimize conflict with their host culture. Doctrine's role of communal differentiation is focused on recalcitrant sects instead of explicitly non-Christian communities. Their ecclesiology has then produced a blindness to the cultural dimension of Christianity and has led them to derive doctrine from the predominant narrative of their surrounding culture. This would be the origin of "doctrines" sometimes found within such communities: "God is nice"; "Christians are people who are nice to the postman."[132]

Lindbeck's perspective is to be preferred because it refuses to play the modern games of epistemology and individualism. Within the cultural linguistic model there is again room for a robust ecclesiology. But does Lindbeck go far enough? I suggested above that he does not, failing as he does to overcome explicitly the modern tendency toward dehistoricization. In what lies ahead I will propose a model that overcomes this weakness. Central to this endeavor will be the development of a different controlling image for Christianity.

A Better Way

In chapter two I will suggest that doctrine is a complex speech act of the church. Lindbeck was on the right track when he turned to J. L. Austin's philosophy of language.[133] He failed, however, to deal with the whole of Austin's theory, leaving himself with an approach to language that is too easily classified as a form of corporate expressivism. This leaves him weak on the question of truth in language, and incoherent on the reality of change. His hylomorphic approach to doctrine—identifying the form as the unchanging, the content as the changing—will be shown to be untenable.

As a speech act of the church, the focus is on doctrine as *action*. Doctrine is always the property of the church before it is the property of the individual. As an action, it takes place through time. It is a thoroughly historical phenomenon and thus dynamic. McClendon and Smith's work on the nature of religious convictions will be useful here as will Wolterstorff's recent work on divine communication in Scripture. The theological doctrine most relevant to this is not Revelation, but Incarnation. In the Incarnation God speaks a Word that is personal and historical, a Word the church claims is truly divine and truly human.

In the third chapter I will briefly consider what the church looks like in this when doctrine is understood as a speech act of the church. Church as "voluntary association," a model so prevalent in modern American Christianity, will be seen to be insufficient. Lindbeck's insights into the church as culture will be compared and contrasted with the recent work of mission anthropologists. While the model of church as culture is attractive, it needs clearer development if we are to account for the fact that this church we confess to be both "One" and "Catholic" is nonetheless quite diverse, with *cultural* difference a major component in that diversity. The church is conceived along lines proceeding from the incarnational model in chapter two. The church is always called to incarnate the Gospel in whatever culture it finds itself. The theological focus here will be an ecclesiology that flows out of soteriology.

In chapter four I will turn more explicitly to the question of history. My objective will not be to prove the historicity of any particular tradition or narrative, but rather to suggest ways history serves as a necessary component of the Christian tradition. At this point, I will develop the suggestion that the best controlling image for Christianity is not science, art, or language/culture, but drama. In Christianity we have not merely a narrative of God's mighty acts from the past, but a still-continuing narrative in which the church today plays a part. I do not want to make any absolute differentiation between narrative taken as a series of events and narrative taken as a relating of these events. Instead, I see these two aspects as complementary. Doctrine *per se* is a natural result of the life of the church through history. Doctrine is generated by the interaction of the still lived out Christian narrative with competing and neighboring narratives.

I will suggest that though they are not the same, there is a close correlation between narrative and tradition. In this context we will see that tradition (in a variety of senses) is essential. Here I will make use not only of Christian reflection on tradition, but also the work of MacIntyre and Gadamer from a more generalized perspective. Key elements of the Christian narrative lie in the past. The church's identity today (and status *as* church) is dependent not merely on its current location, but on its relation to these past events. The guiding doctrine for this chapter is eschatology—not merely a future or individual eschatology, but one relevant to and dependent upon God's actions and intents through all times.

In the final chapter all these strands will be brought together to show that doctrine's key function is to guide the church's life. In this role, doctrine is dependent upon and can never be severed from the Christian narrative. Doctrine identifies the players in the narrative—God, Jesus, church, believers, outsiders, satan, etc. The key actions of these players in the past are summarized to show their continuing relevance for today. Doctrine enables the church therefore to understand the setting in which it finds itself and to identify the plot line in which it lives. Once in this position, doctrine identifies what actions the church as a body and believers as parts of the body should take to live out the narrative in the present. Doctrine that plays these roles will be vital and will resist marginalization.

There are a couple of important consequences to this model. First, the world (the "setting") in which the church lives out the narrative is in constant flux. The flux comes from new neighboring and competing narratives arising that not only "beg" for understanding and evangelization, but also provoke reappraisal of past doctrinal developments. For this reason doctrine must adapt if Christian identity is to be maintained, unbelievers to be won, and the narrative to be faithfully played out.

A second consequence of the adoption of this model would be a shift in ecumenical strategy. If I am right, the major division within the church today is not between various Protestant denominations, or between Protestants and Rome, or even between East and West. Rather, the major divide is between the segments of the church that find their central identity in modernity, and those who, either through reflection on the Christian tradition or through resources from postmodern philosophy, see the necessary role of history. This division is one *within* ecclesial communities and, I believe, is a too often ignored impediment in current ecumenical ventures. For example, conservatives within United Methodism sense a theological chasm between themselves and the church leaders who perform the denomination's ecumenical work at the General Commission on Christian Unity and Interreligious Concerns. When they hear of new ecumenical agreements between denominations they are highly suspicious. They wonder, "Is this the United Methodism to which we adhere or is it liberal activists working together?" One reason local ecumenism seems so much more successful than that on the national level is that this division is more commonly found between than within local congregations. On the side of modernity, cut off from its umbilical relation to history, doctrine will inevitably appear arbitrary, resulting in the marginalization of doctrine in a form of indifferentism or foundationalist apologetics.

Notes

[1] Paul Holmer, *The Grammar of Faith* (San Francisco: Harper and Row, 1978), 2.
[2] William J. Abraham, *Waking from Doctrinal Amnesia* (Nashville: Abingdon, 1986), 12f.
[3] Abraham, *Waking*, 41, 52, 53.
[4] Schubert Ogden, "Doctrine and Theology in the United Methodist Church," in *Doctrine and Theology in the United Methodist Church*, ed. Thomas Langford (Nashville: Kingswood Books, 1991) 41.
[5] Rodney Clapp, *Peculiar People: The Church as Culture in a PostChristian Society* (Downers Grove, IL: InterVarsity Press, 1996), 18.
[6] George Lindbeck, *The Nature of Doctrine: Religion and Theology in a Postliberal Age* (Philadelphia: Westminster Press, 1984), 7.
[7] As commentators have noticed, this is not all Lindbeck's book is about. Though it can be read as a treatise on the nature of doctrine, it can also be read—and perhaps more plausibly—as a polemic against liberal theology. Liberal theology gets it wrong at the very first with a mistaken conceptualization of religion and doctrine. The core difference between Lindbeck and liberalism is not philosophical (as the first part of the book might lead one to believe), but theological. For some who view the theological conflict as primary, see Gordon Michalson, "The Response to

Lindbeck," *Modern Theology* 4:2 (Jan. 1988): 107–20; D. Z. Phillips, "Lindbeck's Audience," *Modern Theology* 4:2 (Jan. 1988): 133–54; David Tracy, "Lindbeck's New Program for Theology: A Reflection," *The Thomist* 49:3 (July 1985): 460–72.

[8]Donald Thorsen, *The Wesleyan Quadrilateral: Scripture, Tradition, Reason and Experience as a Model of Evangelical Theology* (Grand Rapids, MI: Zondervan, 1990), 36ff.

[9] For a view of the Anglican attitude toward doctrine, see Stephen Sykes, "The Genius of Anglicanism," in *The English Religious Tradition and the Genius of Anglicanism*, ed. Geoffrey Rowell (Nashville: Abingdon, 1992), 227–41; and Aidan Nichols, *The Panther and the Hind: A Theological History of Anglicanism* (Edinburgh: T & T Clark, 1993).

[10]The classic example is J. Gresham Machen's, *Christianity and Liberalism* (Grand Rapids, MI: Eerdmans, 1923).

[11]See discussion in Abraham, *Waking*; also, Thomas C. Oden, *Doctrinal Standards in the Wesleyan Tradition* (Grand Rapids, MI: Francis Asbury Press, 1988).

[12]Alasdair MacIntyre and Paul Ricoeur, *The Religious Significance of Atheism* (New York: Columbia University Press, 1969), 24f. See the expansion of this in Stanley Hauerwas, *After Christendom: How the Church is to Behave if Freedom, Justice, and a Christian Nation are Bad Ideas* (Nashville: Abingdon, 1991), 24.

[13]Discussion is in Clapp, *Peculiar People*, 19. See John Shelby Spong, *Rescuing the Bible from Fundamentalism*, (San Francisco: HarperCollins, 1991), 35–36.

[14]Kurt Anders Richardson, "The Contemporary Renewal of Trinitarian Theology: Possibilities of Convergence in the Doctrine of God," in *The Nature of Confession: Evangelicals and Postliberals in Conversation*, ed. Timothy R. Phillips and Dennis L. Okholm (Downers Grove, IL: InterVarsity Press, 1996), 183.

[15]Clapp, *Peculiar People*, 105.

[16]Nancey Murphy, *Beyond Liberalism and Fundamentalism: How Modern and Postmodern Philosophy Set the Theological Agenda* (Valley Forge, PA: Trinity Press International, 1996).

[17]In chapter three I will examine in some detail the relation between church and culture. Needless to say, a work of this kind can only scratch the surface. What must be accounted for is that Christianity has many characteristics of a culture itself, while at the same time finding itself inhabiting a great variety of cultures. While there seems to be an inherent drive in Islam to be monocultural, Christianity seems to glory in multiculturalism.

[18] I came across a resumé recently where an applicant for a ministry position described her *alma mater* as a "secular liberal arts school"—Illinois Wesleyan University. The applicant was from a non-Wesleyan Christian tradition and had no knowledge that "Wesleyan" ought to indicate something Christian.

[19]Charles Taylor, "Philosophy and its History," in *Philosophy in History: Essays on the Historiography of Philosophy*, ed. Richard Rorty, J. B. Schneewind, Quentin Skinner (Cambridge: Cambridge University Press, 1984), 21.

[20]Abraham, *Waking*, 43. See also, Alasdair MacIntyre, *Whose Justice? Which Rationality?* (Notre Dame, IN: Notre Dame University Press, 1988), 394. William Placher speaks of apologetic theology (theology aimed at making itself

intelligible to moderns) as having "gone native" and no longer exhibiting distinctly Christian characteristics in his *Unapologetic Theology: A Christian Voice in a Pluralistic Conversation* (Louisville, KY: Westminster/John Knox Press, 1989), 11.

[21] Lindbeck, *Doctrine*, 63. Of course, no hard and fast distinction can be made between one's "milieu and intellectual conditioning" and one's "science, philosophy, or theological argumentation."

[22] John Milbank, *Theology and Social Theory: Beyond Secular Reason*, (Oxford: Basil Blackwell, 1990), 1.

[23] Alasdair MacIntyre, "An Interview with Alasdair MacIntyre." *Cogito* 5 (Summer 1991): 67. This position is not new for MacIntyre, but is substantially the same as he articulated in *The Religious Significance of Atheism*, 24–29. Colin E. Gunton goes farther and asserts that modernity is essentially characterized by the denial of Christianity. Cf. *The One, The Three, and the Many: God, Creation and the Culture of Modernity, The 1992 Bampton Lectures* (Cambridge: Cambridge University Press, 1993), 1. Too many Christians participated in the development of modernity and have lived their lives in its midst for me to concur in a position this strong.

[24] Stanley Hauerwas and William Willimon, *Resident Aliens: Life in the Christian Colony*, (Nashville: Abingdon, 1989), 19.

[25] Friedrich Schleiermacher, *The Christian Faith*, trans. H. R. MacKintosh and J. S. Stewart (Edinburgh: T. & T. Clark, 1928), 137.

[26] Friedrich Schleiermacher, *On the Glaubenslehre: Two Letters to Lücke*, trans. Francis Fiorenza and James Duke, (Chico, CA: Scholars Press, 1981), 64.

[27] Schleiermacher, *Lücke*, 60.

[28] Ibid., 61.

[29] Ibid., 62.

[30] Ibid., 67. He says, "... As for our doctrine of the canon and of inspiration as a special activity of the Spirit producing the canon, we must take care not to make any claims that conflict with the universally recognized results of historical research."

[31] For an overview see, Paul Deats and Carol Robb, eds., *The Boston Personalist Tradition in Philosophy, Social Ethics and Theology* (Macon, GA: Mercer University Press, 1986) and William John McCutcheon, "Theology of the Methodist Episcopal Church During the Interwar Period (1919-1939)" (Ph.D. diss., Yale, 1960).

[32] Albert C. Knudson, "A Personalistic Approach to Theology," in *Contemporary American Theology: Theological Autobiographies*, ed. Vergilius Ferm (New York: Round Table Press, 1932), 220.

[33] Albert C. Knudson, *The Doctrine of Redemption* (New York: Abingdon-Cokesbury, 1933), 46.

[34] Albert C. Knudson, *The Doctrine of God*, (New York: Abingdon-Cokesbury, 1930), 125.

[35] Alasdair MacIntyre, *Three Rival Versions of Moral Enquiry: Encyclopaedia, Genealogy, and Tradition*. 1988 Gifford Lectures (Notre Dame, IN: Notre Dame University Press, 1990), 69.

[36] Knudson, "Personalistic Approach," 234.

[37] Albert C. Knudson, *The Philosophy of Personalism* (Boston: Boston University Press, 1927), 254. A similar attitude is expressed in his discussion of the immanence of God and the starting place of theology. He claims that

moderns need an immanent God, so that is what he offers (*Doctrine of Redemption*, 469). "In our day theology must be anthropocentric in its starting point. Otherwise is would have no point of contact with modern thought" (*Doctrine of God*, 191f.).

[38] Albert C. Knudson, *Present Tendencies in Religious Thought* (New York: Abingdon, 1924), 56–57; *Doctrine of Redemption*, 467.

[39] Albert C. Knudson, *The Principles of Christian Ethics* (New York: Abingdon-Cokesbury, 1943), 116.

[40] Ibid., 117.

[41] George R. Hunsberger and Craig Van Gelder, eds. *The Church Between Gospel and Culture: The Emerging Mission in North America* (Grand Rapids, MI: Eerdmans, 1996). The demise of Christendom in America is the premise of the whole work.

[42] "The most fundamental and distinctive element in the Christian view of man is its emphasis upon the supreme value of the soul, the sacredness of personality" (*Doctrine of Redemption*, 78). In other words, the most basic thing about real Christianity is that it is personalistic. It is in this light that Knudson can say, "All of these [law, church, etc.] derive their sole justification from the contribution they make to human welfare" (ibid., 80).

[43] Knudson, *Present Tendencies*, 77. Jones notes that Rudolf Lotze, the founder of modern personalism and the teacher of Borden Parker Bowne, was much less interested in theology than his American followers. This lack of strong interest seems to have carried over somewhat, however, into the area of ecclesiology. Curtis Jones says, "The church invisible is for Lotze simply the communion of all men with God and with one another in to which 'everyone may enter of his own free will.' As for the church visible, it is merely a human institution seemingly (from Lotze's brief remarks) having little to do with the church invisible" ("Personalism as Christian Philosophy" [Th.D. diss., Union Theological Seminary, 1944], 46).

[44] Knudson, *Doctrine of Redemption*, 462.

[45] Ibid., 466.

[46] It is ironic that we take the same approach modern critics of Christianity took. These critics were faced with a situation in which modernity was clearly more obvious than Christianity. Some people now find themselves in a place where they have been so enculturated in Christianity and modernity, that they find the former more obvious than the latter. See Alasdair MacIntyre, "Epistemological Crises, Dramatic Narrative and the Philosophy of Science," *The Monist* 61 (1977): 454 for a discussion of the transition from one framework to another.

[47] For various accounts see Jeffrey Stout, *Flight from Authority: Religion, Morality, and the Quest for Autonomy* (Notre Dame, IN: University of Notre Dame Press, 1981); Stephen Toulmin, *Cosmopolis: The Hidden Agenda of Modernity* (New York: The Free Press, 1990); Helmut Thielicke, *The Relation of Theology to Modern Thought Forms*, vol. 1, *The Evangelical Faith*, trans. and ed. Geoffrey W. Bromiley (Grand Rapids, MI: Eerdmans, 1974); Charles Taylor, *Sources of the Self: The Making of the Modern Identity* (Cambridge, MA: Harvard University Press, 1989); Gunton, *The One, The Three, and the Many*; MacIntyre, *Whose Justice?*; David J. Bosch, *Transforming Mission: Paradigm Shifts in Theology of Mission*, American Society of Missiology No. 16 (Maryknoll, NY: Orbis, 1997), 264ff.

[48] Nancey Murphy and James W. McClendon, Jr., "Distinguishing Modern and Postmodern Theologies," *Modern Theology* 5 (April 1989); Murphy, *Beyond Liberalism and Fundamentalism*, chs. 1–3; Nancey Murphy, *Anglo-American Postmodernity: Philosophical Perspectives on Science, Religion, and Ethics* (Boulder, CO: Westview Press, 1997).

[49] For one example see Charles Taylor, "Overcoming Epistemology," in *After Philosophy: End or Transformation?*, ed. Kenneth Baynes, James Bohman, and Thomas McCarthy (Cambridge, MA: MIT Press, 1987), 471f.

[50] William J. Abraham, "Confessing Christ: A Quest for Renewal in Contemporary Christianity," *Interpretation* 51 (April 1997): 126. In a later work Abraham discusses the epistemologization of the canon in the western Christian tradition. If Abraham is correct, the seeds of an overreliance on epistemology lie long before the modern era (*Canon and Criterion in Christian Theology: From the Fathers to Feminism* [Oxford: Clarendon Press, 1998]).

[51] James W. McClendon, Jr. and James M. Smith, *Convictions: Defusing Religious Relativism*, rev. ed. (Valley Forge, PA: Trinity Press International, 1994), 10.

[52] Stephen Sykes comments on the modern view that commitment and rationality are antithetical; cf. *The Identity of Christianity: Theologians and the Essence of Christianity from Schleiermacher to Barth* (Philadelphia: Fortress Press, 1984), 272f. William Placher notes that as far as secularized moderns are concerned, unabashed Christianity, i.e., committed Christianity, is insanity (*Unapologetic Theology*, 84).

Better than commitment is skepticism, the natural correlate of foundationalism. See Charles Taylor, "Explanation and Practical Reason," in *The Quality of Life*, ed. Martha Nussbaum and Amartya Sen (Oxford: Clarendon Press, 1993), 208, 213. For his overview of the role of epistemology in modernity see his "Overcoming Epistemology," 464f.

[53] Ellen Charry, "Reviving Theology in a Time of Change," in *The Future of Theology: Essays in Honor of Jürgen Moltmann*, ed. Miroslav Volf, Carmen Krieg, and Thomas Kucharz (Grand Rapids, MI: Eerdmans, 1996), 118. See also her discussion of the influence of epistemology on theology in *By the Renewing of Your Minds: The Pastoral Function of Doctrine* (Oxford: Oxford University Press, 1997), 6ff.

[54] Charry, *Renewing*, 229.

[55] The marriage to foundationalist epistemologies was pretty much across the board. Liberals and conservatives alike felt constrained to operate within its bounds. For further discussion see, Ronald Thiemann, *Revelation and Theology: The Gospel as Narrated Promise* (Notre Dame, IN: University of Notre Dame Press, 1985), 10ff.

[56] Knudson, *Present Tendencies*, 74. The explicit tie to Descartes is on p. 75. This is a theme that runs throughout his work: "The only condition on which . . . [modern reason] . . . can recognize the authority of Scripture is the proof or conviction that Scriptural teaching is itself rational" (113). Cf. also his *Validity of Religious Experience* (New York: Abingdon-Cokesbury, 1937), 10; *Doctrine of God*, 140.

[57] Albert C. Knudson, "Religious Apriorism," in *Studies in Philosophy and Theology: By Former Students of Borden Parker Bowne*, ed. E. C. Wilm (New York: Abingdon, 1922), 123. Emphasis added.

[58] Procedural rationality found an early home in biblical studies. It was supposed that such an approach would lead to the elimination of the per-

sonal—and thus distorting—element in interpretation. Hans Frei, *Eclipse of Biblical Narrative: A Study in Eighteenth and Nineteenth Century Hermeneutics* (New Haven, CT: Yale University Press, 1974), 78.

⁵⁹Taylor, *Sources of the Self*, 86, 243. See also Hans-Georg Gadamer, *Truth and Method*, 2nd rev. ed., trans. Joel Weinsheimer and Donald G. Marshall (New York: Crossroad, 1989), 277.

⁶⁰Geoffrey Wainwright, *Doxology: The Praise of God in Worship, Doctrine, and Life*, (New York: Oxford University Press, 1980), 80. MacIntyre's comment on ethics is appropriate in theology as well: ". . . Gradually less and less importance has been attached to arriving at substantive conclusions and more and more to continuing the debate for its own sake" MacIntyre (*Whose Justice?*, 344).

⁶¹Paul Holmer, *The Grammar of Faith* (San Francisco: Harper and Row. 1978), 182.

⁶²*The Book of Discipline of the United Methodist Church* (Nashville: The United Methodist Publishing House, 1980), 40.

⁶³*1980 Discipline*, 40. For the entire tract, see Rupert E. Davies, ed., *The Works of John Wesley*, vol. 9, *The Methodist Societies: History, Nature and Design* (Nashville: Abingdon, 1989), 31-46. The statement answers the question of what does strike at the "root of Christianity" by pointing to the Quadrilateral. Supposedly use of the Quadrilateral will make this clear.

⁶⁴*1980 Discipline*, 40–41.

⁶⁵One obvious explanation seems to be that as what would today be called a parachurch organization within the Church of England, Methodism did not need a doctrinal statement or emphasis. Anglicanism included a wide variety of doctrinal positions and Wesley made no attempt to make any one of them the Methodist position.

⁶⁶For further work on the Quadrilateral in Wesley see, Albert Outler, "The Wesleyan Quadrilateral in John Wesley," *Wesleyan Theological Journal* 20 (Spring 1985): 7–18. Ted Campbell responds more critically to the question as to whether Wesley actually used something akin to the Quadrilateral. See his "The 'Wesleyan Quadrilateral': The Story of a Modern Methodist Myth," in *Doctrine and Theology in the United Methodist Church*, ed. Thomas Langford (Nashville: Kingswood Books, 1991), 154–61. The most detailed work on the subject is Thorsen's *The Wesleyan Quadrilateral*. For further work on the development of doctrinal standards in United Methodism, this is a key work. A more recent study of the Quadrilateral seeks to recontextualize the place of scripture, tradition, reason, and experience in Wesley and reconceive ways to use these in United Methodism today. W. Stephen Gunter et al., *Wesley and the Quadrilateral: Renewing the Conversation* (Nashville: Abingdon, 1997). For a study of Wesley's use of reason, see Rex Dale Matthews, "'Religion and Reason Joined': A Study in the Theology of John Wesley" (Th.D. diss., Andover-Harvard, 1986). For a study of the Quadrilateral in Albert Knudson, see William J. Abraham, "How to Dismantle the Wesleyan Quadrilateral: A Study in the Thought of Albert C. Knudson," in *Wesleyan Theological Journal* 20 (Spring 1985): 34–44.

⁶⁷*1996 Discipline* 78, 81. After noting that historically the main standards for doctrine have been the Articles of Religion and the Confession, it goes on to insist that whatever the "standardness" of these documents is, they are "not to be regarded as positive juridical norms for doctrine, demanding

unqualified assent on pain of excommunication" (49).

⁶⁸For literature on both statements see Thomas A. Langford, ed. *Doctrine and Theology in The United Methodist Church* (Nashville: Kingswood, 1991). See also, Jerry Walls, *The Problem of Pluralism: Recovering United Methodist Identity* (Wilmore, KY: Good News Books, 1986).

⁶⁹*The Book of Discipline of the United Methodist Church* (Nashville: The United Methodist Publishing House, 1996), 72–74. For further evaluation see Schubert Ogden, "Doctrinal Standards in the United Methodist Church," in Thomas A. Langford, ed. *Doctrine and Theology in the United Methodist Church* (Nashville: Kingswood Books, 1991), 39–51; and, in the same collection, Thomas A. Langford, "Doctrinal Affirmation and Theological Exploration," 203–7.

⁷⁰*1988 Discipline*, 51.

⁷¹*1996 Discipline*, 52.

⁷²Lindbeck, *Doctrine*, 77. Stanley Hauerwas comments on the impact of modern individualism: "the project of modernity was to produce people who believe they should have no story except the story they chose when they had no story. Such a story is called the story of Freedom...." ("No Enemy, No Christianity: Theology and Preaching Between Worlds," *Future of Theology*, 32).

⁷³Stanley Hauerwas speaks of the price the church has paid for its submission to individualism. Cf. *After Christendom*, 88.

⁷⁴Milbank, *Theology and Social Theory*, 93. Lindbeck, *Doctrine*, 22. For examples of this problem, see Knudson, *Doctrine of Redemption*, 78; *Philosophy of Personalism*, 67; *Doctrine of God*, 173, 309; "The Evolution of Modern Bible Study," *Methodist Review* 93 (Nov. 1911): 903.

Ironically, this individualism is in many ways an outgrowth of Christian thought. Bosch observes, "It is inaccurate to argue—as often happens—that individualism is simply an 'invention' of the West. Rather, the Christian gospel of necessity emphasizes personal responsibility and personal decision: therefore individualism in Western culture is primarily a fruit of the Christian mission" (*Transforming Mission*, 416).

⁷⁵Gadamer, *Truth and Method*, 270, 333ff.

⁷⁶For the clearest account of the traditional nature of "antitraditional" modernity see chapter 17 of MacIntyre, *Whose Justice?* It is this aspect of modernity that Thomas C. Oden finds determinative (*After Modernity....What? Agenda for Theology* [Grand Rapids, MI: Academie/Zondervan, 1990]).

⁷⁷MacIntyre offers useful accounts of this in *Three Rival Versions*, 59; cf. also "Epistemological Crises," 458. He notes that whereas for Durkheim, estrangement from one's community and a feeling of being lost in the world (anomie) was a problem, modernity actually sets it as a goal to be achieved (*Whose Justice?*, 368).

⁷⁸Hans Frei, *Types of Christian Theology*, ed. George Hunsinger and William C. Placher (New Haven, CT: Yale University Press, 1992), 13. Peter Harrison has a fascinating account of the invention of religion in the modern period. He suggests that during this period religion "came to be an outsider's description of a dubious theological enterprise." (*'Religion' and the Religions in the English Enlightenment* [Cambridge: Cambridge University Press, 1990], 1). For further discussion of this issue, see Philip D. Kenneson, *Beyond Sectarianism: Re-Imagining Church and World*, Christian Mission and

Modern Culture (Harrisburg, PA: Trinity Press International, 1999), esp. 53ff. This leads me to doubt the wisdom of beginning a study of doctrine with an analysis of the nature of religion as Lindbeck does.

[79] Knudson, *Validity of Religious Experience*, 187.

[80] Knudson, *Present Tendencies*, 188. For similar examples, see *Doctrine of Redemption*, 388, 412.

[81] For dehistoricization in philosophy, see Stout, *Flight from Authority*, 4. See also Anthony Thiselton, *The Two Horizons: New Testament Hermeneutics and Philosophical Description* (Grand Rapids, MI: Eerdmans, 1980), 64.

[82] Robert T. Osborn, "From Theology to Religion," *Modern Theology* 8 (Jan. 1992): 82.

[83] Taylor, *Sources of the Self*, 267. This also seems to be a universalization of the nominalists' *facere quod in se est*. For a discussion of this in medieval theologian Gabriel Biel, see Heiko Augustinus Oberman, *A Harvest of Medieval Theology: Gabriel Biel and Late Medieval Nominalism*, rev. ed. (Grand Rapids, MI: Eerdmans, 1967).

[84] This clarifies the context in which Schleiermacher essentially set aside the doctrine of creation in favor of a doctrine of providence, or as he called it, preservation (*The Christian Faith*, 142–56). The latter was available to any believer via elucidation from the "feeling of absolute dependence," while the other was an historically remote event (at best).

[85] Taylor, *Sources*, 273.

[86] Harrison, *Religion*, 5.

[87] For examples see Knudson, *Doctrine of Redemption*, 116, 489; Knudson, "Religious Apriorism," 121.

[88] I use Frei's term here. Although I will argue later that actual history is essential, it is not essential at this point of the argument. See the discussion in Nicholas Wolterstorff, *Divine Discourse: Philosophical Reflections on the Claim that God Speaks* (New York: Cambridge University Press, 1995), 232ff.

It is curious that Lessing speaks of the *"regula fidei"* as the content of the creed, and yet at the same time proceeds as if it has no relation to history. Gotthold Ephraim Lessing, *Lessing's Theological Writings*, ed. and trans. Henry Chadwick (Stanford: Stanford University Press, 1956), 62.

[89] Ronald Thiemann suggests that there are two ways narrative has been used in recent theology. The first uses narrative as the latest structure for discovering foundations for theology. The second, which he prefers, sees narrative as a necessary tool for interpreting the Bible. Using this second understanding "Theology . . . is the description or redescription of biblical narrative into a coherent language which displays the logic of Christian belief" (*Revelation and Theology*, 83f).

[90] Langdon B. Gilkey, "Cosmology, Ontology, and the Travail of Biblical Language," in *God's Activity in the World: The Contemporary Problem*, ed. Owen C. Thomas (Chico, CA: Scholar's Press, 1983), 40.

[91] "That in the past Christianity made many historical affirmations that were unwarranted and nonessential to the Christian faith is now generally conceded. The science of biblical criticism has relegated much of what was supposed to be history to the realm of legend and untrustworthy tradition" (Knudson, *Doctrine of God*, 140).

[92] Preachers usually call these "principles."

[93] In addition to previously cited references see also "Personalistic Tendency," 58.

94 Hauerwas, *Aliens*, 90.

95 For more on modern dehistoricization, see Alister McGrath, *Genesis of Doctrine: A Study in the Foundations of Doctrinal Criticism* (Oxford: Basil Blackwell, 1990), chs. 4–5, esp. p. 132ff.

96 From the seventeenth through the nineteenth centuries there were extremely close ties between church and state in western European nations. The State had learned from the Reformation how to keep its people united religiously. For this reason, theological differences were less likely to result in divided churches.

97 Lindbeck is quite aware, however, of the broader incoherences in our culture that result in what MacIntyre speaks of as "interminable debates." George Lindbeck, "The Church's Mission to a Postmodern Culture," in *Postmodern Theology: Christian Faith in a Pluralist World*, ed. Frederick B. Burnham. (San Francisco: Harper, 1989), 49. See MacIntyre's discussion in *After Virtue: A Study in Moral Theory*, 2nd ed. (Notre Dame, IN: University of Notre Dame Press, 1984), chs 1–2.

98 This kind of criticism has come both from those who tend toward propositionalism as well as from those Lindbeck would call experiential expressivists. Those who see a need for a propositionalist corrective to Lindbeck: Colman O'Neill, "The Rule Theory of Doctrine and Propositional Truth," *The Thomist* 49 (July 1985): 417–42; McGrath, *The Genesis of Doctrine*; and for an experiential expressivist response: Tracy, "Lindbeck's New Program," 460–72.

99 Lindbeck, *Doctrine*, 7, 20–21, 112. Nancey Murphy critiques Lindbeck on this as well. Cf. *Beyond Liberalism*, 42.

100 For further discussion of this position in modern theology see Holmer, *Grammar of Faith*, 179.

101 Ronald Thiemann has begun development of a non-foundationalist theory of revelation (*Revelation and Theology*).

102 See Bernard M. G. Reardon, *Religion in the Age of Romanticism: Studies in Early Nineteenth Century Thought* (Cambridge: Cambridge University Press, 1985).

103 Lindbeck, *Doctrine*, 16.

104 Lindbeck identifies Karl Rahner and Bernard Lonergan as exemplifying a third approach, seeking to combine the two other approaches. Their position is dismissed quickly as having the same weaknesses of both its components. Strangely, Lindbeck later relies on them, particularly Lonergan to illustrate the experiential expressive point of view—and even to define the meaning of cognitivist positions. On page 31 Lindbeck claims that he settled on Lonergan as the representative of experiential expressivism ". . . both because in this area he is engagingly succinct and also because his two-dimensional approach takes account of a range of theological considerations, not least Roman Catholic ones . . ." which will be the center of attention at a later section of the book. If one author can so well represent multiple positions, it would seem that Lindbeck's whole schema is called into question. Since Lonergan's position can be so easily assimilated to experiential expressivism, I am not considering it as a true third option.

105 Donald A. Luidens, Dean R. Hoge, and Benton Johnson, "The Emergence of Lay Liberalism," *Theology Today* 51 (July 1994): 249-55 highlights the fact that this understanding has been central even in the thinking of the laity. The larger work of which this is a part is *Vanishing Boundaries: The Religion*

The Modern Marginalization of Doctrine   49

of Mainline Protestant Baby Boomers (Louisville, KY: Westminster/John Knox, 1994).

[106] Lindbeck, *Doctrine*, 32.

[107] Ibid., 33.

[108] Ibid., 20.

[109] Ibid., 19.

[110] Though he is critical of Lindbeck's understanding of the nature of doctrine, Alister McGrath sees the postliberalism that accompanies it as potentially beneficial for his own Anglican tradition. Cf. *The Renewal of Anglicanism* (Harrisburg, PA: Morehouse Publishing, 1993), 113.

[111] James W. McClendon, Jr., *Doctrine: Systematic Theology, Volume II* (Nashville: Abingdon, 1994), 23ff.

[112] Lindbeck, *Doctrine*, 78. At least this is what I take him to be referring to when he says, "The overcoming of the current aversion to doctrinal standards and its replacement by concern for correct doctrine depends much more on social and ecclesial developments than on the solution of the theoretical questions with which this book is concerned, yet theory does have a role to play."

[113] Ibid., 17.

[114] Remember that this absolute propositionalist is, for the most part, an idealized fictional character. It does appear that C.F.H. Henry does come close, however. See George Hunsinger's discussion. "What Can Evangelicals and Postliberals Learn from Each Other?" in *The Nature of Confession: Evangelicals and Postliberals in Conversation*, ed. Timothy R. Phillips and Dennis L. Okholm (Downers Grove, IL: InterVarsity Press, 1996), 142.

[115] Lindbeck, *Doctrine*, 74.

[116] Ibid.

[117] Lindbeck, *Doctrine*, 120–1.

[118] Frei, *Eclipse*.

[119] Lindbeck, *Doctrine*, 121.

[120] Lindbeck, *Doctrine*, 122.

[121] Ibid.

[122] Ibid.

[123] Lindbeck, *Doctrine*, 68.

[124] McGrath, *The Genesis of Doctrine*, 31, 37.

[125] Lindbeck, *Doctrine*, 63–67.

[126] I will treat Lindbeck's philosophy of language and utilization of speech act theory in chapter two.

[127] Lindbeck, *Doctrine*, 67f., 83.

[128] Peter Harrison makes the case that this use of religion as an overarching category is a peculiarly modern phenomenon. Indebted to Wilfred Cantwell Smith, Harrison argues that in the modern period religion "... came to be an outsider's description of a dubious theological enterprise." Harrison, "Religion," 1ff. Stories like the blind men and the elephant come to mind. Several blind people (adherents of various religions in this parable) are feeling an elephant to learn its nature. One feels the trunk and declares the elephant to be a kind of snake. Another, feeling a leg, disagrees, finding it more like a tree. The moral of the story is that only the outsider, the non-participant in the feeling of the elephant knows the truth: they are all feeling the same thing they simply do not know it. For Smith's discussion of

the questionableness of "religion" see his *The Meaning and End of Religion: A New Approach to the Religious Traditions of Mankind* (New York: Macmillan, 1962).

[129] Lindbeck, *Doctrine*, 32–33. Lindbeck takes this phrase from William Christian, *Meaning and Truth in Religion* (Princeton, NJ: Princeton University Press, 1964), 60ff.

[130] Ludwig Wittgenstein, "Lectures on Religious Belief," in *Lectures and Conversations on Aesthetics, Psychology and Religion*, ed. Cyril Barrett (Oxford: Basil Blackwell, 1966).

[131] The "feeling of absolute dependence" and "limit experiences" are, as theorized, intrinsic parts of human life, and thus available for religious reflection regardless of one's setting.

[132] This criticism applies equally to propositionalists insofar as they, too, are functionally unaware of the communally formative role of doctrine. Conservative blindness to culture has in recent years produced an emphasis on how being a "good Christian" is necessary to being a "good American."

[133] J. L. Austin, *How to Do Things With Words* (Cambridge, MA: Harvard University Press, 1975).

Chapter Two

Doctrine as a Complex Speech Act of the Church

IN THE FIRST CHAPTER I IDENTIFIED THE MARGINALIZATION OF DOCTRINE AS A challenge facing American mainline churches, and the United Methodist Church in particular. I suggested that modernity has been a major factor in this process. Modern commitments, namely, the primacy of epistemology and individualism, along with their conceptual children—procedural rationality, individualism, rejection of tradition, and dehistoricization—have worked together in three ways: they bring particular doctrines into question, produce unhelpful conceptualities of doctrine, and have led to poor performance of doctrine in the church. These three dimensions of doctrinal marginalization are dynamically related.

This chapter begins with a demonstration of how the question of language fits with the understanding of Christianity as a play[1] that I introduced in the previous chapter. This model, so foreign to modern sensibilities, fits well with postmodern positions. I will illustrate this with a brief look at some of the features of various postmodern philosophies of language, drawing principally on J. L. Austin, Ludwig Wittgenstein, and Charles Taylor. I will not deal with the entirety of each of their positions, but rather highlight the parts most useful to my project. George Lindbeck in *The Nature of Doctrine* also employs this approach, but key misreadings of Austin[2] make his position unacceptable. The remainder of the chapter will be a dialogue with

Lindbeck about the place of reference, truth, change, and constancy in doctrine.

CHRISTIANITY AS A PLAY

The most helpful and truest controlling image for understanding Christianity is a play. I first picked up this image in N. T. Wright's account of biblical authority. He argues that the way the Bible is authoritative for current believers is analogous to the way the first four acts are authoritative for actors creating a missing fifth act for a five-act play. This authority does not lie in telling actors what to say and do (for those things have already been said and done), but how to continue in such a way as to bring the play to resolution.[3] The beginning of this play is depicted in the Old Testament and continues through the biblical narratives. In the Bible, we see many twists and turns in the plot as well as subplots that sometimes seem difficult to tie into the main story line. That the Bible is at heart one story is a contested theological position, both as to its unity and as to which story line is the center. I will not attempt to demonstrate the unity of the Bible, but will assume the unity (which may be a weak unity) postulated by the canonical tradition of the church. Such a unity is only the beginning point of my position. The larger picture is that it is essential to see that the drama did not end with the last event described or the last book written. Christians today are clearest in their own self-understanding when they see themselves as actors in the continuing story of what God is doing with creation. Thus, it is not only the unity of the Bible that is in view, but the unity of the history narrated there along with the history of the church since then.

Speech as an Act

Given the controlling image of Christianity as a drama, doctrine can be understood as a complex speech act of the church. Actors act. One of their chief actions is speaking. When an actor is asked to perform a role in a play—Polonius in "Hamlet" for example—he does not just pick up the script and start acting. Good acting requires a knowledge of the play as a whole: its setting, atmosphere, plot, and characters. What kind of person *is* Polonius? What are his relationships with the other characters? What motivates him? The questions the actor asks must be drawn out through study, practice, and interaction with the other actors.

The actors are not the only ones necessary for a successful play. The director stands on the edge of the play and keeps an eye on the big picture. While the actors immerse themselves in their own character and place in the story, the director is able to provide guidance and help them work together. The director sometimes will have to overrule an actor's interpretation of a part to bring cohesiveness to the whole.

Characteristics of the Play

What I am calling the Christian play differs in some important ways from this brief sketch of a play by a human author. First, though in a sense we would say God is the author of the play, each actor's role includes a substantial degree of innovation and creative adaptation of traditional material. Second, unlike most plays, this play is open and largely indeterminate. Though scripture gives us some images and descriptions of how the play will turn out, there is much we do not know. Thirdly, the Christian play is totalizing in a way ordinary plays are not. On Broadway it is quite natural for people essential to the play (the producer, the director, and the stagehands) not to be in the play itself. In the Christian play, however, every role is part of the play itself. There is no "outside."

This last point has two important implications. First, it is a claim that Christianity naturally and necessarily pursues a metanarrative. Because of this, it will be necessary to argue against the type of postmodernism some find articulated by Jean-François Lyotard. This argument will be developed in chapter four. Second, claiming there is no outside seems to be a claim for the type of universality sought by modernity, an explicit denial of the diversity we know all too well. Later in this chapter I will deal with the consequences of this for understanding doctrine as a speech act of the church. I will suggest that real diversity must be acknowledged—and maintained, while at the same time seeing language games united not by nature, but by the contingent actions of the people inhabiting them.

At this point, my defense of the totalizing of the Christian play is theological, not philosophical. The Christian tradition teaches that God is the creator of all that is, and all who are.[4] This same tradition claims that God's action from the very beginning has been centered on bringing all people into a perfect relationship with Him. The invitation offered through preaching the gospel is not merely, "Come and be saved," but is also, "Come and become a willing participant in what God is doing in history." A quick glance at the world today shows us that not all *are* intentional participants—clearly many do not appear to be acting in this story. The Christian tradition turns to the biblical narratives that depict the sinfulness of humanity, showing that more often than not, humans prefer to live by their own plans rather than

God's. From this perspective what we see is the Christian play operating alongside numerous other plays—plays that appear to be autonomous and unrelated, yet according to the Christian tradition, as "the world" they are constituted by opposition to God. Not surprisingly, very few, if any, competing plays (if self-reflective) would accept such a characterization. Not only would their self-description *not* be, "We're against God"—they may even deny that they are collectively actors in a play of any coherence. What this shows is that my model is not neutral. It is not the sort of model that will be accepted by any rational person anywhere who simply considers the facts. It is not just a suggestion of how best to understand doctrine, but is at its core the articulation of a position on the nature and purpose of the church.

Doctrine and the Play

In what I have called the marginalization of doctrine, modernity has convinced the church that modernity's metanarrative is the true one. Freedom, justice, and procedural rationality are the most important elements of that narrative. Christianity and other religions can exhibit and illustrate these virtues but a key claim of modernity in its secularized forms is that religion is not necessary and indeed is a hindrance to attainment of these virtues. In this social environment, increasingly dominated not only by the intellectual ideal but by also the political reality of individualism, a propositionalist conceptualization of doctrine could not stand. This is what Lindbeck is getting at when he says,

> Fewer and fewer contemporary people are deeply embedded in particular religious traditions or thoroughly involved in particular religious communities. This makes it hard for them to perceive or experience religion in cognitivist fashion as the acceptance of sets of objectively and immutably true propositions. Perhaps only those among whom the sects chiefly recruit who combine unusual insecurity with naiveté can easily manage to do this.

Many have commented on Lindbeck's inflammatory rhetoric at the end of this passage. What we see here is not a development of his philosophical analysis, but of his Lutheran ecclesiology. It would strengthen his position greatly if he were able to see that Constantinian ecclesiology robbed the church of a major resource to stand against modernity. It is chiefly the "sects'" ability to see themselves as distinct from society at large that enabled them to resist the modern attempt to metanarrate them into submission.[5] Experiential expressivism also accepted the modern metanarrative. While propositionalists still tended to seek universality (in the context of implicit submission to modern ideals), experiential expressivists would admit that Christianity was its own thing, while other religions were their own things, each autonomously operating in the modern world. The ideal goal of each was to seek coherence with modernity.

Although the imagery of the Christian play is totalizing, the place of doctrine is not. Doctrine is a speech act of the church, but not all church or Christian speech is doctrine. In ordinary plays the description of the setting, plot, and characters and the guidance of how to perform the drama are not within the drama itself, but function as adjuncts to performance. Doctrine *is* part of the Christian play and is shaped and formed in the context of the play. Just as there is no human external to the play, there is no external vantage point from which doctrine can be formulated. The church, therefore, is never in a place where it can see the whole of the drama when it makes doctrine.

Postmodern philosophy of language is most helpful at this point because it rejects both the central emphases of modernity—the centrality of epistemology and individualism—while opening new possibilities for an action-oriented perspective. All three scholars I consider in the next section insist that language be seen, not as an adjunct to epistemology—the *form* of our knowledge—but as a characteristically human action. They all see this action as inherently *social*, inexplicable from the perspective of an individual isolated from a linguistic community. In a play, the speech is clearly action, action that makes sense only in the context of the (at least minimally) coordinated actions of others.

DOCTRINAL LANGUAGE AND MODERNITY

> Christ did truly rise again from the dead, and took again his body, with all things appertaining to the perfection of man's nature, wherewith he ascended into heaven, and there sitteth until he return to judge all men at the last day.
> United Methodist Articles of Religion, Article III

The statement above *looks* like a straightforward proposition about the resurrection and future return of Christ. It does not look like it does anything other than state a fact and an expectation. Taken as a proposition, some would judge it true, some false. Some would probably want some clarification before they could say one way or the other, but most would think, regardless of their personal ability to judge, the statement was *either* true or false. Such an approach leaves a number of questions unanswered, though the most interesting of these are questions that would not occur in a modern context.

First: Whose statement is this? Does it make any difference who makes this claim? If we limit ourselves to the Christian church, would it make any difference in our understanding of this statement if it were offered by an individual theologian, by a Sunday School teacher or by a denominational assembly? These are questions of personal contextualization. Modernity would often have us believe that a statement's meaning—and truth or falsity—can be determined apart from any questions of origin and context.

The second question is that of temporal context. Does it make any difference *when* this statement was made? Has it been offered as a once for all statement or merely to meet the needs of a particular time and place? Does it make any difference if this statement originated a thousand years ago or last week? Is it significant that this form of the doctrine was derived from the Anglican form, and so forth, evidencing a rich history of doctrinal reflection?[6] Again, modernity would have us decontextualize the statement and approach it timelessly. Statements deal with facts and facts either are or are not true. Of course, modernity also assumes (though often not at the same time it is articulating this decontextualization assumption) that the more recent a statement, the more likely it is to be true. If pushed, they would say this is because statements that are more recent are more likely to have passed through the critical fires of modern science.

A third unanswered question, and perhaps the most momentous, is whether this doctrine is to be questioned beyond its meaning and truth. What is the doctrine of Christ's resurrection supposed to do? Words like "believe," "hope," and "know" knock against each other, trying to claim exclusive rights to conceptual territory. Pastors come out of mainline seminaries knowing that the official doctrine of their denomination affirms the resurrection of Jesus—and consequently the resurrection of those who belong to him. Their enculturation in the convictions of modern academia, however, often prevent them from saying any more than this.[7] If meaning and truth are the only things to be sought, we are limited in available explanations for the marginalization of doctrine. In chapter one we saw that it was quite possible for the truth of a doctrinal statement to remain unquestioned while that very doctrine was marginalized. We saw also that it was possible to reinterpret doctrine—to change the meaning and maintain the evaluation of its truthfulness—and still have the doctrine marginalized. Although the key way in which doctrine is marginalized in the modern church lies in performance, this lack of performance is rooted in modernity's conceptualizations of doctrine that have not even allowed us to ask what doctrine does.

Such an accusation is easily refuted. Of course, modernity allows such questions. Doctrine states truths—if one is a propositionalist, or doctrine expresses and symbolizes human experience—if one is an experiential expressivist. Being open-minded, I could admit that doctrine (or at least particular doctrines) may well do both of these. But is that all doctrine does?

Postmodern Philosophy of Language

Language, we know, does more than make true or false statements. Perhaps in spite of the fact that this third Article of Religion *looks* like a proposition, it is really more akin to a cheer: "I like Jesus!" or something along those lines. Better yet, perhaps, observant people such as we are, might judge that this is a *religious* statement, and develop a theory of how religious statements work within their own world of linguistic meaning. Perhaps in this way we may be able to say that truth or falsity is still what such a statement is about, but that it may be true for you but not for me. It seems clear that we need to go beyond what appears on the surface to understand what is going on in doctrine. To this end I now consider three postmodern approaches to language.

J. L. Austin

Though unconcerned with "religious" speech, the kind of questions I am asking about doctrine are similar to those which led J. L. Austin to develop his theory of speech acts.[8] The trajectory of twentieth-century philosophy of language began with questions of how language did the work of description and representation. The inadequacy of the conviction that language's central job was to be true or false came to be seen as philosophers both examined language more closely and tried to find a theory of language justifiable in terms of foundationalism. More and more instances of language use seemed not to be true *or* false, leading philosophers to label them meaningless. Problems arose when these theories labeled much of ordinary language meaningless—in spite of the fact that language users seemed to be doing just fine.[9] Austin saw this as a prime indication that the underlying theory was wrong.

In the midst of these problems produced by modern philosophies of language, Austin proposed a different way of looking at language. At the base of his new approach lay a new category of speech acts, "performatives," which are not the stating of some fact, but the doing of an action. The common example given is the "I do" uttered in the context of a wedding. This is neither a description of marriage nor the utterance of feeling about the same. Rather, it is the making of a marriage. It should be immediately obvious how attractive such an approach would be to my model. Knowledge and personal expression have a part in plays, but action is the broadest way to characterize what happens. It is a serious mistake, however, to use Austin's work only to introduce the performative. If we stop here, we fail to get beyond the modern philosophy of language Austin faced: we have simply added one more kind of language. After Austin (if Austin is taken as merely identifying the performative) we now have several types of language: description, expression, nonsense, and the performative. What is most important about Austin's work is not the identification of the performative, but the conclusion that all language use has a performative dimension. Speech is an *action*, done by humans in the context of some social setting to accomplish some goal.

As he investigates the performative (and before he rejects it as an independent category), Austin tries various strategies to set the performative apart from statements (and other forms of speech). The most important qualification he proposes is truth. Constatives are statements whose chief characteristic is being true or false. Performatives, it initially appears, are neither true nor false, but happy or unhappy. A close examination, however, uncovers the fact that constatives can fail in ways other than being false, *and* that one dimension of the happiness of performatives is the way they fit with the world, a component of traditional theories of truth. The details of Austin's analysis are not essential for us to look at in depth, so I will let several examples suffice.[10] "France is a hexagon." Is this true? Well, sort of. Its geographical shape is roughly hexagonal. But how exact must we be? In such a case, it is hard to say whether this is exactly true or not. Or, staying in the same country, how do we assess, "The King of France is bald," when there is no king of France? Do we simply say it is false? Considering some of the ways constatives can fail, Austin concludes that happiness, a broader concept than truth, was highly relevant to non-performatives as well. It also works the other way. Though performatives are not usually strictly true or false, they do frequently rely on conditions in the world for their success. This notion of happiness (or "felicity") is one of the most useful products of Austin's theory, as we will see below.

Austin's analysis of speech acts picks out three kinds of acts that take place in saying something. These acts are to be *logically* distinguished, and are not understood as discrete instances of speech. The first kind he terms a

> *locutionary act*, which is roughly equivalent to uttering a certain sentence with a certain sense and reference, which again is roughly equivalent to 'meaning' in the traditional sense. Second, we said that we also perform *illocutionary acts* such as informing, ordering, warning, undertaking, etc., i.e., utterances which have a certain conventional force. Thirdly, we may also perform *perlocutionary acts*: what we bring about or achieve *by* saying something, such as convincing, persuading, deterring, and even, say, surprising or misleading.[11]

For our analysis, illocutionary acts will be the most important category. I will also need to apply this analysis not only to literal *speech* acts, but also to written acts, since doctrine is often encountered in this form. I will also need to consider this analysis applicable to texts (complex sets of speech acts) and not simply to the individual sentences of which they are composed.[12]

Later in his work, Austin identifies five broadly conceived types of illocutionary act. These five—verdictives, exercitives, commissives, behabitives, and expositives—each have some relation to their subject matter (in some this relation is central to understanding the act, in others much less so), and some kind of relation between the speaker and the hearer (sometimes intimate, sometimes distant). Austin has a useful section not merely defining each type, but contrasting each with the others.[13] John Searle thinks Austin's categories are too artificial—speech acts really are much too varied to fit into only five categories.[14] The definition of each category is not essential to my case, but the notion that they can be differentiated at all will be important later in this chapter when I consider Lindbeck's regulative theory of doctrine.

The most important appropriation of Austin's work for religion is the work on convictions done by James McClendon and James Smith.[15] They consider both individual and communal convictions, but since my position is that doctrine is a communal phenomenon, I will consider that side of their work only. They begin by defining *conviction*.

> A conviction ... means a persistent belief such that if X (a person or community) has a conviction, it will not easily be relinquished and it cannot be relinquished without making X a significantly different person (or community) than before.[16]

Given such a definition, it is easy to see that a person or community can have convictions about any number of things. The language of convictions enables us to move beyond the confines of modern epistemology and to discover new options for understanding religious speech. Since convictions are also communal in nature, this approach opens a way beyond modern individualism. Within modern philosophy of language religious utterances could be understood as pure statements of fact (like the statements we find in science), they could be expressions of personal feeling (or attitudes), or they could be meaningless verbalisms. By approaching convictions from an Austinian perspective, McClendon and Smith are able to consider religious language on its own terms, in all its diversity, without at the same time moving such language into a world all its own.

Clearly, the evaluation of religious statements depends on their classification: we evaluate statements of our attitudes differently than statements of fact. Following Austin's discovery of the performative dimension of *some* speech, widening this discovery to see the performative dimension of *all* speech, and coming to the conclusion that bare fact-stating description is *not* the root function of language, the world is opened to consideration of confession (McClendon and Smith provide a detailed analysis of confession as a speech act), witness, prayer, worship, and other types of speech act found in Christianity. There is no longer a need to assimilate all of these into one category, or find a single (and simple) form of evaluation ("true" or "false" is the most common).

McClendon and Smith are very clear that even in their consideration of the happiness of religious speech acts and the rejection of the adequacy of truth questions *alone*, truth, or some form of connection with the world, still has an essential role to play. In their analysis of the factors contributing to the happiness of a speech act, they speak of this as the "representative" dimension. They say,

> For a speech-act to be *happy*, it is not sufficient that it be a possible speech act in that community and that both speakers and hearers have the appropriate affective states for that speech-act in that community. Language, including religious language, is not only a way of connecting the members of a community with each other—including the connecting of those past others who helped create the linguistic community and those future others who are its heirs. Language also connects its speakers, the members of the community, to the world, and *that* connection must be appropriate if the conventionally permitted speech-act with its successful affective conditions is to be happy.[17]

This quest for a connection with reality, something common to many convictional communities is radically different from the modern quest for certainty. The key difference lies in the contextualization of the connection with reality. No statement is simply and only a description of reality. It is also always a human action in a particular situation. McClendon and Smith's claim is the minimal one: there is more to reality than our language—we are not mired in subjectivism or solipsism—but this connection with reality cannot be completely differentiated from the other things language does.[18]

If doctrine is to be seen as a communal speech act of the church that makes it possible for the church to live the Christian narrative faithfully, these features of Austinian speech-act theory will prove helpful. Beyond the obvious feature—speech as action—the theory offers a way for doctrine to be understood on its own terms, and not merely as a religious kind of proposition or expression of attitude. Though the Christian drama includes others through metanarration, there remains a constant interplay between competing narratives as they are lived out by different communities. If communal discourse is a self-enclosed phenomenon, with no connection to anything beyond—and here I do not speak of something akin to Kant's noumena, but in the most general sense of anything, i.e., cultures, communities, etc.—then we are left with (from a philosophical point of view) Nietzscheanism and its arbitrary will to power, or (from a political-cultural point of view) Bosnia with its "whoever has the strongest army" ethos. I will speak more about doctrine and reality below.

Austin's theory is also helpful in broadening the field of evaluation. Since doctrine is not to be assimilated to other forms of speech, it must be evaluated on its own terms. When the church "doctrines"[19] it aims not only to utter true statements, but statements that forward its mission. Happy doctrine then, at the very least, would aim for truth (in an appropriate sense), coherence (with other doctrine), appropriateness to the situation, capability of being lived—and lived in love. While doctrine serves the broad purpose of forming and directing the church, I would not assume that all doctrines are exactly the same kind of speech act. In other words, doctrine is a broad category containing various subcategories. Using our dramatic analogy, we might speak of the broad category of "direction," which in turn contains various kinds of instruction, description, command, suggestion, inquiry, etc.

Finally, Austin enables us to understand speech—and therefore, doctrine—as a communal activity.[20] Doctrine, like all speech, is to be understood in the context of a community. Doctrine is to be evaluated not merely on the basis of how it fits with reality, but with how it functions in the community. This latter point is essential. Austin's term (which McClendon and Smith appropriate) is "uptake." Doctrine is one of the kinds of speech act that cannot be happy unless it is heard properly—if uptake does not happen. "Reception" is the theological equivalent of "uptake." The nature of doctrine is such that, not only is doctrine unhappy if it is not heard, it also is not doctrine unless at some point it is properly "received" by the church. I will discuss reception in greater detail below. Suffice it to say now that speech-act theory enables us to understand this traditional doctrine in a new light (in fact, in a way impossible in the context of modernity).[21]

Ludwig Wittgenstein

We see in Wittgenstein some of the same contrasts with modernity that we saw in Austin. The most obvious of these is his insistence that language is a human *action*. This is highlighted in his concept of language games. The two models are contrasted when he says, "Giving grounds, . . . justifying the evidence, comes to an end;—but the end is not certain propositions striking us immediately as true, i.e., it is not a kind of *seeing* on our part; it is our *acting*, which lies at the bottom of the language-game."[22] The modern view stemming from Descartes and built on foundationalist epistemology leaves us with the mind in a box *looking* out on a silent world. Wittgenstein, on the other hand, offers us a world based on human action. With language games we find also a reconceptualization of reason. While foundationalism might allow for autonomous or semiautonomous areas of thought, everything had to fit the same methods of justification. If this is what makes something rational, then language games are not rational. Wittgenstein comments, "You must keep in mind that the language game is so to say something unpredictable. I mean: it is not based on grounds. It is not reasonable (or unreasonable). It is there—like our life."[23] This is in direct contrast to the Cartesian system of radical doubt and reconstruction on an indubitable foundation.

If we synthesize Austin's and Wittgenstein's insights, we might say that language games are the arena for speech acts. Language games provide the system of conventions that provide a structure of meaning for human activities.[24] These language games are fractally related: it is not that one level of speech or action is a "form of life," another a "language game," and yet another a "speech act." Though each of these can be logically distinguished, we always find them together, whatever the level of attention to discourse. The key feature of fractals is selfsame structure on all levels of the entity. Shorelines and trees are classic examples. When we look at a map of the east coast of the United States, for example, we see the irregularities of the coast. These irregularities remain no matter the scale on which we consider that coastline. When we look at a tree, we see branching at all levels, from the main trunk through the smallest twigs. Though the language of fractals originated after Wittgenstein's death, it fits well in his analysis of language games. In one place he gives some examples of language games:

> Giving orders, and obeying them—
> Describing the appearance of an object, or giving its measurements—
> Reporting an event—
> Speculating about an event—
> Translating from one language to another—
> Asking, thanking, cursing, greeting, praying.[25]

Notice how many of these actions can include some of the others. For example, reporting an event can include describing an object. Referring to one of his examples of a simple language game (handling building stones), Wittgenstein says,

> We can also think of the whole process of using words in (2) [his sample language game] as one of these games by means of which children learn their native language. I will call these games "language games" and will sometimes speak of a primitive language as a language game. And the processes of naming stones and or repeating words after someone might also be called language games. . . . I will also call the whole, consisting of language and the actions into which it is woven, the "language game."[26]

Not only can each type of speech be considered a language game, but so can the whole. By speaking of a language *game*, Wittgenstein is able to emphasize several features of language at once: action, interlocking systems of conventions, human involvement, and infinite diversity. It is not the case that every language game borders every other; but unlike physical space, there is always room to build new language games or links between existing games.[27]

Language games are extremely flexible. In a fascinating passage Wittgenstein says,

> ask yourself whether our language is complete; —whether it was so before the symbolism of chemistry and the notation of the infinitesimal calculus were incorporated in it; for these are, so to speak, the suburbs of our language. (And how many houses of streets does it take before a town begins to be a town?) Our language can be seen as an ancient city: a maze of little streets and squares, of old and new

houses, and of houses with additions from various periods; and this surrounded by a multitude of new boroughs with straight regular streets and uniform houses.[28]

We see a number of important points in this text. First, it is very difficult to say a language game is complete. On the other hand, it seems that it would also be hard to say it is not complete. The largest scale language game is not like a puzzle with predefined places for each piece. The only time one might be able to say a language game is incomplete (or complete) is when one is in the construction phase. At these times, "complete" means "good enough for the purposes we now intend." Even at this point, however, such judgments are provisional. This brings into the picture an important temporal element. Language games do not remain the same but change through time. Each is what it is through historical development.

A second feature we see in Wittgenstein's image of the city is the diversity and yet ultimate coherence of human language. Like a city, there may be vast animosity between one section and another. Two neighborhoods may even deny the existence (or right to existence) of the other. The coherence that language shows on this larger scale is not a rational coherence but rather a coherence that can only be seen in social relations. It is also highly contingent. It may be the case that two neighborhoods, though in the same city, have never had anything to do with one another; but will next week. This kind of coherence allows for many kinds of incoherence and inconsistency, on the part of both individuals and communities.

Third, the identification of the center of the city is arbitrary. Bankers would identify their district as the heart of the city, while the bishop might suggest the cathedral. Some would suggest their home as the central location. Each group means something slightly different by "center," though each would, I believe, know what the other is talking about even while disagreeing. The location of the center is not a cartographic act, but a communal act.

The image breaks down, however, if we try to take it too literally in terms of space. In an actual city there may be no room for building a new store or neighborhood without tearing down one already in existence. There is no such limitation on developing or extending language games. There is always room for another building. This is another aspect of the fractalicity of language games mentioned above. On one level a fractal may look like a simple curve. When magnified, however, curves within curves are discovered. Though these curves in turn look simple, from the right perspective, further magnification shows yet more curves. We can see this in the act of description, for example. However complete our description of something may appear at a given moment, that description can always be expanded. As people inhabit forms of life and use language games, there is always room for expansion and development.

In our consideration of speech-act theory we noted that one of its strengths is that it allows language to be connected with reality. Though Wittgenstein is frequently considered an antirealist, there are hints in his writing that such an assessment is wide of the mark. In fact, such a view is most likely due either to evaluating his position from the standpoint of modern epistemological convictions—"since foundationalism is the only way to access reality, Wittgenstein's rejection of foundationalism means he rejects realism"—or to a preoccupation with combating modern antirealism. Since antirealism is one outcome of an experiential expressivist approach to religion, it is not surprising that some experiential expressivists might look to Wittgenstein as an ally, while opponents of that position would see Wittgenstein as merely another enemy to be refuted.[29]

What must be avoided in this process is a Cartesian pursuit of realism. That model, in which the lonesome individual begins the search inwardly, stripped of all particularity, leads to a peculiarly modern form of realism. All that an individual standing nowhere has to begin with is a method, a rational procedure to identify reality and differentiate it from "mere appearance." Against this model Wittgenstein insists,

> I did not get my picture of the world by satisfying myself
> of its correctness; nor do I have it because I am satisfied of
> its correctness. No: it is the inherited background against
> which I distinguish between true and false.[30]

While Austin's realism seems characterized by attention to a connection with reality, Wittgenstein's approach is characterized by an awareness that the question of realism is misguided. All speakers grow up in the world, learning to speak and interact, not only with other people, but also with whatever else they run into. In the first example of a language game he offers in *Philosophical Investigations*, the language dealing with building materials, there is no place to doubt the reality of the materials, the contractor,[31] or the building being built. Cartesian doubt and the solipsism it generates are themselves language games, historically contingent, and by no means to be considered normative for all times and places.[32]

The fideism that is often considered characteristic of Wittgensteinians seems to have no place in Wittgenstein himself. One who inhabits a language game is not immune from challenge. He notes, "Certain events would put me into a position in which I could not go on with the old language game any further. In which I was torn away from the *sureness* of the game. Indeed, doesn't it seem obvious that the possibility of a language game is conditioned by certain facts."[33] Wittgenstein's position would, some claim, leave us in a place where we can avoid the modern debates between realism and nonrealism. Such a position, however, seems to ignore our historical location in this debate. Though the two reigning positions are rendered groundless by our rejection of their foundation, we still find ourselves faced with their superstructures. This calls for an anti-antirealist stance, which, for all its inelegance, may prove more rhetorically satisfying than merely denying the problem (which almost inevitably sounds like an antirealist position).[34]

Wittgenstein's work supports my model of doctrine in three key ways. The first two ways are found also in Austin: insofar as doctrine is speech, it is action. Also, the focus on speech does not require either fideism or nonrealism. The third point of support is found in the way language games interrelate. The starting point in doctrine is not any particular doctrine itself (none are foundational) but in living the Christian narrative. It is also the case that not all doctrines will appear to operate on the same level logically. The factor that differentiates doctrine both from theology and from ordinary Christian utterance is not found in the form of the words, but in their role as a speech act of the church. This latter point is not required by use of Wittgenstein, but certainly is permissible.

As a system, doctrine has a unity, yet this unity is not something given once for all. Rather, the quest for unity—for coherence—is a continual work of the church. As the church lives the Christian narrative, encountering competing and neighboring narratives, new development will be necessary. Change would be necessary even if there were no neighbors, since one factor in the development of doctrine is the Christian past—the narrative as it has been lived up until now. One hundred years from now the past that Christians include in the their narrative will include that hundred years not included now. Within the Christian tradition it is not hard to support the position that there is always more of God to know than we know at any moment. Thus there are both external and internal drives toward change. From within, the more we come to know of God, the more we must develop and refine what we say. From without, as the church encounters new questions and new groups who do not know of Jesus, we are compelled to find ways to express doctrine that will ease their way into the kingdom.

As far as Wittgensteinian "realism" goes, we need not see ourselves in the place of a presupposed Kantianism that can get no farther than Hans Vaihinger's *as if*. As we live the Christian story we are not merely acting *as if* there really is a God, *as if* Jesus truly defeated sin and death, *as if* God remains an agent in the day-to-day living out of the story. Though this may be one possible view from outside the narrative, if I read Wittgenstein rightly, there is no reason to suppose it the necessary or best reading. When I consider Charles Taylor's "Best Account Principle" below, we will see a further reason to move in this direction. What I am providing is a view of Christianity from inside, not from a neutral point outside. That a neutral point is an artificial construct, a masquerade, in fact, seems indisputable. I see no reason to join the pretense.

Charles Taylor

A theme that has run through Charles Taylor's work over the past thirty years, impacting both his methodology and his substantive positions, is the need to dialogue with modernity. Taylor writes as one who is consciously at odds with many characteristically modern positions, yet with a less polemical attitude toward modernity than many have expressed. He recognizes that modernity has not been entirely bad. A key tool Taylor relies on is historical narration, showing how the positions we take for granted today developed. The best example of this is his *The Sources of the Self*.

Taylor's approach to the question of language is to consider the competing proposals coming out of modernity, the "designative" and the "expressive," as he terms them. Though there is a connection between Lindbeck's and Taylor's uses of "expressive"—their common rootage in Romantic philosophy—there is much difference in focus. As Lindbeck explicates his analysis of experiential expressivism he shows that it retains a focus on designation. The *designata* of religious language are not in the world outside, but are found in experience. Taylor's focus is on the action of expressing, and thus he explicitly avoids the modern dichotomization.[35]

For Taylor, any account of language must account for both the designative and expressive dimensions. Taylor sees the expressive dimension as, in a sense, more fundamental, since it is the expressive that focuses on language as action.[36] Modernity has a strong tendency toward the designative or representational dimension, intimately connected with the epistemological stance of modern science. As he puts it, early theorists of language were not so much looking to understand language *qua* language, but language *qua scientific* language. What designative/representationalist theories made possible was the elimination of the humanity of the scientist so true objectivity could be achieved. Taylor says that for moderns

> A representation ... is of an independent reality. ... There are all kinds of knowing, from knowings how, to knowing people intimately, which do not have to be construed representationally. We have a temptation to do so when we reflect, because we are inheritors of this modern movement in philosophy which made representation basic. I am suggesting that one of the stronger motives for making it so basic was the desire to overcome projection, and what we later call 'anthropomorphism,' that promiscuous mixing of our own intuitions of meaning, relevance, importance with objective reality.[37]

Taylor's position, then, is based on a rejection of the epistemology, individualism, and decontextualization dominant in modernity. This leads him to base his theory on the expressive dimension, not in contrast to designation or representation, but as the broader and more inclusive category.

From within a view of language as human action, Taylor identifies three main functions language serves. These functions slice up the subject much differently than the designative/expressive division. In fact, each of the functions depends on holding both these dimensions together. The first two functions are fairly easy to explain: articulation and the creation of public space. The third is built on these two and requires fuller explanation. I turn first to articulation.

The best way to understand what Taylor means by articulation, a concept prominent not only in his philosophical papers, but also in *Sources of the Self*, is to consider some of his descriptions. He says, "In language we formulate things. Through language we can bring to explicit awareness what we formerly had only an implicit sense of. Through formulating some matter, we bring it to fuller and clearer consciousness."[38] Such formulation, or articulation, arises when we find the need to say something and cannot. It arises from a focused attention to the features of some thing or situation, specifically as we relate to them. We find ourselves in a web of relationships: with other people, with the world, with ourselves. Taylor's focus in *Sources of the Self* is on ethics, so there he speaks of articulacy as the making of a map of the moral universe.[39] One way to describe what the church does in doctrine is the drawing of a map of the theological universe, or better, the

Christian narrative in which we live. The map analogy breaks down, however, because we not only want to know where we are situated and how to move on to our desired location, but also we need to articulate the relations among the other participants in the narrative community: other Christians, non-Christians, God.

In this emphasis on articulation, Taylor's expressivism is differentiated from that of the Romantics. The key difference is in what is being expressed. For the Romantics,

> Expression was self-expression. What comes to full expression are my desires, my aspirations, my moral sentiments. What comes to light in the full development of expressive power is precisely that what was striving for expression all along was the self.[40]

But the focus on language as expressive action allows for other possibilities. It is this possibility we see in the act of formulation.

> What comes about through the development of language in the broadest sense is the coming to be of expressive power, the power to make things manifest. It is not unambiguously clear that this ought to be considered as self-expression/realization. What is made manifest is not exclusively, nor even mainly, the self, but a world.[41]

The Romantics, Taylor suggests, were able to avoid the subjectivist tendencies of their own approach only through a sort of pantheism that served to unite the world and the selves in it. This seems to be what is at work in Schleiermacher's hermeneutics, for example. Gadamer claims that Schleiermacher's work presupposes that "all individuality is a manifestation of universal life and hence 'everyone carries a tiny bit of everyone else within him, so that divination is stimulated by comparison with oneself.' Thus he can say that the individuality of the author can be directly grasped 'by, as it were, transforming oneself into the other.'"[42] As interest in pantheism waned, those who look to expressivism were faced with the choice: either a self *or* a world, not both. Taylor's focus is, as we have seen, on the latter. He suggests that in our linguistic expression we are "responding to the reality in which we are set." Against modern decontextualization he emphasizes that we ourselves are part of this reality, but that it is not "reducible to our experience of it."[43]

Taylor's image of articulation will prove especially powerful as we consider the role of doctrine in the church. Chapter five will tie this together. Before I can do that, however, I need not only consider other dimensions of doctrine as a speech act, but also attend to the nature of the speaker (the church) and of the narrative.

The second function of language is "to place some matter out in the open between interlocutors." This is what Taylor terms "the creation of public space."[44] As an example, he has his readers imagine traveling with him through the desert. He remarks to the other, "Whew, it's hot." This utterance does not serve to inform the hearer of something he or she did not already know. What is going on here is the creation of

> a rapport between us, the kind of thing which comes about when we do what we call striking up a conversation. Previously I knew that you were hot, and you knew that I was hot, and I knew that you must know that I knew that, etc.: up to about any level you care to chase it. But now it is a fact between *us* that it is stifling in here. Language creates what one might call a public space, or a common vantage point from which we survey the world together.[45]

The epistemology and individualism of modernity have produced an approach to language that is unable to account for such public space. According to most modern accounts, communication is all about the transfer of information from one person to another. As Taylor describes it, such a view "deems all states of knowledge and belief to be states of individual knowers and believers. Communication is then the transmittal, or attempted transmittal of such states."[46] This public space is essential to understanding not only conversations, but also the place of institutions in human society. Important dimensions of the narratives we live in are constituted by this kind of speech action.

The third function of language is to provide "the medium through which some of our most important concerns, the characteristically human concerns, can impinge on us at all."[47] Some examples of these things include the theories of science and our moral language, especially with regard to standards. Some uses of language clearly set humans apart from the rest of creation:

> Anger we can attribute to (some) animals, in at least some sense. But indignation we cannot.... The difference is that we can only ascribe indignation to a being with something like the thought: this person has done an injustice. One is only indignant at a wrongdoer.... But what are the conditions for some agent's having a thought like that? It must be that he can make discriminations of the form right/wrong, as against advantageous/disadvantageous, or hurting me/helping me. But this requires that the agent have some notion of standards that hold of a given domain; here it is a matter of moral standards, which hold of human action.... For many living things can be said to 'apply standards' in some loose sense: the cat turns up its nose at sub-standard fish, and only goes for the best. There are some

> standards, in the sense of criteria of acceptability, which will help explain its behavior.... The cat does not recognize that it is applying standards, has not focused on or articulated the standards *qua* standards.[48]

This account gives us further reason to avoid the tendency to reduce theological language to mere personal expression. Theological concepts like salvation seem to fit here. We can imagine a cat being saved—from starvation, from the cold, from a cruel owner. But the salvation the biblical narrative depicts is much more complex than this.[49] Inasmuch as salvation in the scriptures entails a changed relationship (a relationship that provokes reflection and attention through worship and discipleship) and the creation of a people, it seems to be one of those things that require language to exist fully.

Taylor's understanding of the functions of language is very helpful for understanding doctrine's status within the church. First, using his terminology, we can say that doctrine is first of all an articulation of what we live in the Christian narrative. Doctrine is always dependent on that narrative. When we articulate doctrine, we are setting up an account of how the narrative fits together and explicating its logic, which is the logic of our lives together as Christians. This account serves a threefold function. First and most simply, we articulate an idealized account of the narrative itself. Second, Taylor suggests, it enables us to locate ourselves on the map. Such articulacy is a major element in providing our notion of who we are, of our identity. Third, once we have accomplished the first task, we use the map for guidance in the living of our lives. The first action seeks to answer the question, "What is the narrative?" The act of self-identification boils down to a placing of ourselves into the narrative. The third action is acting out the story. The contrast between this and typically modern conceptions of ethics is profound. Articulation is a way of "giving reasons," but is always done in the context of a particular background. It is not an analysis of the basic concepts upon which a position is built, but rather a demonstration of a coherence and fit that was not previously apparent.

Essential to this account of articulacy is what Taylor calls the Best Account or BA Principle. He claims,

> What we need to explain is people living their lives; the terms in which they cannot avoid living them cannot be removed from the *explanandum*, unless we can propose other terms in which they could live them more clairvoyantly. We cannot just leap outside these terms altogether, on the grounds that their logic doesn't fit some model of 'science' and that we know a priori that human beings must be

> explicable in this 'science'... The terms we select have to make sense across the whole range of both explanatory and life uses.... The result of this search for clairvoyance yields the best account we can give at any given time, and no epistemological or metaphysical considerations of a more general kind about science or nature can justify setting this aside.[50]

When we aim to articulate our theological world, our aim is not an absolute and eternally verifiable account that is acceptable and believable by everyone. We see, instead, an account that makes best sense of the totality of who Christians are and of the world they live in—from a perspective internal to the Christian narrative. It must be remembered that we are always already participants in some narrative when we reach the intellectual maturity to reflect on our "options."

Once we see this we can see another reason that doctrine may have become marginalized in modernity, a reason based not so much on specifically modern commitments, but rather the conjunction of such commitments with certain practices in the church. In periods when Christian doctrine has been most successful, it has tended to make Christianity seem obvious to those living within it. This obviousness, however, has led to an emphasis on doctrine itself, rather than the narrative on which it is based. As the narrative recedes in proximity—which it does especially in the context of modern dehistoricizing—doctrine comes to stand on its own.

Why is this a problem? There is always some unarticulated background to our lives, whether it be the Christian narrative we are living or a naturalistic scientific worldview, with its courageous and autonomous moral agents. Inhabiting the latter environment, doctrine has come to be seen as arbitrary, inducing those who hold to it to find some justification for it. But since justification is always internal to some framework of understanding,[51] Christian doctrine finds itself in the uncomfortable place of seeking justification in an alien framework. As we have seen in the past two hundred years, this is a hard, if not impossible, task.

This is one way we can read what has happened. First, the combination of a focus on doctrine with the dehistoricization of modernity led to a marginalization of the narrative. Next, as doctrine operated in an increasingly foreign environment, it became less and less obvious—and this to Christians! The movement we see is from a place where doctrine is obvious, then becomes taken for granted, and finally is marginalized. This can happen because we never live purely and solely within the Christian narrative. When we take doctrine for granted we overidentify the Christian story with the story of the world. Doctrinal decay was combined, of course, with a decay of church life—the performance of doctrine—that came with the rise of individualism.[52] So by the eighteenth-century doctrine had been abstracted from both of its essential settings: the Christian narrative and the church. It is not surprising that the only way left to understand doctrine was as individual beliefs. Taylor does not discuss this process in terms of doctrine, but in terms of misunderstanding.

> Why can someone always misunderstand? And why is it that we do not have to resolve all these potential questions before *we* understand? The answer to these two questions is the same. Understanding always occurs against a background of what is simply relied on and taken for granted.... If the misunderstanding stems from a difference in background, what needs to be said in order to clear it up has the effect of articulating some aspect of the explainer's background that may never before have been articulated.[53]

Therefore, Christian doctrine is not simple articulation—even *Christian* articulation—pure and simple, but must always be tied to the Christian narrative. In chapter four I will further develop both the reasons for the modern rejection of narrative as well as some ways to recover this essential element. The American church today is composed of people who find their basic enculturation in American culture—in the American narrative of success—and not in the Christian narrative. Thus for doctrine to do this work of articulation properly, the role of the church as formative community must also be recovered. That will be the task of chapter three.

So far, I have shown the value of understanding doctrine as articulation.[54] Insofar as doctrine is an articulation, there is always more work to be done: there is no such thing as a once for all articulation of doctrine. This application of Taylor parallels what I said above of Wittgenstein on the fractalicity of language games. But articulation is not the only valuable element in Taylor's model. The second helpful feature is his development of the idea of a corporate subject for speech acts.

We saw above that one function of language is to create a common space. Modernity, with its radical individualism and universalism, has been able to understand only the individual's space and the universal space. The latter is the realm in which we moderns speak of human rights, for example. If we follow Wittgenstein (with his recognition of multilevel, fractally related, and widely diverse language games) and Taylor (with his recognition that the public space created by language ranges from the merely interpersonal to the communal, national, and international), we can find room for a space peculiar to a given community, which in our case is the church. Within a community there are what Taylor calls *mono*logical and *dia*logical acts. The former are the acts of single agents while the later are characterized by a multiplicity of agents. This multiplicity, Taylor insists, is more than a mere coordination of atoms. Ballroom dancing is an example of a dialogical act. Ballroom dancing can never be the act of a single agent. It is what it is through the joined action of two or more people. Taylor notes, "Such dialogical acts only succeed when we place ourselves in the common rhythm that subsumes our individual contributions to the shared action."[55] He continues,

> An action is dialogical . . . when it is effected by an integrated, nonindividual agent. This means that for those involved in it, its identity as such and such an action essentially depends on the agency being shared. Thus, these actions are constituted by the shared understanding that exists between those who make up the common agent.[56]

When we see doctrine as a dialogical act, we see it as a function of the church united—not merely institutionally or structurally, but primarily in terms of common life in the Christian narrative. This could be a helpful point for ecumenists. The locus of unity is not in submission to the Bishop of Rome (the *sine qua non* of Roman Catholic unity), in institutional unity (as in some mainline ecumenism), or simply in shared mission (which is what we see in grass-roots ecumenism). Rather the unity in the living of the Christian narrative looks backward to our common location in salvation history and forward to our continued life in the Kingdom of God. Because doctrine is not simply "belief," it cannot be seen as a monological act.

Dialogical action makes it possible to claim that doctrine is the speech act of the church. When doctrine is so described, I am not claiming merely that it belongs to the church, but that in a real sense the church itself is speaking. As a Christian, my experience of the Christian narrative is not something I have by myself. Taylor observes,

> The background understanding involved in the first section, which underlies our ability to grasp directions and follow rules [key elements in doctrine], is to a large degree embodied, and this in turn helps to explain the combination of features that it exhibits: it is a form of *understanding*, a making sense of things and actions, yet at the same time it is entirely unarticulated, just as it can provide the basis for new articulations. . . . My embodied understanding exists

in me, not only as an individual agent, but as the co-agent of common actions.[57]

Our common living together of the Christian narrative makes both the production of doctrine and the understanding of Christian teaching possible. If all we have is the modern view of communication as information exchange, we must admit that it seems rather strange to think of the church as the communal agent of doctrine: in effect, the church talking to itself. That the church doing doctrine is more than a crazy person—self-marginalized from the universal discourse of humanity—is a real possibility when we work within Taylor's model. One piece is missing, however, a detail mentioned above in my discussion of Austin's concept of "uptake." I turn now to a discussion of "reception."

RECEPTION

Earlier in this chapter I referred to McClendon and Smith's development of Austin's concept of "uptake." Uptake is "simply the recognition that utterance involves a receiver as well as a sender and calls attention to the necessity that the hearer grasp . . . [the speaker's] intentions and wants as a result the employment of the convention."[58] My suggestion is that doctrine *qua* doctrine requires uptake, or, using the theological term, reception.

The concept of reception has been of long-standing importance in Christian theology. William Rusch defines reception as including:

> all phases and aspects of an ongoing process by which a church under the guidance of God's Spirit makes the results of bilateral or multilateral conversation a part of its faith and life because the results are seen to be in conformity with the teachings of Christ and of the apostolic community, that is, the gospel as witnessed to in Scripture.[59]

Beginning in the bible itself, reception of God's grace has been an important point. The reception of grace has become, even in the biblical text, the reception of God's revelation.[60] In the time before Constantine, reception played the role of unifying the church. Churches received one another (through their representatives), recognizing one another as true churches. When the era of the great councils began with Nicea, reception came to focus on the acceptance of the formulations of these councils. As the merging of church and society continued over the next thousand years, the nature of reception changed radically. Rusch summarizes:

> A new ecclesiology appeared in the West that did not see the church as a community of local churches in fellowship

> but rather saw it as a universal corporation in which clergy and laity gave advice to the pope on important issues. When an agreement was reached on matters of doctrine and discipline by the appropriate representatives, this was regarded as the inspiration of the Spirit and the consensus of the faithful. The responsibility of all was to accept the decision, and no other form of reception was believed to be needed. . . . One part of the church was considered active and the other passive.[61]

In our own time, reception has been hindered not so much by a hierarchical ecclesiology or even a continuing commitment to Constantinianism, but by an antipathy to *any* authority. The centrality of individualism and concomitant neglect of Christian community has undermined reception within the church.

It is essential to keep in mind that reception is the act not merely of the individual but of the church itself. Speaking not of doctrine but of Scripture, Ronald Thiemann says, "The biblical narrative functions as God's promise only in relation to a believing community, but that function further depends upon an assertion of God's priority as the sole initiator, guarantor, and fulfiller of his promise."[62] In the same way, the reception of doctrine through the ages has been an act of ecclesial communities responding in faith under the guidance of the Spirit. One thing United Methodism needs to consider is its reception of the common Christian doctrinal heritage.[63] Claims that United Methodism is not a creedal church, though true on a certain level, entirely miss the point of reception.

My use of reception (in conjunction with uptake) shifts the meaning a bit. My claim that doctrine requires reception to be doctrine is the key way of distinguishing theology from doctrine. This way of making the distinction looks to the role each plays in the church, not to any logical relation between them. Theology can become doctrine if it is received as such by the church. An example of this would be Augustine's development of the doctrine of original sin. In the centuries after his death, the church came to receive his theological development, and in the course of propagating it, it became a doctrine.[64] This action of reception is similar to what Nicholas Wolterstorff refers to as "appropriated discourse."[65] He comments, "If one person appropriates another's discourse by such words as 'I agree with that' or 'that speaks for me too' or 'I second that,' then the appropriated discourse counts as the appropriator's discourse."[66] In the act of reception the church appropriates discourse, regardless of the form, and says, "We see this as true guidance in living the Christian narrative."

Doctrine is a complex speech act of the church, spoken to the church and *heard by the church*. Seen this way doctrine can be on almost any level of generality and can take a variety of forms. Poor performance of doctrine, then, can result either from a failure to speak (which can, in turn, stem from a number of factors) or a failure to hear. Subversion by modern epistemology has led the church to refrain from speaking out of fear of not measuring up to accepted standards of rationality; subversion by modern (autonomous) individualism has made the church oblivious to its own voice. Individualism affects reception further by disinclining hearers to receive doctrine as part of the church, instead inclining them to hear it as a modern, and thus autonomous, individual. Any recovery of doctrine in our churches today will require attention to both speaking and hearing.

I have looked so far in this chapter at three positions in the philosophy of language that seek to get beyond the convictions of modernity. Austin, Wittgenstein, and Taylor agree on several points against modern views. First, language is a human action, not merely an adjunct to epistemology. Second, language is a social phenomenon, understandable only in the context of community. Third, the subjectivism and solipsism implicit in so much modern thought (and explicit in the rest), are unnecessary. We live together in the context of a world that we shape and interact with through language. A fourth commonality is that language is infinitely flexible; new developments and change are the norm.

As we saw in chapter one, George Lindbeck has proposed an understanding of doctrine that seeks to build on some of these features of the postmodern philosophy of language. In the next section I will examine three counterintuitive conclusions he draws with relation to the nature and function of doctrinal language. I will argue that these conclusions are unnecessary and result from a misreading and misapplication of Austin and Wittgenstein (Lindbeck makes no appeal to Taylor). Underlying this misreading seems to be a continuing and unacknowledged commitment to some modern convictions about language.

LINDBECK ON LANGUAGE

Lindbeck's advances over modern positions in his *The Nature of Doctrine* are clear. He has rejected both the epistemological focus and the individualism characteristic of modern theology (both conservative and liberal) that led to the marginalization of the church (again, among both liberals and conservatives). The development of a cultural linguistic model of religion allows a recovery of some important dimensions of ecclesiology that have been eclipsed not merely in modernity, but throughout the dominance of Constantinianism in the church. In spite of these advances, three of Lindbeck's convictions run counter to what one would expect.

The Difficulty of Reference

The first, and perhaps most surprising of Lindbeck's counterintuitive positions is that reference (the main—if not sole—job of language in modern theories) is a hard thing to achieve. I speak here of his assertion of the "informational vacuity" of "modern physics utterances" as well as "religious utterances."[67] This follows his analysis of the Christian claim "God is good." Relying on David Burrell's analysis of Aquinas, Lindbeck claims that we cannot understand what "good" means in reference to God. He says, "When we say that God is good, we do not affirm that any of our concepts of goodness (*modi significandi*) apply to him, but rather that there is a concept of goodness unavailable to us, viz., God's own understanding of his own goodness which does apply."[68] In the same way, the nonscientist, who has no inkling of the math involved, would run into similar problems when saying, "Space-time is a four-dimensional continuum."[69] It is unclear exactly what classes of speech Lindbeck is including in his discussion of informational vacuity. Is he speaking of "ordinary" religious utterances? Doctrines? Theological discourse? If he is including all these forms of speech, one is left wondering if there is such a thing as information in religion at all. It is also a curious feature that the nature of religious language is decided on the analysis of a statement about the being of God. Surely many important religious utterances/assertions—ordinary, doctrinal, and theological—are about something other than God's being. One might wonder why a person who has already based his work on Wittgenstein and comparable philosophers, would turn now to a position that seems to find the individual human mind as the arbiter of meaning. Instead of simply retorting to Lindbeck that the boundary of meaning is not in the individual but in the linguistic community, it is useful to see where he goes with this. The main consequence of the elusiveness of language about God[70] is that it leads Lindbeck to a performative theory of religious language. There are other reasons for his pessimism about reference to be considered as well.

For a statement to be a proposition—and this seems to be what Lindbeck requires for reference to succeed—a determinate context is required. His example is the statement, "This car is red."[71] In the course of reading a theological monograph we are unaccustomed to hearing about red cars. Not being in Lindbeck's location we have no means to test the claim about the car. But why would we want to test the claim? We would desire a test only if we had some stake in the matter, something few of Lindbeck's readers will have. There are a few ways to respond to Lindbeck's point.

First, we can say he is not talking about a red car but about a sentence. Though the car in question may be long gone (or even imaginary to begin with), the sentence "This car is red" remains. In the context of a treatise on the philosophy of language such sentences make perfect sense, however odd they may appear elsewhere. "The cat is on the mat," as far as I know, is rarely used to say anything about cats, but is instead used to point out features of language. To ask about the referentiality of "cat" and "mat" is, then, to miss the point of the sentence.

Second, we can grant his point that given its placement in his book, the sentence lacks the necessary specificity to refer. But how much specificity of context does a sentence need? *"This* x" as an ostensive marking, requires a very specific relationship between speaker and hearer for reference to work. Since we are not in Lindbeck's automotive community, we cannot tell if his speech act "This car is red" refers.[72] But we *are* in Lindbeck's philosophical community and understand his usage quite well. Reference is not a problem here: it simply is not reference to a red car. The role of interpretive communities is central in Stanley Fish's *Is There a Text in This Class?* He says, "In order to grasp the meaning of the individual term [in this case 'red car'], you must already have grasped the general activity . . . in relation to which it could be thought meaningful; a system of intelligibility cannot be reduced to a list of the things it renders intelligible."[73] Fish is often accused of relativism, but a position like Lindbeck's seems more susceptible to such a charge.

The same point can be illustrated by Wittgenstein's story of the five red apples. When a shopkeeper contemplates a written order for "Five red apples," he or she does not work out the meaning of each word and then combine them to make sense of the sentence. The shopkeeper simply understands the convention of ordering apples. We understand the convention of talking about sentences to make points about language.[74]

Red cars are not the problem, of course. My concern is with doctrinal sentences, or, more generally, religious sentences. On the strength of his analysis of "this car is red" Lindbeck claims,

> The same point holds *mutatis mutandis* for religious sentences: they acquire enough referential specificity to have first order ontological truth or falsity only in determinate settings, and this rarely if ever happens on the pages of theological treatises or in the context of doctrinal discourses.[75]

Lindbeck is in good postmodern company in emphasizing the role of context.[76] I claimed in chapter one that decontextualization was a defining feature of modernity. One must ask, however, why determinate contexts are so hard to come by. It seems that making the criteria for a "determinate context" sufficiently determinate leads us to another form of foundationalism. Instead of having a proper relationship to an indubitable proposition, a statement will have a proper relationship with a determinate context. Unlike moderns, who look for a universally determinate context, all we need is one determinate enough to work in a given community of discourse. Lindbeck demonstrates an all-or-nothing approach to referentiality that is simply unrealistic.

Red cars are not the only questionable paradigms of reference that Lindbeck considers. In a different context, he mentions the difficulty of referring to "The 8:02 to New York." We can speak of such a train and yet the actual train could be different every day. "The 8:02 to New York," he suggests, only has meaning by "its function within a particular transportation system."[77] The feature of reference to which Lindbeck points is real: but ought this kind of reference be considered paradigmatic? What if instead of talking about "The 8:02 to New York" we speak of "Old Rustbucket?" "Old Rustbucket" may be the "8:02 to New York" on Mondays, but the "10:22 to Providence" on Tuesdays. "Old Rustbucket" succeeds in referring in a particular context and system of meaning, but has a different kind of relationship to the world than "The 8:02 to New York." Train riders and employees inhabit the same world, so successful reference either to train schedules or to individual trains should not be too surprising. If reference in this world did not work, I think we would read more complaints about our nation's rail system. Are there any good reasons to assume that all religious language (or doctrinal language) is more like "this car is red" or "The 8:02 to New York" than it is like "George Lindbeck wrote *The Nature of Doctrine*" or "Old Rustbucket?" If so, this gives us less reason to despair of reference.

When we turn to "religious" utterances[78] we find sentences that appear very different from "this car is red" in terms of their specificity.

Lindbeck himself considers one: "Jesus rose from the dead." The first thing he notes, however, is that this sentence is in the same place informationally as "God is good." He speaks of the "impossibility of specifying the mode in which" resurrection stories signify. Is this a claim that we have never seen a resurrection and simply do not know how it was done? His argument is a little hard to follow since after referring to the resurrection of Jesus, he goes on to speak simply of "resurrection." Are we talking about a concept ("resurrection") or an event ("the resurrection of Jesus")? The reference of a concept seems quite different in nature from that of an event. Perhaps this is another illustration of his all-or-nothing approach: either we have a complete understanding of "resurrection" or our language about resurrections fails to refer.

But this language *is* doing something, Lindbeck avers. Propositionalism was wrong—it is not about reality. Experiential expressivism was wrong—it does not flow from inner religious experiences. It is performance, more specifically, the performance of a religious community. To understand this, Lindbeck turns to Austin's concept of performative utterance. Despite having read Austin, Lindbeck demonstrates that he retains the notion that propositionality is the root function of language and that the performative is a somehow subsidiary kind of use by making a hard contrast between performatives and what Austin would call constatives.[79] Whether this misstep is due to a mere second-hand acquaintance with Austin's work or an incomplete reading of Austin himself, the results are the same. By suggesting that religious language is performative, Lindbeck blunts the postmodernity of Austin's position, and creates a position that sounds like a variant of some of the liberal strategies to soften the consequences of the apparent failure of the propositionality of religious language.[80]

But is reference such a hard thing to achieve? The work of Austin, Wittgenstein, and Taylor that I discussed above makes clear that reference is not the center of language. The Cartesian image of the self standing in silence pointing at things is inadequate. The work of all three is better described as contextualizing reference than as eliminating it. Contributing to Lindbeck's position on reference is another conviction—that there are different "realms of discourse." Language functions differently in each realm (at least it functions differently in the realm of religious language).[81] Lindbeck claims, for example, "The ontological truth of religious utterances, like their intrasystematic truth, is different as well as similar to what holds in other realms of discourse."[82]

Just when Lindbeck's readers thought they might have a new theory available, they get another version of the "religion has its own kind of language" approach. Just as his use of the performative can be characterized as a misreading of Austin, the "many realms" position can be characterized as a misreading of Wittgenstein. The strategy of claiming that religion has its own kind of language seems to be a variant of the position that language games are autonomous.[83] If religion *is* a language game, it is a game separate from other games. Though fideism is one possible outcome of such a view, my greater concern is that such a position negates Lindbeck's recovery of ecclesiology and doctrinal authority. A better reading of Wittgenstein leads us to the position that language games are contingently related, and that the relationships between them are diverse, numerous, and changing.[84]

That different realms of discourse are not connected is not a new idea. It is interesting to consider its place in the biography of Alasdair MacIntyre. When he gave the lectures that became *The Religious Significance of Atheism*, he identified something like the "different realms" theory as one of the possible responses to modernity.[85] As modern science and philosophy left less and less room for religion to be counted as rational, it became common to consider religion its own domain. In *The Religious Significance of Atheism* MacIntyre does not tell us that under the influence of Barth and Wittgenstein that was his own position for a time.[86] When he came to reject that "solution," he rejected Christianity.[87] Only in his later work, especially *Whose Justice? Which Rationality?* does he fully adopt a position similar to what I have articulated.

It is interesting that MacIntyre's discussion of the different realms theory is in the same context as his contention that modern theology was giving the atheist less and less to disbelieve. As religions came to be understood as autonomous language games, or, using "theological language," enclaves of faith, one could maintain the same positions as atheists and find no conflict. Seeing language games as autonomous, therefore, will not aid us in getting beyond the marginalization of doctrine.

If Christians today, as members of the church, are living in the continuing Christian narrative, their doctrinal language, insofar as it guides them in relating to God and the world, requires real reference. This is not a lapse back into propositionalism: for propositionalists the purpose of doctrine was to state facts. For doctrine, reference is necessary, but not sufficient: it requires reference in order for it to guide us in living the Christian narrative.[88] The Christian narrative presupposes interaction with real agents (including God) who have determinate character, as well as a determinate plot line, part of which is the history of those agents' actions up until the present. Austin comes close to this position in his discussion of "ordinary" language:

> When we examine what we should say when, what words we should use in what situations, we are looking again not *merely* at words (or 'meanings,' whatever they may be) but also at the realities we use the words to talk about: we are using a sharpened awareness of words to sharpen our perception of, though not as the final arbiter of, the phenomena.[89]

The belief that Lindbeck needs to pay greater attention to propositionality is widespread.[90] Ronald Thiemann asserts throughout his work that real reference is necessary for the coherence of Christianity. He points out that

> questions of truth and reference arise in the interlocutionary context. In order to respond to this invitation the reader must recognize this narrative as God's personal promising address. To recognize the gospel as God's personal address the reader must further acknowledge that God is an existent promising agent in actual communication with the human recipient.[91]

This is very close to the position I am articulating. If we are to see ourselves as players in the Christian narrative, there are certain features we must count as real for the narrative to make sense. As Thiemann says, the narrative does not make sense if God is not seen as a player in it. One might think the better strategy is simply to describe what the Christian community believes without making any assessment of truth or referentiality. Thiemann counters that such a proposal presupposes a

> characteristic of revelation which the nonfoundationalist rejects. It assumes that the relation between Christian claims and God's reality is *extrinsic*, so that claims about the church's faith *cannot* be claims about an external God who stands outside all human language.
>
> Nonfoundational theology, however, denies that God is *extrinsically* related to Christian belief, because it rejects the common picture of God as external causal agent.... God's reality is *intrinsically* related to Christian belief and practice, if Christian claims about God are true.[92]

What we have then is not an examination of the Christian narrative from without, from a neutral vantage point, but a view from within, seeking to make the best sense of where we stand. This is, it seems to me, an application of Taylor's BA Principle. It provides the best account of what we see in the church and how the faith is actually lived.

Reference is an act of a speaker in a particular social context before it is a feature of language. Language is the chief means by which speakers refer. If we see doctrine as a speech act of the church, the church is referring to the features of the reality in which it lives. Except in certain cases, the church (and religious speakers in general) is not out merely to make realist claims. Theism (a creation of modernity) makes much of the existence of God. As has been noted by numerous authors, Christianity does not claim but rather assumes the existence of God. Christians are much more prone to speak of the actions, character, and purposes of God than merely of God's existence. It is no great surprise that such claims seem extraordinary from the standpoint of modernity, but when one considers that that same standpoint has produced the "problems" of solipsism and "other minds" one sees less reason to give credence to such a point of view.[93] It is also the dubious conviction of modernity that the reality of something can be demonstrated by words alone. The Christian tradition contends that it is not through argument that people come to believe in the reality of God, but through God's action in and through the church, which reaches out to include them within its span.

Doctrines are Rules Only

Lindbeck's second counterintuitive position is that doctrines are rules, and can be described as such without remainder. This is after offering a noncontroversial definition of doctrine: "Church doctrines are communally authoritative teachings regarding beliefs and practices that are considered essential to the identity or welfare of the group in question."[94] The important part here is the "communally authoritative teachings." Given this definition alone, there is nothing unexpected: it is explicitly formulated to account for "traditional characteristics of doctrine" (excluded *a priori* by the experiential expressive understanding of doctrine).[95] It is communal *authority* that is alien to experiential expressive approaches to religion while *communal* authority seems alien to modern propositionalism. Propositionalism sees doctrines as authoritative, but this authority lies in their role in religious epistemology not in relation to the community. One "traditional characteristic" of doctrine *is* communal authoritativeness. But is this the only one? Surely it is not controversial to say that a "traditional characteristic" of doctrine has been to see it as making truth claims.

This is not the claim that propositionalism is traditional. My sense is that premoderns would be loath to confess that doctrines have nothing to do with truth claims. At the very least, traditional doctrines *look* (as explored above) like they are making truth claims.

Appearances are deceiving, however. Doctrines *are* propositional for Lindbeck—their propositionality is simply not about the world. He claims that

> To say that doctrines are rules is not to deny that they involve propositions. The rules formulated by the linguist or the logician, for example, express propositional convictions about how language or thought actually work. These are, however, second order rather than first-order propositions, and affirm nothing about extra-linguistic or extra-human reality. For a rule theory, in short, doctrines *qua* doctrines are not first-order propositions, but are to be construed as second order ones: they make . . . intrasystematic rather than ontological claims.[96]

But what of the propositional appearance of so many doctrines? Lindbeck admits that "a doctrinal sentence may also function symbolically or as a first-order proposition. Insofar as it is employed in these other ways . . . it either cannot or need not be construed as a norm of communal belief or practice: it is not being used as a church doctrine."[97]

If doctrine is a speech act—my claim, not Lindbeck's, though I doubt he would say otherwise—whose speech act is it? To use his own terminology, who is the "user" of doctrine? My contention is that it is the church, while Lindbeck is strangely silent, never referring at all to the user. Does a statement function as doctrine merely because of the logic of relationships between first-order and second-order propositions? Does the intent of the speaker play a role? What about the context in which doctrine is spoken (or written)? Is it possible that the church might see its action as being communally authoritative *and* claiming truth at the same time? Does the church have to say the same sentence twice to accomplish this goal? Perhaps what happens is that some doctrinal utterances of the church can be analyzed into truth claiming and rule-stating components, never the twain shall meet.[98] An alternative is that Lindbeck's approach to doctrine may best be seen as normative rather than descriptive. The doctrinal use simply is the authoritative use of a given sentence. That sentence can be used other ways, but only when it is used authoritatively is it doctrinal. If this is the case, truth stating is conceived as a kind of use clearly distinct from the use (or property?)[99] of being authoritative.

Part of our difficulty may lie in the fact that our epistemological expectations of doctrine have made us less aware of the variety of forms even "traditional" doctrines come in. In the Methodist tradition doctrinal standards have come not merely in the form of a list of (apparent) propositions, but also in the form of sermons and published commentary on the New Testament.[100] Even more influential in forming and guiding Methodist life have been the hymns of John and Charles Wesley, which though never (to my knowledge) accorded the status of official doctrine, have molded the thinking, speech and action of generations of Methodists and other Christian communities.

Doctrine can take a variety of *forms*: the mistake seems to be confusing form with function. The propositional *form* of much doctrine has led many to see its *function* as propositional, i.e., as stating facts. Doctrine may state facts, but its function is not the stating of facts. When Sally asks Bob to pass the bread, the function of her request (the type of speech act she uttered) cannot be seen as a statement about the bread, but if there is no bread (or no Bob), the request does not count as a request. If this is true of a request, surely it is possibly true of a rule as well.

Lindbeck's pessimism about reference seems to find a place in his decision to see doctrine as pure rule. Modern propositionalism can look too much like an extension of the medieval emphasis on metaphysics. The strong emphasis on ontology from that period is transferred to the modern period, though shorn, of course, of secondary qualities and the like. What is known of God in such a view is God's attributes, taken as ontological characteristics. Considering Lindbeck's strong language against "ontological" reference, this seems to be the background to which he is responding. My understanding of reference in Christian discourse, especially with relation to God, goes against the grain of both modern and medieval conceptions in my focus on *action*. Though modernity has pruned ontological assertions about God to a minimum (especially in that modern construct, "theism"), it has eliminated all talk of God as agent. The specific doctrines that must be recovered by the church now are those that deal with God's action—in the present, past, and future. Doctrine is the grammar of the Christian community. He says that doctrine is more fallible and imperfect than the grammar of a spoken language, with multiple exceptions to every rule. "Some rules may reflect temporary features of surface grammar or may even be arbitrary impositions. The deep grammar of the language may escape detection."[101] But how is one to tell the difference between surface and depth grammar? Is this another way to explain the differences that exist among Christians and ecclesial communities? Instead of saying that another community is claiming the wrong position as truth, we simply say they are proclaiming the surface grammar rather than the depth grammar. As far as actual effect, the difference seems slight.

Doctrine regulates Christian speech (and, more generally, action), but my suggestion, in contrast to Lindbeck, is that its function is not best described as regulative. Rather, sticking to the image of dramatic narrative, doctrine's function is directive. Being directive is not contradictory to being regulative, it is simply broader. This reconception carries with it important implications for our understanding of what doctrine is about, and where it comes from. According to Lindbeck's model doctrine is second order discourse which is based on the first order discourse (preaching, prayer, worship, etc.) of the Christian community. This differentiation between first and second order discourse, that is, between doctrines and "normal" Christian discourse needs clarification. Speech acts are used in a complex system of discourse, complex not only in their variety, but also in the types of situation they occur, the ends they accomplish, as well as their ways of relating to the world. Human action, which is constitutive of so much of the world we talk about, is so bound up with *speech* action that it is unhelpful to make a hard distinction between world and talk about the world.[102] In any given case where we are considering a structure of speech acts we can make distinctions about which seem to be reflecting the world and which are better described as being about other (local) speech acts. This complexity could be the source of a lack of clarity in Lindbeck's discussion of doctrines as rules.[103]

For Lindbeck, doctrine both describes and shapes the way the Christian language game works. If the Christian language game is the chicken and doctrine the egg, we find ourselves in a place were we can never say which comes first. The church is shaped from the very beginning by the teaching (doctrine) and ministry of Jesus. Through the Apostles and the early Christian community this teaching was reflected upon and used further to shape the community. Their explanation of the origin of the community, however, is never merely in terms of reflection upon speech acts (or any other current actions of the community). They do not simply say, "Jesus (or Peter, or Paul) taught this and here we are." Their self-interpretation was always referenced to the narrative of what God had done in Jesus. This is, I believe, also the best explanation of Jesus' self-interpretation. That is, his teaching and ministry become clearest when seen as an acted out reinterpretation of what God had done in Israel and, following from that, an enactment of the promises of God found in Old Testament narrative and prophecy.[104]

I am proposing then, an adjustment in the way we conceive the relation between doctrine and the church. Instead of standing in a second order relationship to Christian practice, it stands in a second order relationship to the Christian drama, of which Christian practice is only a part. Such a move allows for greater inclusion of history, both God's action in the past (and future) as well as the church's. When the church "doctrines," it considers its life in this drama in light of questions being asked from within and without the community. Doctrine, in effect, bridges the (apparent) gaps *within* the narrative as well as the gaps between *the* narrative and *our* narratives. This drama includes not only stories (words) but also the agents and their actions that make it what it is. Since doctrine is itself an action of an agent, the church, previous doctrinal formulations (and theology which, though not formally received as doctrine, has been found valuable by the church) are part of what doctrine *now* seeks to articulate. At any given moment, a large part of what the church is doing has doctrinal articulation "behind" it, though also at any given moment, there is the unarticulated background that the church has, up till now, been able to take for granted and perform automatically (without reflection).

Given this reconceptualization, what does it mean to say doctrines are true? Propositionalism gauges the truth of doctrine by the success of its reference, while the symbolic view of experiential expressivism gauges it by how well it symbolizes inner states, attitudes, and experiences. Lindbeck's discussion of truth focuses first on categorial truth,[105] but this seems to be limited to the truth of a religion as a whole. A *religion* is categorially true (or adequate) when it has the categories necessary to refer to what is really real. The primary way in which religious *utterances* are said to be true is intrasystematically—how well they cohere with the total religion. Lindbeck discusses truth as correspondence, but this correspondence focuses not on religious language corresponding to anything, but on the use of religious language to make the speaker correspond to God's will.[106]

That doctrines must cohere with the totality of Christianity is essential for any theory of doctrine. Whether categorial truth is a useful concept depends on just what Lindbeck means. He explains his position using analogies with math and geometry, two abstract systems.[107] If this position depends on Christianity being seen as an abstract system (which is possible if the analogy between religions and languages is pressed too far), then it is not useful to a theory like mine that emphasizes the strong historical dimension of Christianity. The better choice is a form of evaluation that is broader than one considering truth (of whatever kind) alone.

When doctrine is seen as the speech act of the church, truth is a necessary component. There must be a true (faithful) relation of the Christian narrative. This narrative, as something we live in, is seen as something true as well, though "actual" would be a better evaluative term.[108] If we are to relate to the other actors, including God, we must hear the truth about them—about their character, intentions, and actions. The kind of truth we need is not reducible to the simple either/or characteristic of so many modern discussions of truth, based as they are on mathematical logic. Charles Taylor puts it well:

> We cannot but operate with a notion of truth; that the way we live our transitions, and struggle with potential redescriptions, unfailingly makes use of these notions of overcoming distortion, seeing through error, coming to reality, and their opposites. We can't function as agents without some such language.[109]

As inhabitants of a historical narrative, Christians continually find themselves in a place where they must make the kinds of distinctions and evaluations to which Taylor refers. Our location in this narrative is never pure—we also inhabit other narratives (those belonging to American culture, our locale, our families, etc.)—so such evaluations are inescapable if we are to understand who we are, where we stand, where we are going, and what we do next. The coherence we seek *can* be described as a coherence with—or correspondence to—God's will, but the complexity of the world in which we live requires a kind of coherence that is more than simply internal, but includes a relation to the rest of what there is.[110]

Austin insists that whatever the value of seeing truth as coherence, coherence does not work apart from some sort of correspondence. He says,

> There is much sense in 'coherence' (and pragmatist) theories of truth, despite their failure to appreciate the trite but central point that truth is a matter of relation between words and world, and despite their wrongheaded *Gleichaltung* of all varieties of statemental failure under the lone head of 'partly true' (thereafter wrongly equated with 'part of the truth').[111]

Truth is a much more complex evaluation than modernity has allowed and correspondence to reality is much more complicated than the picture Lindbeck draws. Consider Austin's comments in this regard:

> Is it true or false that . . . the galaxy is the shape of a fried egg? . . . That Wellington won the battle of Waterloo? There are various degrees and dimensions of success in making statements: the statements fit the facts always more or less loosely, in different ways on different occasions for different intents and purposes.[112]

Obviously this gets us into the question of happiness, a discussion I am putting off until later in this chapter. Let it suffice now to say that there are at least some senses in which it is essential to speak of the truth of doctrinal statements.[113]

Doctrinal Hylomorphism

Lindbeck's third counterintuitive position results from the combination of his understanding of reference and truth with convictions regarding doctrinal change and permanence, and supports his regulative theory of doctrine. This position is that doctrine must be understood in terms of form and content, with the former changing, and the latter unchanging. Or is it the other way around? Lindbeck uses the example of a computer program remaining the same while producing differing output in response to differing input (83). Which is the form, which the content? Lindbeck's objective is to explain how doctrine can change and remain the same at the same time. He notes that within Christianity there has always been a conviction that "the same faith, the same teaching, and the same doctrine" could be expressed in a variety of ways. He illustrates this with the multiplicity of titles for Jesus in the New Testament, claiming that though each title represents a different "form," each has the same underlying content.[114] Only a reductionist account,[115] however, would see these titles as different ways of saying the same thing. Each title fits into the narrative a different way and serves as a bridge to another part of the Biblical narrative or to a neighboring community.[116] Each title has a similar function: to answer the question, "Who is Jesus?" Since this question is always asked from a particular context, the question is not merely about Jesus' "inner being" but could be paraphrased as, "Who is Jesus with respect to X?" where X is some aspect of the asker's context: "the fact that Israel is under the domination of the Romans," "The God who brought Israel out of Egypt," "the Kingdom of Israel" are some possibilities. Therefore, the diverse titles are best understood as complementary, not synonymous. The church has retained them because in their richness they provide a depth and cohesion to the narrative otherwise unavailable. This is in spite of the fact that some of the original contexts in which the question was asked are quite foreign to the church's current experience. The church today is tied to these "fossilized" (I do not mean this in a pejorative sense) identifiers because their original context is continually presented to the church through the biblical narratives. In the past couple of decades, biblical theology has shifted away from the preoccupation, common to earlier twentieth-century biblical theology, with christological titles.

Lindbeck claims that form and content are more easily distinguished if doctrines "are taken as expressing second-order guidelines for Christian discourse rather than first-order affirmations about the inner being of God or of Jesus Christ."[117] To address his separation between form and content, we must remember two suggestions I made above. First, the distinction between first and second order discourse is always local to particular discourse and cannot be understood absolutely. Second, I reject the claim, as strenuously as Lindbeck, that the function of doctrine is to make "affirmations about the inner being of God or of Jesus Christ." The Nicene claim about the relation between Father and Son to which Lindbeck is referring must be understood in its narrative context. Nicea did not simply make the statement that Jesus is "of one substance with the Father," but that through this Jesus God was performing certain acts resulting in our salvation.

Analyzing language into form and content seems to rely on the propositional understanding of language that Lindbeck is rejecting. The propositional content can be stated in a variety of ways. Adopting a speech act analysis instead, we can still find a representative dimension (which will be different in different doctrines), but the way this works will be affected by the illocutionary force of the sentence (text) in question. My suggestion is that doctrine, varied as it is, is its own kind of illocution. I will develop this more fully in chapter five. Instead of focusing on what is different in two doctrinal utterances that "say the same thing" (where Lindbeck's answer is "the content"), I find it easier to come from the other direction, from the side of difference. What changes in doctrine is the context in which the question is asked. In chapter three I will deal with the agent of doctrine, the church, and consider some details of its relationship with its context, or better, its culture. Suffice it to say now that the questioning that results in doctrine is dialectical. The context in which the church lives leads to new questions (and new answers to old questions) while at the same time the context is questioned by the church using current doctrinal formulations.

This approach will allow us to keep the strength of Lindbeck's position—that Christians believe a given doctrine can be expressed in a variety of ways—while not rejecting referentiality (though taking it in nonpropositionalist terms).¹¹⁸ It is possible to maintain the conviction of variety and some degree of propositionality. The past of the Christian drama has a fixedness to it insofar as it is the history of God's interaction with creation. The church's access to this past history is through the scriptures that it deems canonical. These narratives are not mere reports of events told *wie es eigentlich gewesen*, but inseparably include interpretation of the meaning and significance of those events. Considering the variety of ways the story of Jesus is told in the four canonical Gospels, the tradition has held from the very beginning that more than one perspective on the events (and actors) is not merely possible, but also desirable. Though I do not have room to discuss it here, my suggestion is that the best evaluative term for these narratives, just as for doctrine, is happiness, not truth.¹¹⁹

A second conviction leading Lindbeck to espouse doctrinal hylomorphism is that there is an essential continuity in Christian doctrine. He claims that in the midst of these "shifts in Christological affirmations and in the corresponding experiences of Jesus Christ, the story of passion and resurrection and the basic rules for its use remain the same."¹²⁰ Languages, cultures and religions are

> the lenses through which human beings see and respond to their changing worlds, or the media in which they formulate their descriptions. The world and its descriptions may vary enormously even while the lens or media remain the same. Or, to change the simile, just as genetic codes or computer programs may remain identical even while producing startling [sic] different products depending on input and situation, so also with the basic grammars of cultures, languages and religions. They remain while the products change.¹²¹

When we turn to these examples—genetic codes and computer programs—what is the form and what is the content? Instead of relying on a hylomorphic metaphor, he would have been better off drawing from these metaphors. The continuity of a religion is likened to a language that "remains the same" in the midst of change. The problem, of course, is what does it mean for a language to stay the same? We speak of *Old* English, *Middle* English, *Elizabethan* English, *Modern* English and *American* English as all being English. But how can we say the language has not changed? Most of the people I know are fluent in English. None, as far as I know, would understand Old English. Just because we have decided to call all these languages "English," does not mean they are the same language in any meaningful sense. If all we have is the historical relationship (and this *is* important, as I will show in chapter four), then it seems that just about anything could pass for a Christianity whose continuity was conceived along the same lines.

Lindbeck's position is not original with him. It is a variant of the position of early ecumenist Jan Comenius who "felt that when the 'terms of meanings' in such [religious] disputes were examined, differences would be found to exist 'not in fundamentals,' but 'only in the manner of expressing them.'"[122] Lindbeck's problem is twofold: he has carried his analogy—religion (Christianity) is like language—beyond the breaking point, and his scheme treats the form as too neutral and detachable from the content. Christianity is *unlike* a language in that there are controls on what is said and not said, not merely on *how* things are said. Christianity is *more* than a language in that it is the combination of actions done through time, so the sameness that is required concerns more than a present "product."[123] Paul Holmer says,

> Unlike the popular everyday view that theology must always adapt and must always be contemporary, we must insist that theology proposes something that is timeless and eternal. Instead of using popular causes and ideas of the day and then clothing them in the language of faith, the task of theology is to construe those causes and ideas, their feasibility and truth, in relation to God and his way among men.[124]

With a hylomorphic view of doctrine, content seems to be entirely neutral and inert. The unchanging doctrinal form plays the active part in this relationship. There seems no substantial difference between this position and Bultmann's position that Christianity is really an ancient form of Heideggerian existentialism standing in need of demythologization, that is, a separation from the archaic cultural husk.[125] Bryant rightly insists that even rules are expressed in words and are sociohistorically shaped. Thus not even a purely negative regulative approach is unchangeable.[126]

CHANGE, CONSTANCY, AND THE CHRISTIAN NARRATIVE

The task Lindbeck set for himself was far from a simple one. It is much easier for me to stand at a distance and criticize his work than it is to propose a replacement. In the rest of this chapter I will briefly outline the advantages there are in following the lead of Wittgenstein, Austin, and Taylor and seeing doctrine as a speech act of the church.

Doctrine Beyond Epistemology

Most importantly, like Lindbeck, I eschew the position and epistemological focus of modernity. Doctrine is not something that can be evaluated without consideration of the Christian narrative. Although my detailed discussion of this narrative and its relation to history will have to wait until the fourth chapter, I can say at this point specifically that doctrine makes our life in the Christian narrative intelligible. MacIntyre says of intelligibility: It "is a property of actions in their relationships to the sequences within which they occur. . . . To learn to act is one and the same as learning to participate in such sequences."[127] Doctrine is that which enables us to understand the narratival sequence in which we live and know how to move within it. This sequence is much more complex than a simple concatenation of "facts." It is the multifaceted interplay of many characters, some individual, some communal, some divine, and some demonic. Inasmuch as the sequence is constantly changing, doctrine must change as well.

It would be a mistake, however, to see this change as drastic or wholesale. Lindbeck is correct when he says the main change comes in how we seek to say the same thing. The challenge is that there is no simple test to know we are saying the same thing. It is tempting to stop at this point and say the only sameness we need is sameness of effect: if formulation *A* and formulation *B* have the same effect, they are "saying the same thing." This fails, however, because there is no metaperspective where the description of "same effect" can be kept undefiled by the sociohistorical and linguistic changes that also affect doctrine. The test of faithfulness is, therefore, whether or not what doctrine says fits with the Christian narrative, and there is often no simple way to do this. Many modern positions fail this test, not merely because their claims are counter to the traditional reading of the narrative, but because the dehistoricization inherent in modernity denies the narrative itself.

The continuing and abiding element in doctrine is necessary because certain features of our life in the narrative are constant. The biblical witness claims that God's character is unchanging—God is always good, faithful, merciful, and holy. God has performed certain actions in the past, most importantly the events surrounding the Incarnation. The way the church has lived the narrative for close to two thousand years has identified this event as indispensable. Though interaction with new communities will require new ways of speaking about the Incarnation and the Incarnate Son, the One of whom we speak remains the same. This sameness does not lie in the fact that Jesus is a historic personage whose life is fixed in history. As for the past alone, this is accurate. But according to his promise Jesus is with the church now, and thus is a continuing actor in the play.

Doctrinal change is also slowed by the fact that it is a communal speech act. For an articulation to become doctrine it must be spoken by the church *and* received by the church. This is a process that can take years, even centuries, for official doctrine. Nonofficial but still operational doctrine can arise much more quickly, but is more ephemeral. It lies beneath the surface (in what Taylor calls the "unarticulated background") until the fires of controversy or conflict (internal or external) bring it to the surface.

The Process of Regulation

Any theory of doctrine must account not only for change and continuity, but also for exclusion. Is it possible that some doctrinal and theological formulations could be wrong? A rule theory alone finds it difficult to exclude any position as non-Christian. Considering the three rules Lindbeck discovers in Nicene Christology, Terrence Tilley claims they fit Arianism as well as orthodoxy,[128] while Barrett finds they are just as compatible with Nestorius and Apollinaris as they are with the position finally accepted as orthodox.[129] The function of rules is even more complex than this. Wittgenstein comments:

> This was our paradox: no course of action could be determined by a rule, because every course of action can be made out to accord with the rule. The answer was: if everything can be made out to accord with the rule, then it can also be made out to conflict with it.[130]

What makes the difference in my model is that language games are seen as contingently connected with each other and with reality. In speaking doctrine, the church is making truth claims *and* regulating our life in the narrative. With any given doctrine we have not only the effect of the doctrine itself, but also the narrative background from which it has been articulated and in which we live.

Lindbeck's hylomorphism ultimately has no explanation for a phenomenon he himself points out: that official doctrine becomes nonoperational. Because he regards language games as essentially autonomous, he is unable to move completely beyond modern dehistoricization. It is the modern conviction that we stand nowhere (or, all stand in the same place) that accounts for the marginalization of doctrine. With such an account, truth claiming doctrine cannot but be seen as heteronomous, and thus not worthy of consideration.

The Happiness of Doctrine

The key consideration of doctrine is not truth, but happiness. Lindbeck's account was marred in many ways by his failure to consider Austin's mature position. Doctrine itself, like direction in a play, is a complex speech act expressible in a number of forms, each of which influences the evaluation of its happiness.[131] In chapter five I will consider more closely how the happiness of doctrine can be evaluated. Chapter three will consider the nature of the "speaker" of the speech act of doctrine, the church. In addition, I will consider the relationships the church has with its host culture as well as surrounding cultures to see how these influence the formulation of doctrine.

NOTES

[1] I am not entirely satisfied with any of the available terms (play, drama, narrative) and so will use them interchangeably, not because there is no difference between them, but because each has important connotations. The key features of the image will be brought out as I develop the model.

[2] I would say misreadings of Wittgenstein as well, but the issues involved are less clear than they are with respect to Austin.

[3] N. T. Wright, *The New Testament and the People of God*, vol. 1, *Christian Origins and the Question of God* (Minneapolis: Fortress, 1992), ch. 5; N. T. Wright, "How Can the Bible Be Authoritative?" *Vox Evangelica* 21 (1991): 7–32. The image also seems implicit in James W. McClendon's concept of the "baptist vision." *Doctrine: Systematic Theology, Volume II* (Nashville: Abingdon, 1994), 36, 45f. I will have much more to say about the "baptist vision" in chapter four.

[4] Francis Watson discusses the relation between the doctrine of creation and the metanarrativity of the Christian story in chapter 8 of *Text, Church and World: Biblical Interpretation in Theological Perspective* (Grand Rapids, MI: Eerdmans, 1994).

[5] Lindbeck, *Nature of Doctrine: Religion and Theology in a Postliberal Age* (Philadelphia: Westminster Press, 1984), 21.

[6] For the history of the form of this doctrine, see Thomas C. Oden, *Doctrinal Standards in the Wesleyan Tradition* (Grand Rapids, MI: Francis Asbury Press, 1988).

[7] In study on the relation between faith and knowledge in postmodern theology, W. Stephen Gunter tells a tragic story of a pastor facing just this problem. Cf. *Resurrection Knowledge: Recovering the Gospel for a Postmodern Church* (Nashville: Abingdon, 1999), 10f.

[8] J. L. Austin, "Performative Utterances," in *Philosophical Papers*, 3rd ed., ed. J. O. Urmson and G. J. Warnock (Oxford: Oxford University Press, 1979), 233ff. See also his *How to Do Things With Words* (Cambridge, MA: Harvard University Press, 1975).

[9] One thinks back to David Hume who took foundationalist epistemology to its logical conclusion—leaving nothing secure as real knowledge. Hume found his own arguments philosophically compelling but practically irrelevant, turning instead to enjoying his friends over beer and pool.

[10] One of the key tests he proposes is the "hereby test," as in "I hereby christen this ship *Phantom of the Aqua*." The "hereby test" breaks down rather quickly as a way to distinguish performatives from constatives once one tries saying "I hereby assert...." *How to Do Things With Words*, 57–61.

[11] Ibid., 109.

[12] Anthony Thiselton uses speech act theory as one of the key models in his

hermeneutical theory. Cf. *New Horizons in Hermeneutics: The Theory and Practice of Transforming Biblical Reading* (Grand Rapids, MI: Zondervan, 1992).

[13] Austin, *How to Do Things With Words*, 151–64.

[14] John Searle, *Speech Acts: An Essay in the Philosophy of Language*. (Cambridge: Cambridge University Press, 1969), 64–71. He also has a more extensive discussion of the types of illocutions in "A Taxonomy of Illocutionary Acts," in *Expression and Meaning: Studies in the Theory of Speech Acts* (Cambridge: Cambridge University Press, 1979), 1–29. I am inclined to think that Searle would get no serious argument from Austin on this. Austin's writing here is aimed more at illustration than comprehensiveness.

[15] *Convictions: Defusing Religious Relativism*, rev. ed. (Valley Forge, PA: Trinity Press International, 1994). Donald Evans is another who bases his work on Austin. Cf. *The Logic of Self-Involvement: A Philosophical Study of Everyday Language with Special Reference to the Christian Use of Language about God as Creator* (New York: Herder and Herder, 1969). Evans' work is less useful because he does not consider the entirety of Austin's theory of speech acts, stopping only with the performative. In a recent work on divine speech Nicholas Wolterstorff uses Austin's work to analyze the complex speech act that scripture would be if it is taken to be both the word of the author and the Word of God. Cf. *Divine Discourse: Philosophical Reflections on the Claim that God Speaks* (New York: Cambridge University Press, 1995).

[16] McClendon and Smith, *Convictions*, 5.

[17] McClendon and Smith, *Convictions*, 77.

[18] They claim that "if it turns out that the representative, primary, and affective elements of our utterances are intertwined as it seems to us they are, then saying what is true will sometimes be an elusive goal. The history of convictional controversy (political and social as well as religious) seems to offer reasons for believing that just collecting facts or thinking up new arguments . . . is insufficient to resolve such controversies" (*Convictions*, 78).

[19] Since doctrine is an action of the church, it makes sense that there be a verbal form. "Indoctrinate" is an option, but has so many negative connotations I would rather avoid it.

[20] McClendon and Smith speak of doctrinal convictions, but their analysis compares doctrinal convictions with particular convictions, with the former being more general than the latter. They also claim that this is a relative distinction. While this position seems accurate, it does not investigate the corporate nature of doctrine. Their discussion is in *Convictions*, 92–96.

[21] For more on appropriating Austin, see Nancey Murphy, "Textual Relativism, Philosophy of Language, and the baptist Vision," in *Theology Without Foundations*, ed. Stanley Hauerwas, Nancey Murphy and Mark Nation (Nashville: Abingdon, 1994), 245-270.

[22] Ludwig Wittgenstein, *On Certainty*, ed. G.E.M. Anscombe and G. H. von Wright, trans. G. H. von Wright and Denis Paul (New York: Harper and Row, 1969), ¶204.

[23] Ibid., ¶ 559.

[24] These patterned human activities are what Wittgenstein means by "forms of life." For the clearest discussion of "forms of life", see his *Philosophical Investigations*, 3rd ed., trans. G.E. M. Anscombe (New York: Macmillan, 1958), ¶19, ¶23. (Henceforth, *PI*.)

[25] Wittgenstein, *PI*, ¶23.
[26] Ibid., ¶7.
[27] One way to understand metaphor is as a bridge built from one language game to another. Sometimes the bridge does not quite reach the other side. Sometimes it works well for a time but becomes so wide and broad that its status as a bridge (a metaphor) drops from sight. See also *PI*, p. 224.
[28] Wittgenstein, *On Certainty*, ¶18.
[29] This is the challenge all postmoderns face. Their key positions cannot be evaluated from within a modern framework—they simply do not fit on the map, or as Murphy and McClendon suggest, they occupy different conceptual space. "Distinguishing Modern and Postmodern Theologies," *Modern Theology* 5 (April 1989). Until one position comes out the winner for the dominant postmodern philosophy (not assuming, of course, that one must), we will continue to face the fact that claimants will inevitably be called by critics both premodern and ultramodern. Either assessment could be true, but is usually part of a rhetorical strategy. For an example of this issue in relation to Wittgenstein, see D. Z. Phillips, *Wittgenstein and Religion*, Swansea Studies in Religion (New York: St. Martin's Press, 1993), 22-32.
[30] Wittgenstein, *On Certainty*, ¶94. See further development of this issue in ¶105 and in *PI*, ¶241-42.
[31] Not Wittgenstein's term, but it makes sense here.
[32] For more on Wittgenstein, realism, and antirealism, see Fergus Kerr, *Theology After Wittgenstein* (Oxford: Basil Blackwell, 1986), ch. 6; Fergus Kerr, "Idealism and Realism: An Old Controversy Dissolved," in *Christ, Ethics and Tragedy: Essays in Honour of Donald McKinnon*, ed. Kenneth Surin (Cambridge: Cambridge University Press, 1989), 15-33.
[33] Wittgenstein, *On Certainty*, ¶617. On change within language games see also ¶256.
[34] This seems to be the source much of the current emphasis on "critical realism" in evangelical works. It is not so much a desire to maintain foundationalism as it is to overcome antirealism. For an example of such a position see N. T. Wright, *New Testament*, 32-37.
[35] For an analysis of Schleiermacher that moves in this direction see Georg Behrens, "Schleiermacher *contra* Lindbeck on the Status of Doctrinal Sentences," *Religious Studies* 30 (Dec. 1994): 399-417. If we read Taylor as a postmodern (which I suggest is the way to read him), we find that some important roots of postmodernity are already present in the Romantic reaction to the Enlightenment. For a similar claim in the context of a very different position, see David Bloor, *Knowledge and Social Imagery* (London: Routledge and Kegan Paul, 1976).
[36] Charles Taylor, "Language and Human Nature," in *Philosophical Papers* 1 (Cambridge: Cambridge University Press, 1985), 220f.
[37] Charles Taylor, "Theories of Meaning," in *Philosophical Papers* 1 (Cambridge: Cambridge University Press, 1985), 249.
[38] Ibid., 256f.
[39] Taylor, *Sources of the Self: The Making of Modern Identity* (Cambridge: Harvard University Press, 1989), 41.
[40] Taylor, "Language and Human Nature," 238.
[41] Ibid.
[42] Hans-Georg Gadamer, *Truth and Method*, 2nd, rev. ed., trans. Joel Weinsheimer

and Donald G. Marshall (New York: Crossroad, 1989), 189.
⁴³Ibid., 238.
⁴⁴Taylor, "Theories of Meaning," 259.
⁴⁵Ibid., 259. Gadamer makes a similar point. See *Truth and Method*, 260, 392.
⁴⁶Ibid., 259.
⁴⁷Taylor, "Theories of Meaning," 260.
⁴⁸Ibid., 261. This idea of standards that go beyond mere desire or preference is what Taylor elsewhere terms "strong evaluation." This entails a form of evaluation that examines things in terms of higher and lower, better and worse. This is contrasted (not surprisingly) with *weak evaluation*. Taylor comments: "(1) In weak evaluation, for something to be judged good it is sufficient that it be desired, whereas in strong evaluation there is also a use of 'good' or some other evaluative term for which being desired is not sufficient; indeed some desires or desired consummations can be judged as bad, base, ignoble, trivial, superficial, unworthy, and so on. . . . It follows from this that (2) when in weak evaluation one desired alternative is set aside, it is only on grounds of its contingent incompatibility with a more desired alternative. . . . But with strong evaluation this is not necessarily the case. Some desired consummation may be eschewed not because it is incompatible with another. . . . For strong evaluation deploys a language of evaluative distinctions, in which different desires are described as noble or base, integrating or fragmenting, courageous or cowardly, clairvoyant or blind, and so on. But this means they are characterized contrastively." It is exactly this contrastive characterization that differentiates weak and strong evaluation. Taylor, "What is Human Agency?" in *Philosophical Papers* 1 (Cambridge: Cambridge University Press, 1985), 18–20.
⁴⁹Though we must admit that some segments of the church do seem to offer a fairly reductive and individualistic account of salvation.
⁵⁰Taylor, *Sources*, 58.
⁵¹"All testing, all confirmation and disconfirmation of a hypothesis takes place already within a system. And this system is not a more or less arbitrary and doubtful point of departure for all our arguments: no, it belongs to the essence of what we call an argument. The system is not so much the point of departure, as the element in which arguments have their life." Wittgenstein, *On Certainty*, ¶105.
⁵²Alister McGrath is aware of this feature of doctrine as well: "Doctrine cannot be regarded as an isolable aspect of the Christian faith, as if it could be detached from the community of faith and treated as a purely ideational phenomenon." *The Genesis of Doctrine: A Study in the Foundations of Doctrinal Criticism* (Oxford: Basil Blackwell, 1990), 193.
⁵³Charles Taylor, "To Follow a Rule," in *Rules and Conventions: Literature, Philosophy, Social Theory*, ed. Mette Hjort (Baltimore, MD: Johns Hopkins University Press, 1992), 169. See also, Taylor, "Philosophy and its History," in *Philosophy in History: Essays on the Historiography of Philosophy*, ed. Richard Rorty, J. B. Schneewind, and Quentin Skinner (Cambridge: Cambridge University Press, 1984), 23f. Lindbeck seems to allude to this when he notes that reality is different for catacomb dwellers and astronauts, Platonists and Whiteheadians. George Lindbeck, *The Nature of Doctrine*, 121. He does not, however, allow this recognition to influence sufficiently his theory of doctrine, handicapping his understanding of doctrinal change and con-

stancy and rendering his hylomorphic theory of doctrinal language unacceptable.

[54] William Abraham's explanation of what doctrine does fits this as well. He claims that the chief functions of doctrine are: (1) the articulation of communal convictions that provide communal identity and differentiate it from other communities; (2) the explication of this identity to outsiders; (3) to "provide road maps for sorting out who we are;" (4) the identification of the content of the Gospel for proclamation. Cf. *Waking from Doctrinal Amnesia* (Nashville: Abingdon, 1996), 38. The main difference from my position is that mine includes the narrative more centrally and thus sees doctrine as more dynamic. Doctrine not only lays out the current reality—our identity, the gospel—but also directs the church on where to go, i.e., how to play the next act of the drama.

[55] Taylor, "Rule," 175.

[56] Ibid., 176.

[57] Taylor, "Rule," 177.

[58] McClendon and Smith, *Convictions*, 60.

[59] William G. Rusch, *Reception: An Ecumenical Opportunity* (Minneapolis: Fortress Press, 1988), 31. See also Frederick M. Bliss, *Understanding Reception: A Backdrop to Its Ecumenical Use*, Marquette Studies in Theology (Marquette, WI: Marquette University Press, 1993).

[60] Rusch, *Reception*, 33–36. The discussion in this paragraph is drawn from Rusch's second chapter.

[61] Rusch, *Reception*, 44.

[62] Ronald Thiemann, *Revelation and Theology: The Gospel as Narrated Promise* (Notre Dame, IN: University of Notre Dame Press, 1985), 148.

[63] Abraham, *Waking*, 91.

[64] The doctrine of original sin has in recent times and in some sections of the church, been reduced in status. Rusch speaks of nonreception and dereception, but these developments focus on changes for the sake of ecumenism. Rusch, *Reception*, 71. What we see in the rejection of doctrinal status for original sin is something different. This simply shows that while reception is necessary in an account of doctrine, it is not sufficient.

[65] Wolterstorff, *Divine Discourse: Philosophical Reflections on the Claim that God Speaks* (New York: Cambridge University Press, 1995), 51ff. This concept adds a further dimension to how we can understand a speech act to be corporate in nature.

[66] Ibid., 186.

[67] Lindbeck, *Nature of Doctrine*, 66–67.

[68] Ibid., 66.

[69] Ibid.

[70] See Nicholas Lash, "When Did Theologians Lose Interest in God?" in *Theology and Dialogue: Essays in Conversation with George Lindbeck*, ed. Bruce D. Marshall (Notre Dame, IN: University of Notre Dame Press, 1990), 132f.

[71] Lindbeck, *Nature of Doctrine*, 68.

[72] This ignores the fact that the convention of using ostensive reference depends on certain spatial relationships existing between interlocutors. When speaking (or writing) to someone not present, one simply does not say, "This car is red." Instead, one finds another way to specify the car in question: "Bob's car is red," or "The car I bought yesterday is red."

⁷³Stanley Fish, *Is There a Text in This Class? The Authority of Interpretive Communities* (Cambridge, MA: Harvard University Press, 1980), 304.
⁷⁴For more about talking about sentences, see J. L. Austin, "The Meaning of a Word," in *Philosophical Papers*, 3rd ed., ed. J .O. Urmson and G. J. Warnock (Oxford: Oxford University Press, 1979), 55–75.
⁷⁵Lindbeck, *Nature of Doctrine*, 68.
⁷⁶Just one other example is Stephen Toulmin: "It is unnecessary . . . to freeze statements into timeless propositions before admitting them into logic: utterances are made at particular times and in particular situations, and they have to be understood and assessed with one eye on this context" (*Uses of Argument* [Cambridge: Cambridge University Press, 1958], 182. See also p. 240).
⁷⁷Lindbeck, *Nature of Doctrine*, 114.
⁷⁸Below I will question the practice of splitting the world up into "realms of discourse."
⁷⁹Lindbeck is not alone. See McClendon and Smith, *Convictions*, 47. This seems to be the most common way of misreading Austin. The pattern suggests an agenda aimed at avoiding having to posit a connection with the world in religious language.
⁸⁰See the discussion of Bultmann's existentialist reinterpretation of biblical texts in Thiselton, *The Two Horizons*, 281, 292.
⁸¹Talk about the realms of language is scattered throughout his discussion of truth and reference. *Nature of Doctrine*, 65–67.
⁸²*Nature of Doctrine*, 65.
⁸³See the discussion in William Placher, *Unapologetic Theology: A Christian Voice in a Pluralist Conversation* (Louisville, KY: Westminster/John Knox, 1989), 65.
⁸⁴For further discussion of the interrelatedness of language games and their openness to each other, see Thiselton, *New Horizons*, 541-42; and, McClendon and Smith, *Convictions*, 108.
⁸⁵Alasdair MacIntyre and Paul Ricoeur, *The Religious Significance of Atheism* (New York: Columbia University Press, 1969), 15f.
⁸⁶Karl Barth had emphasized the radical discontinuity between God and humanity, between Christianity and culture. Perhaps Lindbeck's position, like MacIntyre's old one, has been shaped by a commitment to Barth combined with Wittgensteinian talk of language games. John Milbank sees a connection here, characterizing neoorthodoxy as a form of liberal Protestantism insofar as it sees no connection with the world. Cf. *Theology and Social Theory: Beyond Secular Reason*, (Oxford: Basil Blackwell, 1990), 101. Neoorthodoxy certainly envisions the connection with the world differently than mainstream liberalism. I believe Milbank is correct, however, in his understanding that Barth, for all his criticism of Kant, never gets beyond his dualism of phenomena and noumena. See Barth's discussion of Kant in *Protestant Theology in the Nineteenth Century: Its Background and History*, trans. B. Cozens and J. Bowden (Valley Forge, PA: Judson Press, 1973).
⁸⁷Giovanna Borradori, "Interview with MacIntyre," in *The American Philosopher: Conversations with Quine, Davidson, Putnam, Nozick, Danto, Rorty, Cavell, MacIntyre and Kuhn*, trans. Rosanna Crocitto (Chicago: University of Chicago Press, 1994), 142.
⁸⁸Wittgenstein recognizes the complexity of the situation. "Here one must, I believe, remember that the concept 'proposition' itself is not a sharp one"

(*On Certainty*, ¶320). The great advantage of a position like that of Austin and Wittgenstein is that we speak of propositionality, a characteristic of many types of language use, instead of "proposition," one kind of language use.

[89] J. L. Austin, "A Plea for Excuses," in *Philosophical Papers*, 182.

[90] Milbank says against Lindbeck's reduction of religious language to the performative: "While every dimension of religious practice, including the articulation of a theology, is 'performative,' it is also the case that no performance could be staged without the assumption . . . of a historical and mythical scene within which that performance is set" (*Theology and Social Theory*, 383). Lindbeck must, he says, pay greater attention to propositionality. Miroslav Volf makes a similar point: "Phenomenologically, at the level of the self-perception of religious actors, propositionality seems built into the very fiber of religious belief" ("Theology, Meaning and Power" in *The Future of Theology: Essays in Honor of Jürgen Moltmann*, ed. Miroslav Volf, Carmen Krieg, and Thomas Kucharz [Grand Rapids, MI: Eerdmans, 1996], 107). Also, "If God and *God's grace* are the proper objects of religion and theology (rather than religion and theology just being efficacious talk about God), then religion and theology must be at their core propositional" (108). William Placher, "Paul Ricoeur and Postliberal Theology: A Conflict of Interpretations?" *Modern Theology* 4:1 (1987), 46f; Colman O'Neill, "The Rule Theory of Doctrine and Propositional Truth," *The Thomist* 49 (July 1985): 417–42.

[91] Thiemann, *Revelation and Theology*, 145. Elsewhere he shows that this is also true in Christian worship: "Analysis of the force and propositional content of the eucharistic prayer shows that this liturgical act presupposes the prevenience of God. Indeed, this act is unintelligible if God's prior gracious reality is not presupposed" (100). See also p. 108.

[92] Thiemann, *Revelation*, 81.

[93] As Austin notes, it only makes sense to ask about reality in certain settings. "Other Minds," in *Philosophical Papers*, 86–87. It is simply not something one can question of everything, either taken as a whole or in its particulars.

[94] Lindbeck, *Nature of Doctrine*, 74. See also ibid., 18. In the earlier definition, he explicitly contrasts this definition with the notion that doctrine functions symbolically or to make truth claims.

[95] Ibid., 79.

[96] Ibid., 80. Lindbeck's use of the distinction between first order and second order propositions seems to rely on Wittgenstein, who says, "Everything descriptive of a language-game is a part of logic." *On Certainty*, ¶56. Lindbeck seems to have in mind something like Wittgenstein's discussion of "physical object." Wittgenstein says, "'A is a physical object' is a piece of instruction which we give only to someone who doesn't yet understand either what 'A' means, or what 'physical object' means. Thus it is instructive about the use of words, and 'physical object' is a logical concept. (Like color, quantity. . . .) And that is why no such proposition as: 'There are physical objects' can be formulated. Yet we encounter such unsuccessful shots at every turn" (*On Certainty*, ¶36). The thought may be that doctrinal language is akin to talk about "physical objects." Much doctrinal language, however, resists the tendency toward generalization, holding doggedly to

contingent historical events of eternal significance. I do not see how "Jesus rose from the dead" could be reduced to rules without a prior reduction along the lines of liberalism in the direction of dehistoricized generality.

Lindbeck could read further and find that the distinction between logic and fact is not at all as hard as Wittgenstein is sometimes read to claim. In relation to questions of doubt, Wittgenstein says, "'The question doesn't arise at all.' Its answer would characterize a *method*. But there is no sharp boundary between methodological propositions and propositions within a method."

"But wouldn't one have to say then, that there is no sharp boundary between propositions of logic and empirical propositions? The lack of sharpness *is* that of the boundary between *rule* and empirical proposition" (*On Certainty*, ¶318–19).

[97] Ibid. Lindbeck's style is frustrating. His frequent use of the subjunctive and conditional clauses makes it hard to tell sometimes exactly what he is asserting. In this case, the phrase "it either cannot or need not" seems to leave open the possibility of "can." The tenor of Lindbeck's position is that he wants to exclude such a possibility; so he ought to just come right out and say so.

[98] Lindbeck's hard distinction between rule and truth claim seems to be another case of his conviction regarding the autonomy of language games and misunderstanding of the performative dimension of language. These come together in his discussion of theology, doctrine, and truth. *Nature of Doctrine*, 69.

[99] It is odd to identify "be authoritative" as a kind of use.

[100] See the discussion in Oden, *Doctrinal Standards*.

[101] Ibid., 81–82. This must also be seen in light of his claim that "Religious" is a very hard language to learn. "For Christians, even mature Christians, this process has just begun. They have only begun to confess Jesus as Lord, to speak the Christian language, the language of the coming kingdom.... In terms of this analogy, all human beings are toddlers, whether Peter, or Paul, or the veriest infant in Christ" (Ibid., 60–61). This example seems more influenced by Lindbeck's appropriation of his Lutheran heritage and its doctrine of *simul iustus et peccator* than by attention to languages and their speakers.

[102] That there would be a dichotomy here seems to be the recurrence of the same tendency toward dualism that we see in other areas. See the discussion in "A Panel Discussion: Lindbeck, Hunsinger, McGrath and Fracke." In *The Nature of Confession: Evangelicals and Postliberals in Conversation*. Ed. Timothy R. Phillips and Dennis L. Okholm (Downers Grove, IL: InterVarsity Press, 1996), 246–53.

[103] "Most doctrines illustrate correct usage rather than define it.... Faithfulness to such doctrines does not necessarily mean repeating them; rather, it requires, in the making of any new formulations, adherence to the same directives that were involved in their first formulation." Lindbeck, *Nature of Doctrine*, 81.

[104] This was at the very center of what Jesus was doing. See N. T. Wright, *Jesus and the Victory of God*, vol. 2, *Christian Origins and the Question of God* (Minneapolis: Fortress Press, 1996).

[105] Lindbeck, *Nature of Doctrine*, 48–52.

106. Ibid., 65.
107. It does not help that he sometimes speaks of categorial adequacy and sometimes of conceptual truth.
108. There is a necessary ambiguity in the word "narrative." I use it to refer to both the enacted drama and to the stories that relate this drama. We find it much easier to speak of the truth of the latter than of the former.
109. Charles Taylor, "Rorty in the Epistemological Tradition," in *Reading Rorty: Critical Responses to Philosophy and the Mirror of Nature*, ed. Alan Malachowski (Oxford: Basil Blackwell, 1990), 272. Taylor makes this point against Rorty and pragmatist theories of truth that see truth as nothing more than usefulness.
110. John Milbank makes some useful points along these lines. First, there is always an infinite number of coherences. Coherence alone is not enough. Second, and because of this, doctrine requires a substantive anchor in reality. Cf. *Theology and Social Theory*, 342. Again, this is not a claim that there is a neutral and objective view of reality.
111. Austin, "Truth," in *Philosophical Papers*, 3rd ed., ed. J. O. Urmson and G. J. Warnock (Oxford: Oxford University Press, 1979), 130. See also 123.
112. Ibid., 130.
113. For more on truth in a Christian and postmodern context, see Nancey Murphy, *Anglo-American Postmodernity: Philosophical Perspectives on Science, Religion, and Ethics* (Boulder, CO: Westview Press, 1997), ch. 6.
114. Lindbeck, *Nature of Doctrine*, 92.
115. Something like, "Jesus sure is a great guy!" except, perhaps, with more religious overtones.
116. For example, "Son of David" connects with the narrative of monarchy, and "Logos" connects with the creation and wisdom parts of the story.
117. Lindbeck, *Nature of Doctrine*, 94.
118. Ibid., 80.
119. "Accuracy" seems like a useful term for the world-fitting dimension of the relation between the biblical narratives and the drama they depict: as long as we remember that accuracy is always a "more or less" relation. See Austin, "Truth," 126ff.
120. Lindbeck, *Nature of Doctrine*, 83. Where are the definite articles? Are we talking about *the* passion and *the* resurrection? These do not come to us as mere concepts. Within the narrative they are heartily described: *the* passion was a real suffering that led to a real death. *The* resurrection was an event that led to an empty tomb and a risen Jesus who fellowshipped with his disciples.
121. Ibid. On p. 82 he has said, "The first-order truth claims of a religion change insofar as these arise from the application of the interpretive scheme to the shifting worlds that human beings inhabit.... In one world, for example, the origin of things is pictured in terms of a Babylonian myth; in another, in terms of Plato's Timaeus tale; and in a third, in terms of a scientific account of cosmic evolution. The descriptions of God as originator change correspondingly." For a discussion of this feature, see Lee Barrett, "Theology as Grammar: Regulative Principles or Paradigms and Practices," *Modern Theology* 4 (Jan. 1988): 159.

This sounds like the "translation theology" against which Hauerwas and Willimon speak. "The theology of translation assumes that there is some kernel of *real* Christianity, some abstract essence that can be preserved even while changing some of the old Near Eastern labels. Yet such a view distorts the nature of Christianity. In Jesus we meet not a presentation of basic ideas about God, world, and humanity, but an invitation to join up, to become part of a movement, a people." Stanley Hauerwas and William Willimon, *Resident Aliens: Life in the Christian Colony* (Nashville: Abingdon, 1989), 21.

[122] Peter Harrison, *'Religion' and the Religions in the English Enlightenment* (Cambridge: Cambridge University Press, 1990), 148.

[123] Barrett makes this point as well, "This distinction of formal syntactical rules and their instantiation in practice is misleading. Most importantly, the identity of Christianity should not be attributed to the continuity of formal doctrinal principles apart form the continuity of particular first-order truth claims, behavioral patterns and truth experiences" ("Theology as Grammar," 161). Gadamer says, "Verbal form and traditionary content cannot be separated in the hermeneutic experience. If every language is a view of the world, it is so not primarily because it is a particular type of language ... but because of what is said or handed down in the language" (*Truth and Method*, 441).

For a claim that Lindbeck's approach is profoundly ahistorical, see Milbank, *Theology and Social Theory*, 386.

[124] Holmer, *Grammar of Faith* (San Francisco: Harper and Row, 1978), 12. Lindbeck is *not* saying that theology (or doctrine) must adapt to contemporary demands. His language implies, rather, that this adaptation simply happens and is a completely neutral development. I do not think, however, this is a position he would want to defend.

[125] See discussion in MacIntyre and Ricoeur, *Atheism*, 27.

[126] David Bryant, "Christian Identity and Historical Change: Postliberals and Historicity," *Journal of Religion* 73 (Jan. 1993): 40.

[127] Alasdair MacIntyre, "The Intelligibility of Action," in *Rationality, Relativism and the Human Sciences*, ed. J. Margolis, M. Krausz, and R. M. Burian, Studies in the Greater Philadelphia Philosophy Consortium (Dordrecht: Martinus Nijhoff, 1986), 64.

[128] Terrence Tilley, "Incommensurability, Intratextuality and Fideism," *Modern Theology* 5 (Jan. 1989), 103.

[129] Barrett, "Theology as Grammar," 168.

[130] Wittgenstein, *PI*, ¶201. See also, Barrett, "Theology as Grammar," 162.

[131] Murphy, "*Textual Relativism*," 249. See also, Austin, "Performative Utterances," 250f.; "Truth," 130.

Chapter Three

The Church as Agent of Doctrine

> It is my thesis that questions of the truth or falsity of Christian convictions cannot even be addressed until Christians recover the church as a political community necessary for our salvation. . . . Our beliefs, or better, our convictions, only make sense as they are embodied in a political community we call church.[1]
> Stanley Hauerwas, *After Christendom*

STANLEY HAUERWAS IS EXACTLY RIGHT. DOCTRINE DOES NOT MAKE SENSE— let alone "work"—as a free-floating set of propositions, but exists in a symbiotic relationship with the community called church. In chapter two I claimed that doctrine is a speech act of the church. In this chapter I will investigate the character of the church insofar as it is the subject of this speech act. The primary modern obstacle to healthy doctrine dealt with in chapter two was epistemology: here I will confront the impact of modernity's individualism. If the church is not living as church, but merely as a collection of individuals (a voluntary association), doctrine will inevitably fail to function as doctrine. I will also argue that individualism has contributed to the marginalization of doctrine within the church, not merely through the neglect of the church itself, but also through the covert substitution of an alternative interpretive community. Finally, the rest of this chapter will focus on the relation between church and culture. Hauerwas' argument that the church itself is a cultural alternative to the world is suggestive in this regard. I will consider his claim and suggest some ways we can understand the many dimensions of relationship between church and culture.

What must be said about the church if we are to make progress in understanding the nature and role of doctrine? In chapter two I claimed that doctrine is better understood as a speech act of the church than as the epistemological dimension of religion. This chapter claims that the problem of doctrine as it is now experienced is, to a great extent, a problem in the area of ecclesiology. The problems faced in ecclesiology parallel those faced by doctrine. If we are to "recover the church" as Hauerwas suggests, such a recovery will require both a reconceptualization of what the church is and better performance on the part of the church. My aim here is to make some progress in the former dimension.

My claim that Christianity can best be understood as an ongoing dramatic narrative has definite implications for ecclesiology. From this perspective the necessary starting point is not with an analysis of modernity, politics, communities, or culture, though these elements are important. Rather, we must begin with soteriology. How these other aspects figure into the question will be dealt with later in the chapter. Starting with soteriology allows us to see how the church fits into God's action in history and why doctrine might function to guide the church in living out this continuing history. When the church is understood from a soteriological perspective, the tendency to interpret ecclesiality from the standpoint of individualism—leading to a reduction of ecclesiality to sociality—is reduced. If the church owes its very existence as church to the action of God, then there is a fundamental difference between Church and other social groupings.

THE ECCLESIAL COMPONENT OF SALVATION

When God called Abram to leave his country and family behind and move to a new place, we see nothing about an explicit offer of salvation. What we find instead is a twofold promise: God would bless Abram (by giving him children and making them into a mighty nation) and make this nation a blessing to all nations.[2] By the time of the Exodus, Israel is great numerically, but enslaved, a condition hard to conceive of as a blessing. Exodus tells us that the Israelites cried out from their oppression and that God remembered the promise to Abram and delivered Israel by the hand of Moses. In Exodus 19:3–6, God restated (in a different form) the promise given centuries before to Abram. God's intent was not merely to make Israel a great nation or to bless them. They were to be God's "treasured possession" and "a kingdom of priests." Each individual Israelite experienced the salvation of deliverance from slavery in Egypt. This salvation was, in its very essence, corporate. They were not merely saved *from* slavery, but they were also saved *to* a life as the people of God.

Modernity Misses the Corporate Element of Salvation

That modernity has missed this point is all too evident in the way the very next chapter of Exodus has been used. The Ten Commandments, in a culture defined by individualism, are all too easily read as universal rules for personal morality. In the context of Exodus, however, the natural way to read them is to hear God saying, "You see how I have saved you. I brought you out so you could live as my people. Here are the markers that will identify you as such."[3]

The connection between salvation and church is not merely an Old Testament phenomenon.[4] Popular evangelistic preaching in America has often featured reference to Ephesians 2:1–10. This passage is typically used to demonstrate the horrible reality of sin and its deadly consequences, the gift of God's Son to overcome this sin, and our appropriation of this gift by faith, not by works. This approach fits quite nicely with our individualistic convictions. But what do we do with Ephesians 2:11ff.? This passage, following immediately after the last one, has the same structure (i.e., problem–"but God"–solution–consequences) so it is natural to read the two sections together. While the first section (v. 1–10) can be used legitimately to refer to the individual dimension of salvation, the second section clearly speaks of a communal dimension that must also be counted as part of what salvation is about. Formerly the Gentiles were beyond the scope of God's salvation: now, through Christ, they can enter the people of God and experience salvation—as one people.

No Salvation Outside the Church

It is in this context, I believe, that Cyprian's dictum, "*extra ecclesiam nulla sallus*" is best appropriated.[5] I say "appropriated," because this is clearly not his (or the usual) understanding of the phrase. The meaning traditionally attributed to this phrase is that the Church is the only place where one can receive the grace necessary to salvation (usually understood as being through the sacraments).[6] Though this position may be correct, it is substantially different from what I am claiming. I want to claim that the church is not merely the place where people find salvation, but it is itself part of that salvation. Salvation so conceived is much more than the believer going to heaven after death. It is very much something experienced by the believer here and now, which finds its ultimate fulfillment in the presence of God in eternity.[7] In this light Cyprian's dictum is analytic, defining the relation between salvation and the church. Part of being saved is being in the church, so it makes no sense to speak of being saved outside the church.

This seems to be the direction Hauerwas is heading, though there are some echoes of the traditional position in his work. He claims that

> Salvation is a political alternative that the world cannot know apart from the existence of a concrete people called church. Put more dramatically, you cannot even know you need saving without the church's being a political alternative.[8]

It is not difficult in our culture to have at least a bastardized notion of individual salvation, culminating in heaven, which is something like: this life we now live is envisioned as continuing *ad infinitum*, with no sickness or defeat. Knowing one needs some form of salvation in order to "go to heaven" is mostly a conceptual issue: getting beyond seeing God as nice enough to save me for my sincerity, to a place where one recognizes the need for faith. But salvation is more than this—it includes membership in the Body of Christ, the church. It is to this latter dimension of salvation (a major dimension, if we consider the entire biblical witness) that individualism has blinded us, crippling the church in its attempts to live as church and demonstrating in its life the reality of God's salvation. Living in our culture it is not difficult to come to know we need to be saved from sin to go to heaven; however, we rarely see evidence that we need to be saved from sin and be joined to the people of God.

Ecclesiology and Soteriological Universalism

If the church is not merely necessary for salvation but is itself *part* of salvation, the commonly raised question regarding the salvation of non-Christians takes on a different light. Soteriological universalism (the view that all will be saved) seems most commonly associated with an implicit conception of salvation as knowledge. The tie between salvation and knowledge is evidenced by frequent claims in the same context that other religions have some truth within them, that is, that Christianity though it may be the truest religion, does not have a "corner" on all truth. This view of salvation fits nicely with epistemological universalism (the view that real knowledge is equally accessible to all since one's location cannot be epistemically relevant). That people in other religions might come to acquire such knowledge seems completely logical. Further confusing the issue is the notion that in a pluralistic world we ought to be tolerant of other points of view, including religions, and that it is somehow intolerant to suppose that only in one religion can one find salvation. I have already questioned the usefulness of the category "religion" to encompass Christianity, Islam, Hinduism, etc. (a category seemingly presupposed by many discussions of this issue), and will not pursue that part of the question here.

Schubert Ogden criticizes the Christian tradition (which is, for the most part, not universalist in this respect) for seeing the church as the locus of salvation. Instead, he claims, the church should be seen as the *sign* of salvation (of all).[9] All are saved and the reality of the church proclaims this. If, to the contrary, we take the biblical claim that the church is *part* of salvation the universalist position simply is not available. Whatever we might say about the future salvation of all, the biblical picture, with its tie to the church, does not allow us to say that all are now saved. Though it may be possible to imagine an "anonymous Christian," it is nearly impossible to image an "anonymous church member" without etherealizing the church beyond recognition.

The Recovery of the Biblical Picture

The "recovery of the church," therefore, will require a recovery of the full biblical picture of salvation. One dimension of this recovery will necessarily be of the church as a historical (and eschatological) community, which I will show in chapter four. Doctrine, therefore, is much more than a list of beliefs for autonomous individuals to believe, but is closely tied to salvation itself. In chapter two I claimed that doctrine is a speech act of the church. Once we see that salvation includes joining the historically particular people of God, we can imagine how this speech act can function as guidance in living within this continuing history. When conceived this way, doctrine requires a church living as the community of the redeemed. The individualism of modern American Christianity depicts spirituality as intensely (and purely) private, with little place for community.[10] Doctrine is left not only with no role other than the epistemological, but also with no community to speak and hear. At this point, it will be helpful to consider more closely the impact of individualism on church.

INIDIVIDUALISM AND ECCLESIOLOGY

It may sound strange to say that individualism has hurt the church. Churches are full of individualists are they not? The problem lies in the fact that individualism has brought about a redefinition of church so it can be included under the genus "voluntary association." Community is nice, but dispensable. The polemic against individualism must be tempered, however, by an admission that not all elements of individualism stem from modernity or are harmful to the church. The stance modern epistemology leads us to take in relation to the world is radically individualist, leading to an equally individualist conception of religion. This stance, however, has roots in specifically Christian thought.[11] The harmfulness of specifically modern individualism lies in the combination of individualism with atomism and a kind of universalism that leads to a view that all individuals are essentially alike. Thus, although we find doctrines of the church in the modern period, it is all too common to find in them a reduction of ecclesial community to a collective sociality.[12]

The distinction between "collective" and "community" is not absolute. The former relies on political atomism and tends to see the social as nothing more than an extension of the individual. The latter sees community as composed of yet irreducible to individuals. Community is more than a collection of individuals. Within community individuals are considered different from each other, in contrast to the atomism of the collectivist approach. The character and health of each community is dependent upon the harmonious diversity of its members.

Individualism and Salvation

The biblical picture of humanity is of people who are defined by their brokenness with respect to God, themselves, other people, and creation. God's goal in salvation is the overcoming of all these dimensions of brokenness.[13] As one who is being saved, the Christian is no longer defined by broken relationships, but by a host of new relationships, most importantly with God, but also with other people (in the church). Radical individualism and the collectivist view it engenders looks like the rationalization of the biblical picture of sin: a person so cut off from all relationships and utterly alone that nothing impinges on him or her. Colin Gunton describes it like this: "Individualism is a non-relational creed, because it teaches that I do not need my neighbor in order to be myself."[14] The biblical story of salvation, on the other hand, is intensely relational. Christians do not find their identity in the beliefs to which they adhere—though they do adhere to certain beliefs—nor in their world view—though at least some elements of a world view are implicit in the gospel—nor, finally, in their religious experience—though they will share many experiences in common. Rather, Christian identity is based on relationships: a renewed relationship with the Triune God, with fellow believers (and prospectively with future believers), and with creation.[15]

Individualism and the Function of Doctrine

Modern individualism not only blinds one to the social dimension of salvation, but also to the role doctrine plays. The communal nature of doctrine is incomprehensible—rejected as heteronomous, irrational, external authority. My beliefs are my own, the result of my reason and experience. Adopting beliefs through some other means would be inauthentic. But this assumes that religion is a kind of science or aesthetic enterprise, not a drama in which I (and we together as the church) play a part. Within my model, the authority of doctrine is not primarily something that makes us believe things we would not otherwise believe, but something that directs us in living our lives as the church. The dramatic model will bear directly on *what* we believe, since within the church doctrine will direct our attention to things and put us in a place where we can perceive realities we cannot perceive from other vantage points.

A dramatic conception of Christianity is contrary not only to individualism, but especially to the modern variety of individualism that insists that as humans we all stand in the same place, which, as it so often turns out, is nowhere in particular. When people stand nowhere, a community's main strategy is apologetics: offering such a person reasons to join or consider such a community. MacIntyre describes this situation strikingly:

> The individual human being confronts an alternative set of ways of life from a standpoint external to them all. Such an individual has as yet *ex hypothesi* no commitments, and the multifarious and conflicting desires which individuals develop provide in themselves no grounds for choosing which of such desires to develop and be guided by and which to inhibit and frustrate.[16]

This position, a social variant, perhaps, of Locke's *tabula rasa*, is relevant to questions of the truth of Christian doctrine. Since modernity is committed to the position that questions of truth are most important, *and* that such questions are to be answered foundationistically, doctrine in the modern era has found itself incessantly faced with questions of its own justification. Doctrine, however, cannot be justified from nowhere—and, as repeated attempts over the past couple of centuries have shown, neither can anything else. This fact has been the bane of foundationalists for most of this century. Reality, though accessible from all locations, is not accessible from none (the place moderns think they are standing). This has profound implications for doctrine.

In the face of Christian doctrinal claims, moderns protest that their beliefs are not under their control. What one believes, it is thought, is a matter of the reason, not of the will. The claims of Christian doctrine, if true, must be equally available for all to judge. If, however, everyone does, in fact, already stand within an interpretive community, then it is simply not true that everyone is in a place to judge those claims or even to see rightly the realities to which they refer. The question, "How do you know?" when asked of the church in its act of making doctrine will likely not be answered the same way in each and every situation.

In talking about the human act of reasoning, Stephen Toulmin turns to this very question, though outside of the theological context. Questioning foundationalism, he investigates the sense of asking how someone knows something. In many cases it simply does not make sense to ask the question.[17] Say, for example, that I tell someone my wife's name is Christina. In what context would it make sense for them to respond with, "How do you know?" If, on the other hand, I say that my great-great-great-great grandfather was Ephraim Doty, a fellow genealogist may rightly ask for some evidence.

This is not a fideistic approach to doctrine. Fideism is a bogeyman of foundationalism—once we move beyond foundationalism, the bogeyman departs. The problem remains to a degree, however, because foundationalism is so deeply engrained in our culture. We are schooled in the science of detachment. This is, as I noted in chapter one, a major cause of the marginalization of doctrine and its cousin theological indifferentism. So often our relation to doctrine is similar to that of the emotivist moral agent as described by MacIntyre.

> To be a moral agent is ... precisely to be able to stand back from any and every situation in which one is involved, from any and every characteristic that one may possess, and to pass judgment on it from a purely universal and abstract point of view that is totally detached from all social particularity.[18]

If we seek to understand doctrine from a perspective detached from the ecclesial community we will find ourselves in the same predicament as the emotivist. We will be unable to understand doctrine as anything other than an expression of the individual religious person.

The question may arise: what about prospective converts, the outsiders who are investigating Christianity? Where do they stand? How can they understand doctrine? These people always stand somewhere, inside some community, and it is from this community that they will seek to understand Christian doctrine. For them an understanding will require some relation to the church. From this perspective evangelism is not merely the transfer of information from one mind to another, the work of an individual, but is always the work of the church. The one who is seeking to obey Jesus' command to make disciples of all nations must live in such a relation with the prospective convert that that person can be close enough to the Christian interpretive community to borrow its resources to discern the work of God in his or her life. This kind of evangelism is clearly process rather than event oriented.

Another consequence of the modern individualist intention to stand nowhere can be seen when we remember Charles Taylor's discussion of the function of language. One function of language is to constitute public space and make dialogical action possible. As long as we are in thrall to modern individualism, we cannot see the church as the locus of dialogical action. Both doctrine and the conception of ministry in the model of church as Body of Christ depend on such dialogical action.

ONE FUNCTION OF COMMUNITY

So far I have claimed that a "recovery" of the church requires a reconnection of soteriology and ecclesiology. This reconnection helps establish the historical dimension of the church—it is God's action in history that brought the church into being and continues to sustain it today. I also claimed that in so doing, we must overcome modern individualism and its attendant atomism and reductionism. Once we do this, we will be able to understand the church as a community and not simply as a collective.

One function of community that has been ignored through most of modernity has been its role in interpretation. As long as knowledge and understanding were seen as the work of the autonomous individual, any contribution to the knowing process from the community in which the individual was situated could only be seen as truth-defeating bias. I have already suggested above, following Charles Taylor, that one important function of language is the creation of public space. It is in this public space that the church speaks and interprets. In what follows, I claim that if we are to understand the place of doctrine in the church we must rediscover the church as an interpretive community while at the same time overcoming the pretensions of modernity that there is no such thing.

Why is the question of interpretation so important? Doctrine relies on the act of interpretation in two closely related ways. First, the church interprets its place in the narrative of God's continuing action. It is an act of interpretation just to see this communal history as part of this broader history. Discerning this history includes both the recent history of the community as well as the narrative of scripture. In my discussion of the baptist vision in chapter four, these two dimensions (the scriptural narrative and the communal narrative) will be brought together. Interpretation also comes into play with the use of doctrine. When we speak of someone's performance of a play, "Hamlet," for example, we speak of his or her "interpretation" of the play. Any performance requires not only an interpretation that looks backward (what does the text say? what happened?) but also forward in a projective sense. The act of directing a play is interpretation in this sense.

The Church as Interpretive Community

Epistemology and individualism have worked together in the modern period to produce a distinctly monological approach to language and interpretation. Understanding is objective and absolute in the sense that any usage of language is potentially understandable by anyone anywhere. Reflecting on the nature of language gives us a number of reasons to think this modern approach is insufficient.

I suggested above that Hauerwas is correct in his claim that the church must communally live out the reality Christians call salvation if outsiders are to have any inkling they need salvation. It is necessary to posit further tasks of the church, related to this one. As the community in which God's Kingdom is demonstrated and lived out in concrete communal relationships, the church is also the primary interpretive community for the understanding of Scripture and doctrine.[19]

I find Lindbeck's concept of "intratextuality" attractive in this regard, though in the end it seems to neglect some important factors. Lindbeck discusses intratextuality in *The Nature of Doctrine*, but the clearest exposition of intratextuality (in contrast to *intertextuality* and *extratextuality*) can be found in an article written two years afterward. Intertextuality has a focus on texts, but claims that "all texts interpret each other on the same level" while the intratextualist position claims that a single central text "functions as the comprehensive interpretive framework."²⁰ It is this latter position that Lindbeck identifies as Barth's and claims as his own. In *The Nature of Doctrine*, Lindbeck's polemic is directed not against *intertextuality* but against *extratextuality*.²¹ Extratextuality looks for the meaning of the text outside the semiotic system of the text, and is more congenial to propositionalist views of religion. Propositionalist extratextuality seems to see the world as a whole as a semiotic system to be approximated by other semiotic systems. Read this way, the extratextualist position requires the epistemological neutrality and universality that Lindbeck and I reject. How does the intratextually created semiotic system relate to the ecclesial community and the historical drama in which it participates? In other words, what is the connection between the semiotic and the nonsemiotic? Considering only the semiotic dimension, my position fits nicely with Lindbeck's version of intratextuality. My concern is that the case against extratextuality not be combined with his aversion to referentiality in doctrinal language, resulting in a reduction of doctrine (or Christianity) to a mere semiotic system.

Lindbeck's explication of intratextuality appears to rely on his convictions that language games are autonomous and that doctrinal language is best understood hylomorphically. Such a position seems not too different from foundationalism except that the foundation is found in the text's implicit world and not in external "reality" or truth statements.²² The understanding of doctrine I am proposing requires the concrete community living in the context of a real history. As this community lives the drama and interacts with other communities, unreflected upon aspects of this drama (and of its plot and characters) come to be articulated (or rearticulated) in doctrine.

There are two key differences between Lindbeck's intratextuality and the controlling image I have offered for our understanding of Christianity, which focuses on continuing life in the Christian narrative. First, my model, in its thoroughgoing commitment to the centrality of community, questions whether pure intratextuality is possible. Miroslav Volf approaches this issue from another angle, suggesting that intratextuality as propounded by Lindbeck requires a "pure" place to stand, a single interpretive community that can guide one in understanding the world of the text without interference. Such a world simply does not exist. Volf contends that we are never simply the people of God; we are always also the people of "Corinth" or America or some such location.²³ It is partly this lack of a pure place to stand that makes doctrine necessary. Since we cannot take our identity for granted, we must continually refine and reassert that identity in light of inter- and intracommunal developments. Secondly, the life of the ecclesial community in the ongoing narrative must be central. Intratextuality is too easily conceived in an ahistorical fashion.[24]

Doctrine finds its intelligibility in a particular kind of communal context, the church. This does not mean that no doctrine can be found intelligible outside the church, or that the "biblical world" resides solely in the community. Rather, doctrine finds its home in the church and as a whole fits there, while at the same time the church finds its home in the Christian narrative, the ongoing world constructed by scripture. It is exactly as a whole that doctrine cannot be fit in other communities. If this is indeed true, a second point is that as modernity has denied the necessity of community in the act of interpretation, it has not merely been mistaken, but has blinded interpreters to the role their community plays in their actions. Interpretive actions they performed were taken to be the actions of autonomous rational agents responding to a text with clear and indubitable meaning (if only the correct technique were applied).

Though not writing with the church in mind, Stanley Fish's conception of "interpretive communities" is helpful here. Fish insists that it is within a communal framework that things and events are found intelligible. No actions can be understood—either as intelligible or as unintelligible—apart from the interpretive structure provided by a community. Fish tells of writing the words "Private Members Only" on the board one day in class. He then asked his students to interpret this phrase. Not surprisingly, his literature class came up with a number of possibilities before a student broke in, objecting that the meaning was obvious. Fish notes that in its context on the outside of the faculty club at Johns Hopkins, such a meaning might be obvious, but his action had blurred the interpretive framework that led to such "obviousness." Fish says,

> Constituting their [the students'] perception is not the knowledge of what to do with signs on faculty club doors but the knowledge of what to do with texts written on blackboards by professors of English literature. That is, professors of English literature do not put things on boards unless they are to be examples of problematic or ironic or ambiguous language. Students know that because they know what it means to be in a classroom, and the categories of understanding that are the content of that knowledge will be organizing what they see before they see it.[25]

Fish's students were, in a sense, members of two interpretive communities. Inasmuch as they walked by the faculty club on a regular basis and were familiar with the nature of clubs in general, the meaning was easy to discern. But that day in class Fish did not take them outdoors and show them the sign on the building—he showed it extracted from its original context and inserted into a new one. Supposing that the message was written on the board as the students assembled, how would they try to understand it? Would they assume that, contrary to prior experience and established practice, literature class was now an exclusive club? Knowing something about Fish and understanding his methods would likely lead them to believe that he had some point in mind. Although either context could make the words intelligible, the meaning thus construed would be different. The words "Private Members Only" do not constitute an action: placing them on a sign outside a club or writing them on a classroom blackboard are actions. Because the text never stands apart from some such context, it is not purely the "same" text in each case. For this very reason doctrinal faithfulness requires more than holding to doctrinal substance. Performance of doctrine within the context of the Christian community is an essential component.

This action of interpretive communities is Fish's answer to the charge of subjectivism, and works equally well with regard to doctrine. No one is left on his or her own to say what a doctrine means. Such a person is always a member of some community that (1) assigns the piece to the category "doctrine;" and (2) determines a range of possible approaches to the doctrine.[26] Since communities have a continuity through time, interpretations of doctrines can be considered stable, though still not permanent. This model of interpretation does not provide, however, all we need. In chapter four I will suggest a particular stance toward history that will enable us to identify more clearly the historical continuity of the community and thus face the question of the continuing role of *ancient* doctrine within the contemporary church.

In this section I have claimed that the church must be the primary interpretive community when it comes to doctrine. The other side of this claim is developed in the next section where I suggest that that doctrine has been marginalized not merely because individualism has led to a neglect of the church as church, but because an alternative community, let us call it "enlightened modernity," has instead served too often as the matrix of interpretation for doctrine. When I speak of modernity as an alternative community, I do not want to suggest that it has produced a monolithic interpretive community. Even within this era there have been a wide variety of ways of honoring a fundamental commitment to epistemology, individualism, reductionism, and dehistoricization. These characteristics take a different form and are variously emphasized in different communities. It does seem that these are commonalties found in most distinctively modern communities.

Modern Communities

If the postmodern conviction regarding the role of communities in world view formation and living of life are true, the modern commitments to individualism and universalism are not merely wrong, but blind us to the degree to which modern communities, varied as they are, have fulfilled this role. The complexity of society today virtually guarantees that any given person will be a member of multiple communities, all seeking to constrain interpretation in a particular direction. These two points (the covertness of modern community and the multiplicity of communities) are key elements of Alasdair MacIntyre's argument in *Whose Justice? Which Rationality?*[27] In a later work he contrasts philosophers in the Thomistic tradition with those whose work is institutionalized in the modern university. He says of the latter that they

> characteristically, although not always, come to it bringing with them commitments to some extra-philosophical standpoint. In modern philosophy these have been as various as Tolstoyan morality, the aesthetic *weltanschauung* of Bloomsbury, and scientific materialism. . . . These ideological *weltanschauungen* cannot be provided with support by this type of philosophy and they are permitted to enter into it only insofar as theses abstracted from them can be brought to bear in a piecemeal way on the acknowledged problems of philosophy. But it is they which furnish, to their adherents, what the philosophy itself cannot furnish, a standard of evaluation and of preference whereby the costs and benefits of each particular rival solution to some particular problem can be assessed. And the range of consequent disagreement within philosophy of this kind will then be as great as the range of prephilosophical disagreement in ideological standpoint.[28]

The "standard of evaluation and of preference" that comes from these other traditions borne by communities of which these philosophers are participants has an analogy both within the church and within academic theology. On this analysis these two problems (lack of self-understanding and consequent blindness to the effects of multicommunality) lie behind the incoherence MacIntyre exposes in *After Virtue*.[29]

McClendon and Smith recognize this phenomenon as well.[30] Their approach, drawing on the work of Willem Zuurdeeg,[31] tends to approach the issue on more neutral terms than MacIntyre, emphasizing the complexity of the relationship between various conviction sets. They suggest that when these interacting conviction sets exist in an individual they tend to be held hierarchically. If there is a conflict or area of overlap, one set of the whole will be the dominant set, putting others in a subservient role.[32]

Modernity, with its universalism and individualism, looks for a neutral place to stand, a place free of all prejudice, tradition, and commitment. It is tempting, as we seek a place for Christian doctrine that both overcomes individualism (without eliminating the individual) and also allows the church to function as an interpretive community, to seek a place that is "pure" church. We find ourselves in a difficult position. We want to say that Christian doctrine is to be understood on its own terms, in light of Christian convictions and not subservient to so-called universal convictions. As much as we castigate modernity for corrupting Christianity, we find it difficult, however, to rid ourselves of all the "corruption" of modernity.[33] When we submit to academic training in theology, we submit to the standards and convictions of modern academia, convictions which are often unfriendly to Christianity. It is not a silly question then to ask whether one can be both a Christian and an academic theologian at the same time.[34]

CHURCH AND CULTURE

I agreed above with Miroslav Volf that the church is never a pure community capable of a perfect semiotic unity of interpretation. Wherever the church is, it finds itself immersed not only in the particularities of God's action in history, but also in geographical and cultural particularities as well. When this claim is combined with Lindbeck's view that religion is a cultural linguistic system and Hauerwas' view that the church *is* its own culture, it becomes necessary to ask how the question of culture relates to doctrine. The concept of culture is of recent vintage, born in the disciplines of sociology and anthropology in the past two hundred years. Where today we might ask the question of church and *culture*, Christians may once have spoken of church and *world*. In the mid-twentieth century H. Richard Niebuhr framed the question as the relationship between Christ and culture.[35] His treatment, regarded as definitive by some, misguided by others, has been highly influential.[36] This is not the place for an analysis of his work: however, I do wish to note that the discussion has moved beyond his position, most significantly in rejecting his monolithic approach to both Christ and culture. As I investigate the relations between church and culture in the rest of this chapter, Niebuhr's typology is not my point of departure.

At least two new possibilities for understanding the relationship between church and culture have arisen in recent years. One of these, which is defended explicitly by Hauerwas and Clapp[37] (and implicitly by Yoder) is that the church *is* a culture. The other possibility, closely related to the first, is Lindbeck's claim that the church is a cultural-linguistic system. Both of these positions recognize the full complexity of the relations between church and culture. My position is more in line with the first, because it seems to allow more room for the necessary historical dimension. This view can perhaps best be framed as not only an explicit rejection of Constantinianism, but also as a claim that the time in which we could understand the church in Constantinian terms has passed.[38] If, as John Howard Yoder suggests, the essence of Constantinianism is a denial of the difference between church and world,[39] it can be seen why its passing is so helpful.[40] Once we reject the monolithicity of both church and culture, allowing each to stand apart, what sense does it make then to suggest that church is a culture?

That the church *is* a culture seems to be contradicted by the vast variety of churches, or expressions of Christianity. Personifying the tradition it seems as if Christianity takes an almost perverse joy in cultural diversity, becoming incarnate in a wide array of cultures. Christianity has also made itself at home in numerous languages. Unlike the case of Islam, one does not have to be a speaker of a single language to be a true Christian. If Christianity is indeed incarnate in these cultures, in what sense can it be said that Christianity is a *separate* culture? This question is sharpened when we notice that all these Christians are always already—and continue to be—members of other cultures. When a Tamil becomes a Christian, he or she does not then cease to be a Tamil. Cultural pluralism has always been reality, but our setting is similar to the New Testament era in that we find other cultures next door and even within ourselves competing for our attention.

I claimed above that normal human existence in the West is multicommunal.[41] It is normal for us to find ourselves participating in a number of communities, each with their own conviction sets. Constantinianism, in its conviction that society itself is Christian, weakened the differentiation between the Christian community and its host culture. As long as Christianity was central, doctrine could function as a list of propositions to be believed. Formation into the Christian community was unneeded since mere enculturation in the Constantinian order accomplished that. When missionaries took the gospel to other cultures, it was common to assume that as people in those receptor cultures became believers, they would, in some way, leave their own culture and become participants in Western civilization. Western style Christianity did not work well in non-Western settings, however, so questions about the indigenization of Christianity began to occupy missionaries as early as the mid-nineteenth century.

These questions of culture are essential, even though I am suggesting that my own dramatic image is better than a cultural-linguistic one. The focus on Christianity as a drama, as God's action with God's own people through the passage of time, does not negate the cultural dimension, but rather takes it up and contextualizes it in the historical. Doctrine is that which shapes a people, giving them identity. It is, as Lindbeck says, the grammar of their "language." What it is also, and what I will focus on in chapter four, is that which guides the church and its members in living the Christian narrative. As such, doctrine can never be abstracted from that narrative. It is all too easy to understand a culture ahistorically and nonteleologically (or, as I will show in the next chapter, noneschatologically).

There are many ways to discuss the nature of the church.[42] The account that follows, therefore, is far from exhaustive. In focusing on the nature of the church's relation to culture I will deal with three key convictions regarding the church. First, within the church there is a fundamental unity. Second, the church, as a social institution, is fundamentally different from ordinary social institutions because its origin lies in the activity of God. Finally, the church is what it is through its purposive participation in history—its mission is central to its identity. I will show that each of these features has implications for the church's relationship with culture. Additionally, I will suggest that these characteristics must be held in balance lest the church be led astray.

The Fundamental Unity of the Church

Diversity within the bounds of the church is as ancient as the church itself. Jesus' band of disciples in the New Testament is depicted as made up of Galileans and Judeans. By the time of the events recounted in Acts 2 we see visitors to Jerusalem from all over the world hearing and responding to the gospel. Acts 6 describes a controversy between the Christians of Palestinian and Hellenistic backgrounds. Before the account in the Book of Acts is over there are not only Jewish believers, but also Syrian, Asian, Greek, and Roman believers. Ephesians 2–4 explicitly declares the oneness of Jew and Gentile in Christ. The Apocalypse pictures innumerable multitudes of every tribe, language, and nation joining in heavenly worship. At the very least we see here an instance of unity in diversity.

This fact of diversity gives pause to any easy conviction that the church is itself a culture. Diversity within the church has two origins. In the first place, there is diversity because people from a multitude of cultures have responded to the Gospel and bring with them elements of their culture. The Jerusalem Council (Acts 15) set an early precedent that Christians were not required to become Jews culturally before they could truly be Christian. This is not a claim that the early Christians understood the concept of "culture" in the same way we do today. Rather, the cultural pluralism in which they lived enabled them to make distinctions between church and something roughly equivalent to what we would today call "culture." Secondly, diversity arises within the life of the church itself, and this diversity goes deep enough to lead even to doctrinal diversity. It is a commonplace that doctrine is formulated in the fires of controversy. In the last chapter I suggested that the way this worked was in terms of Christian articulation of the background of their lives in the Christian narrative. As anomalies arise—as conflicts with neighboring communities arise or as internal conflicts arise from the living of the narrative—doctrines are developed to overcome the anomalies. Inasmuch as the communities on which a church borders will differ from region to region, and different aspects of the unarticulated background narrative in which the church lives are questioned, doctrine will develop differently.

The *unity* in the midst of this diversity also has a complex origin. First, it lies in the common participation in the Christian narrative. While the Bible pictures cultural differences remaining in heaven, it also pictures all those varied cultural expressions as participants in God's action in history. Although my branch of the church may be acting one way in the drama, simultaneously another branch of the church is playing a different role in their own location.

Second, the church has an institutional unity. Individuals relate to one another in concrete social structures both within and across cultural boundaries. Most major denominations today exhibit this kind of unity. The church as a whole exhibits unity in the institutions of worship, prayer, preaching, evangelism, and mission. Though each of these is conceived in a multitude of ways, each has a place in each community.

The third locus of unity grows out of the first and is found in doctrine itself. Since doctrine functions to guide us in living the Christian narrative and one of the most fundamental practical doctrines is love of fellow Christians (John 13:35, I John 4), there is an internal drive to fellowship. Doctrine thus conceived, though logically separable from Christian life, in practice becomes part of that life. Though doctrine originates in local conflicts, it is always prospectively available globally through the act of reception that is not merely the reception of *doctrine* but also the reception of other *churches* as full fellow participants in the narrative. This unity is prospective, since full reception has not yet taken place—and given the fact that all branches of the church are in constant development, this unity is best conceived as being achieved in the Eschaton. Thus, though doctrine is generated locally, it is only as it is received as doctrine by other branches of the church that it truly becomes doctrine.

It is always conceivable that doctrine will not be received. This may happen for three reasons. First, the receiving community may find the proposal to be untrue to previous doctrine received or contradictory to life in the narrative. Second, it may be the case that the receiving community has itself been corrupted and is thus unable to see the truth of the proposed doctrine. Between these two there is no simple and instantaneous way to tell which is the case. Both types of doctrinal nonreception tend to lead also to nonreception of the community that propounds the doctrine in question. A third possible reason is that the doctrine is perceived to be relevant to particular communities only. In this case nonreception of doctrine may accompany reception of the other community.[43]

Consider an example of nonreception. Wesleyan Methodism had some central convictions (that one could have assurance of salvation, that the Christian could be made perfect in love in this life, for example) that were, to the larger church in England, simply regarded as instances of enthusiasm, or as we might say today, fanaticism. These convictions, among others, served to differentiate Methodism from Anglicanism, as the nonreception of these convictions became permanent.[44] Similarly the early baptist communities had a conviction that the church should be distinct from the world (and the State). This conviction brought them not reception but persecution and exclusion for centuries. Now, however, people outside the baptist tradition are beginning to receive their condemnation of Constantinianism. It is likely that the reception of this teaching by whole churches is still farther off.[45]

It is possible to overemphasize the oneness of the church. This is characterized by a concern for uniformity that seems unaware of cultural differences.[46] In *Christianity in Culture* Charles Kraft suggests that what Christians are concerned to do is make Christian *use* of the cultural forms with which they are presented. Writing from an anthropological perspective, Kraft identifies four components of culture. *Forms* are "the observable parts of which it is made up": things, objects, institutions, etc. *Functions* are discernible on at least three levels: they may be personal, universal, or pertaining to a particular group. Forms and functions are related—each form *has* at least one (possibly more) function. *Meaning* in culture refers to the "totality of subjective associations attached to the form." Each form not only has a function, it also tends to convey more than one meaning. Finally there is *usage*, which "makes explicit the active part that human beings take in the operation of culture."[47] Kraft uses marriage to illustrate how these components come together in usage:

> The culturally patterned use of the wedding ceremony to legitimize the setting up of a new family may be intersected by a number of other culturally approved (or, at least, allowed) individual usages, and also by certain culturally disapproved usages. It is approved, for example, for the organist and the preacher to use such a ceremony to earn money. It is culturally allowed (and sometimes approved) for certain participants to drink in excess in many American wedding celebrations. It is not unknown, though never culturally approved, for certain persons or groups to use a wedding celebration as an occasion for revenge or stealing.[48]

Once culture is so conceived, it is clear why culture is inescapable—why a consistent application of Niebuhr's "Christ against Culture" position is impossible.[49] That which remains the same from culture to culture seems to be the functions: marriage, child-rearing, coming of age, acquiring food and shelter. It would certainly seem odd to think of Christians not being engaged in these activities.

Culture shapes people, but it does not strictly determine their action. Instead of offering a single track to operate on, culture offers a set of boundaries, sometimes and in some places narrow, in others, rather broad. Within these boundaries individuals (and groups—though here Kraft's focus is individualistic) have various options from which to choose. Even a single culture encompasses diversity.[50] An illustration of this feature of culture (which Kraft does not mention) is Jesus' relationship to the Judaism of his day. Jesus' words and actions fit within Judaism so that they could be understood, yet they were seen as radical moves within that system.[51]

Where "Christianness" lies, Kraft claims, is "primarily in *the 'supracultural...functions and meanings* expressed in culture rather than in the mere forms of any given culture."[52] The supracultural is Kraft's way of bringing relations with God (and the supernatural) into the picture. When people become Christian they "live pretty much according to the same patterns and processes as before. . . . But now they use them with a new allegiance, for the sake of a new master."[53]

The advantage of Kraft's position is that one can readily conceive ways in which churches can truly inhabit their local culture and yet remain Christian. The basic function or goal fulfilled by worship can be done in a number of ways. There is a world of difference between the worship styles in ancient Israel, fourth-century Christianity, downtown "First Church" in 1960, and charismatic praise gatherings. In each case Christian worship has been indigenized in a particular cultural setting and made meaningful to people enculturated in popular culture. It is thus possible to stand against the urge to uniformity.

Kraft's position is not without its problems, however. Two stand out. First, his position remains individualistic. The church is a collection of individuals, an assemblage of users of cultural forms. Second, though a logical distinction can be made between forms, functions, meanings, and usages, we inhabitants of culture never find ourselves in a place where we experience any one of these in abstraction from the others. I think these problems could be overcome if he were more attentive to the role of narrative and the teleology it implies. Such a shift would fit with his use of Kingdom of God language, but is impeded (as was Lindbeck) by the ahistoricism of the social science models on which he is building.

The Church is of God

The church is not of its own making. It is not a natural assemblage of people (I Corinthians 1:18–30) any more than was Israel (Deut. 7:6ff.). This distinctiveness of the people of God lies behind the biblical claims that first Israel, and later the church, are holy. The church is to live as a distinctive people, different from the world around it. This is not a lifestyle of absolute difference but rather of invitational difference. Only as the church fulfills its calling to be holy and different will the nations be attracted to come and see what God is doing. The ethical holiness of the church is based first on its origin in the work of God, and only derivatively on its performance. This characteristic has important consequences for the church's relationship with culture.

In an insightful article on the unity of the church across cultural and historical boundaries, anthropologist Andrew Walls suggests that what characterizes the true church in all ages (and provides the context in which it relates to varying cultures) is adherence to two principles: the Pilgrim Principle (PP) and the Indigenizing Principle (IP). I will speak about the IP below, under the head of Apostolicity, but the PP relates primarily to the God-ward dimension of the church. The essence of the PP is that the church is going somewhere: this world is not its home.[54] It is easy to see the tie to eschatology here. Prior to Constantine, when it was easier for the church to see in daily life the difference between itself and the surrounding culture (however much it was always *in* that culture), the PP dominated. The PP is also what prevents the church from being swallowed up by its host culture as well as what structures its critique of culture.

It is possible to overemphasize the otherness of the church, or in Walls' terms, the PP. The result of taking this feature too far is withdrawal. Withdrawal takes two forms. It can be institutional: when the church seeks to be an entirely self-contained community unsullied by contact with the evil world. Withdrawal can also be an individual action, where the individual believer seeks to cultivate his or her soul inwardly through increasing detachment from the world, and lives only for the eventual consolation of heaven. Those communities most affected by individualism take this latter route, while those that have been most successful at retaining true community take the former. This shows that a mere retention of functioning community is not sufficient for the church to be the church, but that such a community must always be contextualized in the Christian narrative that includes God's mission to the nations.

The Church is Apostolic

My use of the term "apostolic" is a bit idiosyncratic, but not wholly so. Within Catholicism apostolicity has meant a strict and closely determined succession from the apostles, most notably Peter. As such, apostolicity is tied to the properly performed acts of ordination that have continued from the days of the apostles. Protestants move from this position (they have to, do they not, if they want to defend their own ecclesial status?) to one closer to my own, emphasizing not the apostolic ordination and authority, but apostolic *teaching*, which their communities now share with the first church.[55] The problem here is that apostolicity seems to be reduced to the ideational—a claim that we have the same beliefs that the first church did.[56] I have already made the claim that a focus on doctrine as *belief* is too indebted to modern epistemology and individualism to be of much use to us. Apostolicity is not merely institutional (though it is tied to the institution of the church) or theoretical (though it does entail common convictions), but is ultimately narratival and missional.

Taking apostolicity as narratival is not meant to make it passive. Rather, inasmuch as the narrativity is ongoing, it is constituted by action.

The church is always and everywhere on the move, seeking to incarnate the gospel in new settings so that Jesus' Great Commission might be fulfilled. In other words, the church is partially constituted by its relation of witness to other cultures.[57] This is the point of Walls' Indigenizing Principle. He claims that the church is composed of people who are always already part of some culture, a people who here and now are working together to express their faithfulness to God and live in the narrative in a way that also fits with their host culture. As the church proclaims the Gospel, it seeks to include others in the flow of events that constitute this dramatic narrative. This act of proclamation requires attention to indigenization so that members of other cultures can hear the Gospel as good news.

I have just suggested that the distinctiveness of the church must always be tempered by its full inclusion in the ongoing drama of God's action. This narratival or dramatic[58] dimension is what I will mean by apostolicity.[59] Jürgen Moltmann sees apostolicity in a similar light: "The apostolic succession is not only a category of the church's legitimation; it is a category of its commission. It does not only look backwards, but forwards as well."[60] With the demise of Constantinianism the discussion of the marks of the church—including apostolicity—has shifted from a strategy devised primarily to differentiate ecclesial communities from each other to one aimed at specifying the church's role in the world, specifically in relation to other communities.

This approach is based on two biblical factors. First and most important, is the fact that Jesus is considered the first apostle (Hebrews 3:1). Jesus is on a mission from God, to bring life, not condemnation, to the world. The second biblical factor grows out of this. The doctrine of the incarnation claims that in Jesus we see God not only becoming fully human (metaphysical indigenization, one might say) but also fully Jewish. Jesus did not come as an Everyman, abstracted from culture, but was fully immersed in the Palestinian Jewish culture of his time. His audiences, whether Jews like himself, or later Roman soldiers trying him, had no difficulty recognizing him as a Jew—and a Galilean Jew at that! What stood out about Jesus was not his culture, but the moves he made within that culture.[61]

Walls suggests that through the changes we identify with Constantinianism, the church took the IP too far, to the exclusion of the PP. Thus, just as it is possible for the church to overemphasize its unity and distinctiveness, the same is true of apostolicity. The exclusive focus on the IP leads the church to identify itself closely with culture.[62] In addition to denying the church's otherness, the problem with such a close identification is that culture changes. Then the church, still focused on itself as culture, fails to see itself as different. Having forgotten the PP it loses its connection to living history—to the Christian narrative—which was its original impetus. Strangely enough, such an overemphasis on the IP precludes future use of the IP since the church is now so tied to its host culture that any change (indigenization) to incarnate the gospel for or in another culture (even a future version of that same culture) would seem heretical. Churches that are blind to culture fail to see their own bondage to culture, usually a culture of some age past. What such a church is left with is institutionalism and the deep commitment to preserve that institution no matter what.

The modern church seems to be in such a situation. Not only has modern individualism denied its communal logic, but through its own misuse of the IP it has invested itself completely in the wholeness of society resulting from Constantinianism (truth, culture, church, and society are all unified). The additional problem comes in the fact that now within modernity this ancient synthesis is coming apart. The church finds itself in the double bind of either failing to admit that this is the case, or finding that coming from such a location there is no "space" within modernity for it to stand.

Conclusion

The subject, the speaker, of the communal speech act called doctrine, has been shown to be communal in its very essence. It is the community of those who have been and are being and will be saved. The church is not merely the association of those who are saved but is itself part of that salvation. Modern individualism and reductionism sidelined the church and broke the link between soteriology and ecclesiology. A primary advantage of my model is that what had been severed is now joined again.

This church is a communal participant in the ongoing narrative of God's action in history. It is always and everywhere related and relating to a diversity of cultures. As God calls believers out of every race, tribe, nation, and language, these people bring their cultural specificity into the church with them. In spite of this diversity, the church is one. The church is also universal, in the sense that God's action in which it joins is aimed at including all creation.

The church is and is not a culture in its own right. It *is* a culture, in that one becomes a fuller member through the process of discipleship, which can be likened to enculturation in the Kingdom of God. The church has its own forms and practices: the Eucharist and love of enemies, for example. The church has its own worldview rooted in history: God has acted through Israel and through Jesus to bring salvation to the nations. That worldview is not only rooted in history but requires a particular stance toward history. A conception of history as a closed continuum of naturalistic cause and effect with no room for divine action is simply incoherent within Christianity. The action of God continues even now through the church. This is why Lindbeck's claim that Christianity has no cosmology and can work from the perspective of any culture seems inconsistent with his more basic claim that Christianity is a cultural linguistic phenomenon. With the former claim, Lindbeck seems sensitive to the vast differences in the way we moderns understand the nature of the universe—heliocentrism, relativity theory, quantum physics, etc. But what about other features of the modern understanding of the world? Can we accept atheism (or a nonagential god), the conviction that the dead stay dead (no exceptions) and still have something recognizable as Christianity? I do not think so, and my guess is that Lindbeck would see Christian adaptation of culture rejecting these elements. Evidently more work needs to be done on this question.

It is not sufficient to focus on Christian community alone, the cultural dimensions are essential as well. Paul Holmer balances the two nicely: "One of the aims . . . of theology should be precisely to root believers firmly in the Christian life. But this does not mean beliefs are of no significance. For one of the features of much modern theology, *'post mortem dei'* and in the post-Christian era . . . , is that it indeed helps to liquidate whole sets of beliefs. It suggests that we can have the virtues and the way of life without the beliefs and the view of life."[63] Christianity is not a culture, in that it is always "incarnate" in some particular culture. We can intelligibly speak of American, Fijian, Korean, and Kenyan Christianity. American Christians will look like Americans (in many respects) while Kenyan Christians will be unmistakably Kenyan. Nevertheless, no matter where (and when) Christians are, they live a common story, and seek to join in common practices, both of which serve to differentiate them from their host cultures and unify them with each other. When these multicommunal and intercultural relationships are most healthy, the kingdom enculturation relativizes but never obliterates the other enculturations.

Finally, the church that performs the speech act we call doctrine is apostolic. It is active in history, seeking to incarnate the gospel so that the good news of Jesus may become accessible to all nations. It is in this final characteristic of the church that we see the bridge to chapter four. If the modern challenge to the church highlighted in this chapter was individualism, in the next it will be the modern penchant for ahistoricism. The next chapter will look in closer detail at what it means to say the church is now involved in the continuing dramatic narrative of God's action, even in the face of a modernity that not only rejects the usefulness of history, but even questions the coherence of the concept of God's acting in history. We will see the reason this has led to the marginalization of doctrine in the modern church as well as investigate some ways forward based on new possibilities opened up by postmodern philosophy.

Notes

[1] Stanley Hauerwas, *After Christendom: How the Church is to Behave if Freedom, Justice, and a Christian Nation are Bad Ideas* (Nashville: Abingdon, 1991), 26.

[2] Genesis 12:1-3. See echoes of this promise in Genesis 18:18; 22:17-18; 26:4. Bob Sjogren has developed this on the popular level in *Unveiled at Last* (Seattle: YWAM Publishing, 1992).

[3] For a reading of Old Testament ethics that fully considers this attention to context see James W. McClendon, Jr. *Ethics: Systematic Theology*, vol. 1 (Nashville: Abingdon, 1986), especially 177ff.

[4] Exodus 19:5-6 is applied to the church in I Peter 2:9, showing that at least one segment of the early church identified a continuity here.

[5] Cyprian, Epistle LXI: "To Pomponius, Concerning Some Virgins," in *The Ante-Nicene Fathers: Translations of the Writings of the Fathers down to A.D. 325*, ed. Alexander Roberts and James Donaldson, American Reprint of the Edinburgh ed. v. 5, Hippolytus, Cyprian, Caius, Novation, ¶4; Epistle LXXII: "To Jubaianus: concerning the Baptism of some Heretics," ¶21.

[6] *Catechism of the Catholic Church* (Nahwah, NJ: Paulist Press, 1994), 224.

[7] L. Gregory Jones says, "A proper understanding of what Benedict and others like him in the Christian tradition have been up to requires that we reject two conventional assumptions: first, that salvation is either individual or social, but not both; and second, that the border between the secular and the religious is somehow stable. When these assumptions are rejected, a different conception of Church becomes possible: 'The Church . . . is not primarily a *means* of salvation, but rather a *goal* of salvation, insofar as it is nothing other than the community of the reconciled. Our way back to God is through our incorporation into the historical body of the redeemed'" ("Alasdair MacIntyre on Narrative, Community, and the Moral Life." *Modern Theology*, 4:1 [1987]: 65). He is quoting here from John Milbank, "An Essay Against Secular Order," *Journal of Religious Ethics* 15:2 (1987): 204. Jürgen Moltmann makes a similar point in *The Church in the Power of the Spirit: A Contribution to Messianic Eschatology*, trans. Margaret Kohl (San Francisco: Harper, 1977), 35.

[8] Hauerwas, *After Christendom*, 35.

[9] Schubert Ogden, "Doctrinal Standards in the United Methodist Church," in *Doctrine and Theology in the United Methodist Church*, ed. Thomas Langford

(Nashville: Kingswood Books, 1991), 48. How does this differ from Hauerwas' position? Though I think he and Ogden can be harmonized, Hauerwas nowhere that I know evidences any concern at all to be universalistic.

[10] Rodney Clapp, *Peculiar People: The Church as Culture in a PostChristian Society* (Downers Grove, IL: InterVarsity Press, 1996), 40–41.

[11] Julian N. Hartt, *A Christian Critique of Culture: An Essay in Practical Theology* (New York: Harper and Row, 1967), 57. See the discussion in Charles Taylor, *Sources of the Self: The Making of the Modern Identity* (Cambridge: Harvard University Press, 1989), ch. 7; also David J. Bosch, *Transforming Mission: Paradigm Shifts in Theology of Mission*, American Society of Missiology, No. 16. (Maryknoll, NY: Orbis, 1997), 416.

[12] In the liberal model "culture, and religion like it, is confined to the private; both alike are idealized and etherealized. The liberal model ostensibly exalts culture and religion, yet in reality it marginalizes them. I would even go further and say it gnosticizes them. Culture and faith are redemptive, but redemptive only at the cost of being reduced to the knowledge and feelings of private individuals—individuals carefully removed from the world of the social, the economic and the political" (Clapp, *Peculiar People*, 62).

[13] Hauerwas says something similar in *After Christendom*, 37.

[14] Colin Gunton, *The One, The Three, and the Many: God, Creation and the Culture of Modernity*, The 1992 Bampton Lectures (Cambridge: Cambridge University Press, 1993), 32.

[15] This seems to be at least part of what Paul is getting at in II Corinthians 5:16–21.

[16] Alasdair MacIntyre, *Whose Justice? Which Rationality?* (Notre Dame, IN: Notre Dame University Press, 1988), 133. See also the discussion of the Encyclopaedist position in his *Three Rival Versions of Moral Enquiry: Encyclopaedia, Genealogy, and Tradition*. 1988 Gifford Lectures (Notre Dame, IN: Notre Dame University Press, 1990), 117. Charles Taylor discusses this from a different angle: "Since the seventeenth century, the progress of natural science has been inseparable from our separating ourselves from our own perspective, even from the human perspective as such, in order to come as close as possible to 'the view from nowhere,' to use Nagel's phrase. The aim is to identify and neutralize those features of the way the world appears which depend on our particular make-up. Science is only concerned with what is beyond these" ("Comparison, History, Truth," in *Myth and Philosophy*, ed. Frank Reynolds and David Tracy [Albany: SUNY Press, 1990], 39–40). Taylor's reference is to Thomas Nagel, *The View from Nowhere* (Oxford: Oxford University Press, 1986). Though Nagel's title is frequently invoked to describe the modern standpoint, the main argument of his book does not really fit this context. Nagel's goal is to propound a new form of objectivity that is more comprehensive than the "view from nowhere," and thus able to include human subjectivity. See also Alister McGrath, *The Genesis of Doctrine: A Study in the Foundations of Doctrinal Criticism* (Oxford: Basil Blackwell, 1990), 189; Hartt, *Christian Critique*, 42.

[17] Stephen E. Toulmin, *Uses of Argument* (Cambridge: Cambridge University Press, 1958), 216.

[18] Alasdair MacIntyre, *After Virtue*, 2nd ed. (Notre Dame, IN: University of Notre

Dame Press, 1984), 31f.

[19]Hauerwas and Willimon claim that apart from the church, scripture is unintelligible. *Resident Aliens: Life in the Christian Colony* (Nashville: Abingdon, 1989), 128.

[20]George Lindbeck, "Barth and Textuality," *Theology Today* 43 (1986): 361–76 (quote from p. 371). For a broader consideration of the literature on intertextuality, intratextuality and surrounding issues, see the survey in Anthony Thiselton, *New Horizons in Hermeneutics: The Theory of Transforming Biblical Reading* (Grand Rapids, MI: Zondervan, 1992), 38ff., 503ff., 557f.

[21]Lindbeck, *The Nature of Doctrine: Religion and Theology in a Postliberal Age* (Philadelphia: Westminster Press, 1984), 113ff.

[22]For the contested claim that Barth was a revelational foundationalist see James W. McClendon, Jr., *Doctrine: Systematic Theology*, 2 (Abingdon: Nashville, 1994), 455.

[23]Miroslav Volf, "Theology, Meaning, and Power," in *The Future of Theology: Essays in Honor of Jürgen Moltmann*, ed. Miroslav Volf, Carmen Krieg, and Thomas Kucharz (Grand Rapids, MI: Eerdmans, 1996), 103.

[24]John Webster notes that "The terms of the intratextualist's explanation are heavily structured (grammar, code, grid) and its concerns are with the givenness of certain regularities which Scripture imposes on the church. Because of this, its ecclesiology is strongly affiliative and tends to lack the dimension of temporality, possessed of the coherence and stasis of a single system which does not *become*. I am suggesting that the church is necessarily far more mobile and plural than this" ("Locality and Catholicity: Reflections on Theology and the Church," *Scottish Journal of Theology* 45:1 [1992]: 5.

[25]Stanley Fish, *Is There a Text in This Class? The Authority of Interpretive Communities* (Cambridge, MA: Harvard University Press, 1980), 277.

[26]Thomas C. Oden's charge against modernity is that it has led theology to a position of glorifying the doctrinal creativity of the individual. Though I think Oden would be surprised by the claim, Fish makes an effective ally in his counterclaim for the necessity of tradition and rejection of individualism. The main difference is in emphasis. Oden is making normative claims, Fish is making descriptive claims. Thomas C. Oden. *After Modernity . . . What? Agenda for Theology* (Grand Rapids, MI: Academie/ Zondervan, 1990).

[27]See especially chapter 17 where he argues that liberalism is itself a community.

[28]MacIntyre, *Three Rival Versions*, 159–60.

[29]The reality of interpretive communities produces the incommensurability Donald Davidson argues against. Cf. "On the Very Idea of a Conceptual Scheme," in *Inquiries into Truth and Interpretation* (Oxford: Clarendon Press, 1984). When statements are understood atomistically, apparent translation is usually possible. Our problem is that speech acts do not come as simple statements but always inhabit complex social settings.

[30]James W. McClendon, Jr. and James M. Smith, *Convictions: Defusing Religious Relativism*, rev. ed. (Valley Forge, PA: Trinity Press International, 1994), 91ff.

[31]Willem Zuurdeeg, *An Analytical Philosophy of Religion* (New York, Abingdon, 1958).

[32]McClendon and Smith, *Convictions*, 91. See also Clapp, *Peculiar People*, 146.

[33] Charles Taylor, "Justice after Virtue," in *After MacIntyre: Critical Perspectives on the Work of Alasdair MacIntyre*, ed. John Horton and Susan Mendus (Notre Dame, IN: University of Notre Dame Press, 1994), 21.

[34] For discussion of issues along these lines see Alasdair MacIntyre's discussion of the Encyclopaedist tradition in *Three Rival Versions*; and Nicholas Wolterstorff's, *Reason within the Bounds of Religion*, 2nd rev. ed. (Grand Rapids, MI: Eerdmans, 1984). See also William Placher, *Unapologetic Theology: A Christian Voice in a Pluralistic Conversation* (Louisville, KY: Westminster/John Knox Press, 1989), 155–56.

[35] H. Richard Niebuhr, *Christ and Culture* (New York: Harper and Row, 1951).

[36] For interaction with Niebuhr see James W. McClendon, Jr. *Ethics*, 23ff.; John Howard Yoder, Glenn Stassen, and D. M. Yeager, *Authentic Transformation: A New Vision of Christ and Culture* (Nashville: Abingdon, 1996); Charles H. Kraft, *Christianity in Culture: A Study in Dynamic Biblical Theologizing in Cross-Cultural Perspective* (Maryknoll, NY: Orbis, 1984), ch. 6; Clapp, *Peculiar People*, 63ff.

[37] Clapp, *Peculiar People*, 44.

[38] Loren B. Mead discusses this from another perspective in *The Once and Future Church: Reinventing the Congregation for a New Mission Frontier* (Washington, DC: Alban Institute, 1991). Though he uses the term "Christendom" instead of "Constantinianism," he has the same phenomenon in view.

[39] "The most pertinent fact about the new state of things after Constantine and Augustine is not that Christians were no longer persecuted and began to be privileged...; what matters is that the two visible realities, church and world, were fused. There is no longer anything to call 'world;' state, economy, art, rhetoric, superstition and war have all been baptized" (John Howard Yoder, "The Otherness of the Church," in *The Royal Priesthood: Essays Ecclesiological and Ecumenical*, ed. Michael Cartwright [Grand Rapids, MI: Eerdmans, 1994], 57). See also Clapp, *Peculiar People*, 25. For a discussion of the more recent effects of Constantinianism, see William T. Cavanaugh, "'A Fire Strong Enough to Consume the House:' The Wars of Religion and the Rise of the State," *Modern Theology* 11 (Oct. 1995).

[40] Yoder sees this link between church and culture as the root of the separation of ecclesiology and soteriology I spoke of above. Cf. "A People in the World," in *The Royal Priesthood*, 75.

[41] See also McClendon and Smith, *Convictions*, 92; Clapp, *Peculiar People*, 179.

[42] For a good overview of some of these see Avery Dulles, *Models of the Church* (Garden City, NY: Image Books, 1974).

[43] To account adequately for the relativism implicit in this claim is beyond the scope of this work. The way reception and nonreception work in actual church life is very complex, usually taking place over a long period. This is the location for the old maxim "in essentials unity, in nonessentials liberty, in all things charity." The maxim does nothing, however, to help us differentiate essentials from nonessentials. I will make some suggestions in this regard in chapter four.

[44] When I say "permanent" I am not precluding the possibility that Anglicanism as a whole might someday come to receive these teachings. For right now the matter appears closed.

[45] The churches of the West have lived under Constantinianism too long simply to throw it off at once. It is much easier simply to revise it. See Yoder on

neo, neo-neo, neo-neo-neo and neo-neo-neo-neo-Constantinianism [sic]. Cf. "The Constantinian Sources of Western Social Ethics," in *The Priestly Kingdom: Social Ethics as Gospel* (Notre Dame, IN: University of Notre Dame Press, 1984), 141–44.

[46] Albert C. Outler observes that "The unity of the church does not lie in the uniformity of her doctrines and rites, but in the unity of her witness to her common Lord—and to His Lordship in all of life" (Outler, *The Christian Tradition and the Unity We Seek* [New York: Oxford University Press, 1957], 137).

[47] Kraft, *Christianity in Culture*, 64–66. His concept of *use* seems parallel to Ferdinand de Saussure's *parole* within the context of *langue*. Cf. Saussure, *Course in General Linguistics*, ed. Charles Bally and Albert Sechehaye; trans. Wade Baskin (New York: McGraw-Hill, 1959), 13f.

[48] Ibid., 66.

[49] Kraft identifies three key mistakes of Niebuhr's position: (1) It equates culture with *kosmos* as negatively evaluated in the NT; (2) It assumes culture is merely external; (3) It assumes that since Satan is able to use culture to his ends, all of culture is evil. *Christianity in Culture*, 105f.

[50] Kraft, *Christianity in Culture*, 69.

[51] See the discussion of "double dissimilarity" in N. T. Wright, *Jesus and the Victory of God*, vol. 2, *Christian Origins and the Question of God* (Minneapolis: Fortress Press, 1996), 131ff., 226f. Double dissimilarity seeks to consider the differences between Jesus and both Judaism and the early church, recognizing that continuities are to be expected as well.

[52] Kraft, *Christianity and Culture*, 118. Further, he adds "God, being completely unbound by any culture (except as he chooses to operate within or in terms of culture) is 'supracultural'.... Likewise, any absolute principles or functions proceeding from God's nature, attributes, or activities may be labeled 'supracultural'" (120).

[53] Kraft, *Christianity in Culture*, 114.

[54] Andrew F. Walls, "The Gospel as the Prisoner and Liberator of Culture," *Missionalia* 10:3 (1982): 98–99.

[55] *The New Catholic Encyclopedia* (New York: McGraw-Hill, 1967), s.v. "Marks of the Church," v. 9 (Ma–Mor), 240–41; "Apostolicity," v. 1 (A–Azt), 699–700; by Gustave Thils; C. Westphal, "The Marks of the Church," *Anglican Theological Review* 42 (Apr. 1960): 91–100.

[56] McGrath, *Genesis of Doctrine*, 188.

[57] I understand I Peter 2:9 to be speaking of corporate witness.

[58] It is ultimately eschatological, as I will suggest in the next chapter.

[59] Curtis W. Freeman says that "the church is more than simply the people who tell the gospel story. The church *is* the story." ("Toward a *Sensus Fidelium* for an Evangelical Church: Postconservatives and Postliberals on Reading Scripture," in *The Nature of Confession: Evangelicals and Postliberals in Conversation*, ed. Timothy R. Phillips and Dennis L. Okholm [Downers Grove, IL: InterVarsity Press, 1996],164).

[60] Moltmann, *Church*, 312. He also claims that "the church can only appeal to the apostles when it lays hold of its own apostolate and missionary charge" (359).

[61] Moltmann, *Church*, 10.

[62] Hauerwas, *After Christendom*, 70f. Gregory Jones and Michael Cartwright iden-

tify the refusal to "go native" in the host culture as one of the four requirements for vital Christian communities. Cf. "Vital Congregations: Toward a Wesleyan Vision for the United Methodist Church's Identity and Mission," in *The Mission of the Church in Methodist Perspective: The World is my Parish*, ed. Alan G. Padgett. Studies in the History of Missions 10 (Lewiston, NY: Edwin Mellen Press, 1992), 114. For an especially vivid portrayal of mainline American Christianity going native, see Hartt, *Christian Critique*, xivf., 59ff.

[63]Paul Holmer, *The Grammar of Faith* (San Francisco: Harper and Row, 1978), 50.

Chapter Four

The Historical Questions Relating to Doctrine

IN CHAPTER ONE I DISCUSSED SEVERAL FEATURES OF MODERNITY THAT HAVE provided the matrix in which doctrine has been marginalized. The chief of these, a centering on epistemology and a reductive individualism, have been dealt with in chapters two and three respectively. In chapter two I suggested that the models that base their understanding of doctrine on epistemology, whether positively as seen in what Lindbeck calls propositionalism, or negatively, in what he terms experiential expressivism, should be replaced with an understanding cognizant of new options for understanding language that have been offered by recent philosophy. When doctrine is conceived as a speech act, new attention can be given to the sociality of doctrine and to how it functions in Christian community. Chapter three turned then to the speaker of that speech act, the church. Developing Charles Taylor's suggestion (presented in chapter two) that language functions to create public space, I investigated ways in which the communal nature of the church must be recovered for doctrine to function. Such a development, while in line with postmodern philosophy, is also a recovery of a lost dimension of soteriology that provides a needed link between that doctrine and ecclesiology. The rest of that chapter was dedicated to a discussion of the relation between church and culture motivated by Lindbeck's cultural linguistic model of religion and Hauerwas' suggestion that the church itself *is* a culture. The relation between church and culture was seen to be complex, not capable of the sort of monolithic analysis found in Niebuhr's *Christ and Culture*. Saying the church *is* a culture is true, but not sufficient—more must be said. That "more" is what I brought up in my discussion of the apostolicity of the church, focusing on the fact that the church is, in its very nature, actively engaged in history, and thus in a variety of cultures lives as an agent in God's continuing drama.

It is at the point of apostolicity that we encounter the final major impediment offered by modernity: dehistoricization. I had suggested in chapter one that what we needed to deliver doctrine from its marginalization was a new controlling image for what Christianity is. The other proposed controlling images—science, aesthetic enterprise, and cultural linguistic system—are all capable of ahistorical construal. My suggested image, that Christianity is best understood as a dramatic narrative, admittedly can also be construed ahistorically. In fact, as I will show in this chapter, there are ways to construe narrative as completely unrelated to actual history, as instead merely historical in literary form. There is, unfortunately, no absolute position from which to argue the contrary. My strategy instead will be to suggest that the best way to account for the Christian tradition is to articulate a role for real history.

My contention is not merely that of mainstream Christian conservatism, which claims that Christianity depends on certain events having actually happened. I believe this is important and will discuss that point shortly. More important to my argument is the defectiveness of the conception of Christianity that results when history is rejected or considered unimportant.

The goal of this chapter is twofold. First, I will illustrate the necessary tie between doctrine and the Christian narrative. I will argue that the former is dialectically related to the latter. Doctrine is an articulation of life in the narrative and cannot exist apart from it. As an articulation, however, doctrine helps us understand the narrative and continue living within it. When this relationship is severed, doctrine will inevitably be marginalized. Second, I will claim that the Christian community is inextricably tied to a particular narrative that is both verbal and actual. It is *verbal* in the sense that we have the biblical narratives before us (as well as the narratives within our ecclesial communities that tell us how we came to where we are). It is *actual* in the sense that not only are certain events depicted in those narratives essential to what the church believes, but also in the more important sense that we now stand in direct continuity with those events. This continuity is not merely theoretical but actual. Writing about the related problem of the interpretation of biblical texts, Nancey Murphy claims that "the first requirement for a community today to get the point of biblical speech acts is that it understand itself to be addressed by the texts. The second requirement is that the community now be in some sense *the same interpretive community* as that of the writer."[1] Once we see doctrine as a speech act of the church that requires reception *by the church* in order to function as doctrine, the need for such a position seems clear. If the only concern was timeless truths to be existentially appropriated or confessed, the historicity of the narrative would be moot. Since the greater claim is that we now stand in a later place in this same narrative, facticity cannot be easily surrendered.

The link between these two claims is eschatology. I recognize that there is little unanimity about the nature of the eschatological teachings of the bible. Eschatology remains a point of discussion in modern theology, but has for the most part been either individualized into a concern about the afterlife, pushed into the future and limited to an imminent Second Coming or, given that both of these approaches are difficult for moderns to accept, is taken to be a mistake. When the controlling image of Christianity is changed to drama, a full recovery of the biblical picture of eschatology—past, present, and future—is possible.

Modern Dehistoricization

The starting point for my case will be a closer consideration of the dehistoricization brought about by modernity. Though not original, Lessing is the clearest exponent of a position typical of the period, so I will begin with a brief exposition of his views. In his theological work we see a clear conjunction of the typically modern convictions I discussed in chapter one.

G. E. Lessing

Gotthold Ephraim Lessing's famous statements about history are found in his little essay "On the Proof of the Spirit and of Power,"[2] an erstwhile response to the orthodox position on the relation of historical events to Christian truth. His argument is framed as a response to Origen's response to Celsus. Origen had claimed that the miracles Jesus did and the prophecies he fulfilled are adequate proof of the power of the Spirit in him and substantiated the claim that he was the Son of God. It is still popular today to argue for the deity of Christ by appealing to the miracles he performed (who but God could do such things?) and to the prophecies he fulfilled. Lessing's response to Origen can be summarized as a combination of three lines of thought.[3] His first move is to show the great difference between Origen's time and his own. Believers in Origen's time could look around them and see miracles for themselves (or so they claimed). Lessing, however, observed that miracles were no longer happening in the eighteenth century; therefore, he reasoned, not only were the claims based upon miracles suspect, but the claims themselves could no longer be demonstrated. Because the events that support particular Christian claims are simply so far distant in time, we cannot hold to them with certainty. Anthony Thiselton comments, "In effect, if not in intention, Lessing has brought us to the place where the nature and value of historical inquiry is judged in terms of *its relation to the interpreter's present horizons.*"[4]

But what if we could travel back in time to the days of Jesus, or even to the miracle filled days of Origen, would that solve the problem? Clearly such a solution would not work for Lessing. Though he begins with the problem of our accurate knowledge of ancient events, he soon identifies another "ditch," this one derived from his adherence to the philosophical tradition represented by G. W. Leibniz and Benedict Spinoza that claimed that religion (i.e., Christianity) was a rational religion constituted by necessary truths of reason.[5] This view has been very popular with moderns, being easily derivable from the central modern commitments to the centrality of epistemology, procedural rationality, and individualism. It spread beyond philosophy and theology as the new sciences became more widely known. The new view of the world as a completely intelligible place open to science, led to seeing the chain of cause and effect "as being the embodiment of a deductive system and analogous to the sequence of propositions that makes up a mathematical or logical proof."[6] I do not take early modern theologians like Lessing to be subversive agents seeking to undermine Christianity. What drove them to their conclusions was not a conviction that Christianity was untrue, but exactly the opposite. Because they believed it to be true religion (and frequently *the* true religion), *and* they were convinced that as truth it must be a deductive system like mathematics and Newtonian physics, they were compelled to take the steps they did. In chapter one I agreed with George Lindbeck that a solution to the problem of doctrine in the modern era begins with asking what Christianity is all about. Lessing and a great number of his contemporaries agreed that real religion is about truth. They differed on their understanding of and what they counted as true, but the intellectual climate of the time was such that it seemed only natural to affirm that Christianity was rational religion, since the only alternative was that it might be irrational religion. The orthodox retained a focus on the facts of Christian history, but it was all too easy to read these facts as illustrative of general truths. As far as practical results, then, their position was not substantially different from Lessing's. History was irrelevant for religion except as a storehouse of facts also available elsewhere.[7]

As Michalson notes, this is not the last barrier Lessing sees, nor I suspect, the last one other moderns find in claims like Origen's. In the temporal ditch we saw that the location of the current interpreter is all-important. The Cartesian epistemology presupposed in the metaphysical ditch between "contingent truths of history" and the "necessary truths of reason" also leads one to look for the equally Cartesian turn to the subject. One is not disappointed. The third ditch is exactly the point that something ancient cannot have authority *for me* insofar as I am an autonomous individual.[8]

In the next century the approach to history epitomized by Lessing became mainstream. After Schleiermacher the understanding of religion shifted from propositionalism to one focusing on religious experience. As the propositions available to make Christianity a fully deductive system were both reduced in quantity and more and more generalized, the Christianity that was left seemed too anemic and sterile. For Schleiermacher this was clearly unacceptable. This was not a large leap, given the continuing confluence of the epistemological and individualist strands of modern thought. Though the conception of religion changed, the attitude toward the role of history in Christianity did not.

Given Lessing's approach to the nature of religion and the place of history, where does doctrine stand? First, since religion is essentially an individual enterprise, it makes no sense to think of doctrine as communally authoritative. Doctrinal authority, like historical fact, would surely be judged a heteronomous imposition. Second, since religion has to do with necessary truths of reason, doctrines are unnecessary—and perhaps harmful—to the extent that they involve particularities and contingencies. Practical doctrines—like "love one another"—are self-evident and need no dogmatic support.[9] True doctrine tells believers nothing they cannot know from other sources, and is only recognized as true doctrine insofar as it measures up to the religion one has by nature. This kind of analysis ignores the biblical context of the love commands. These are not contextless commands, but are commands from Jesus to "love one another *just as I have loved you.*" Once we turn to the question of how Jesus loved the disciples we find ourselves immersed not only in historical questions but also in doctrinal ones. Once doctrine is conceived as separable from historical context, it has been effectively marginalized.

Beyond Lessing

Since the commitment to epistemology and individualism continued to grow in the century and a half following Lessing, the dehistoricization of Christianity continued apace. Not only does it not matter what actually happened, but scholars were to doubt the factuality of more and more scripturally depicted events. The social sciences arose in the nineteenth century, partly in an attempt to account for religion and religious differences from a naturalistic perspective. From the beginning the social sciences have had a tendency to speak in ahistorical terms, this in spite of their use of history for reductive purposes.[10] Auguste Comte's three levels of development, for example, can be interpreted as an attempt to provide a metanarrative of human religious development. For all their attempts to be objective their fundamental position has been that real religion is a distillation of modern convictions (and always had been, though in ancient times *real* religion was harder to find) and not connected to the particularities of any tradition. Their very conception of what it means to be objective blinded them to the necessarily historical dimension not only of Christianity, but even of their own project.[11]

Alasdair MacIntyre finds a similar turn from history in the broader culture of modernity as well.

> The project of founding a form of social order in which individuals could emancipate themselves from the contingency and particularity of tradition by appealing to genuinely universal, tradition independent norms was and is not only, and not principally, a project of philosophers. It was and is the project of modern liberal individualist society.[12]

Later in this chapter I will return to MacIntyre and use his concept of a tradition to claim that the church understands itself best when it understands itself historically, not merely in its genesis, but in its very essence. The modern church in the West has found it too easy to identify with its host culture and has, as a result, forgotten its own historicity. The title of MacIntyre's book asks whose justice and which rationality moderns have in mind when they universalize those concepts.

Concepts like justice and rationality are just as historically (and communally) rooted, and thus contingent, as theological concepts like love and peace.

The secularization thesis in its most basic form is a claim that as modernity progresses (and progress is inevitable), religion will drop by the wayside, a vestige of a former and less rational age. Though it operates in the guise of a descriptive hypothesis of social science, it is really an apologetic strategy for modern rationalism and individualism. Secularization of this sort depends on the viability of universal concepts that can be separated and maintained independently from particular cultures, traditions, and communities—safely away from the contingencies of history. If people were to come to see these modern virtues and values to be just as historically contingent as those they replaced, the whole structure would collapse. Theology has done the church a disservice by taking this culture of purported universalism with its narrative of never-ending progress as its home rather than the culture of the kingdom with its narrative of a crucified God and his people.

Particularly in the twentieth century, theology has had a love-hate relationship with facts. Conservatives have focused much of their energy on proving the facticity of the bible, while liberals have either rejected such facticity or simply denied its relevance.[13] One sign of this is the supposed opposition between the "Jesus of history" and the "Christ of faith." The Jesus of history is unapproachable—either too remote to be accurately known or too strange to be a real option for us. Either way the facts of the matter are not relevant to where believers stand today. John Howard Yoder critiques the separation between the "Jesus of history" and the "Christ of faith" as jumping too quickly from Jesus' birth to his death and missing the political significance of his life and ministry. Helpfully, a current trend in New Testament studies is a return to history in the form of a broad based attempt to understand Jesus in his historical, and specifically Jewish, context. As the church appropriates (receives) this study the political significance of Jesus' teaching may also be recovered.[14] Another illustration of the problem theology has had with facts is the mid-twentieth-century movement within biblical studies that saw an emphasis on the "Great Acts of God" while at the same time refusing to speak of historicity. As I turn to a discussion of "real history" Langdon Gilkey's seminal essay is a good point of departure.[15]

Gilkey and the Biblical Theologians

Gilkey's gaze is set on the so-called biblical theologians of the last fifty years. These scholars focused on what they called the "Great Acts of God," which according to Gilkey's reading of their texts, they took to be neither acts, nor of God. As historians, the position of these scholars on both the historicity of these events and the nature of religion is essentially the same as Lessing's. Gilkey says that they rejected special revelation because it "denied that ultimately significant religious truth is universally available to all mankind, or at least in continuity with experiences universally shared by all men."[16] Like Lessing, Christianity is a religion, religion has to do with truth, and truth is unrelated to the "accidental truths of history," but rather is tied to the necessary, and thus universal, truths of reason. This position says that "Whatever the Hebrew believed, *we* believe that biblical people lived in the same causal continuum of space and time in which we live, and so one in which no divine wonders transpired and no divine voices were heard."[17] So how could they combine a commitment to using biblical language with an equally strong commitment to what Gilkey calls liberalism? Their strategy was to redescribe what they were doing. As biblical theologians they were not seeking truths from scripture for the church to live by today. Rather, they were describing the faith of ancient Israel. Therefore, in spite of the apparent turn to history in these writers, the categories they think in fit better with ahistorical social science. Gilkey describes their attitude:

> These narratives represent not so much *histories* of what God actually did and said as much as *parables* expressive of the faith post-Exodus Jews had, namely, belief in a God who was active, did deeds, spoke promises and commands, and so on ... the biblical accounts of the post-Exodus life—for example, the proclamation and codification of the law, the conquest, and the prophetic movement—are understood as the covenant people's interpretation through their Exodus faith of their continuing life and history. ... Thus the Bible is a book descriptive not of the acts of God but of Hebrew religion.[18]

By such an approach the biblical narratives are seen as wholly mythological, mere interpretive frameworks for understanding current reality.

By now, this position ought to look familiar. From the perspective of the individual believer, it looks amazingly like what Lindbeck terms experiential expressivism projected back onto Israel. Biblical events are not really events, any more than doctrines are *about* anything in the world. Both are symbolizations or expressions of internal feelings, attitudes, commitments, and experiences.[19] Thus Hebrew religion is just a unique way of talking about universal human religious experience. If experiential expressivism is suspect as a way to understand what religion is and in its conceptualization of contemporary doctrine, should we expect it to be more accurate when applied to ancient Israel?

But what if we keep all but the individualism and universalism of this approach? If we read just the surface of these biblical theologies, finding handbooks of Hebrew religion, what is the difference between these positions and Lindbeck's own cultural linguistic view? Both are centered on a theory of religion. Both grew out of the theology of Karl Barth (though this is not the place to discuss the legitimacy of their birth in his thought). Both eschew a connection with a reality that is other than the enclosed system. It is time for a better way.

NARRATIVE: THE BETTER WAY

Saying that narrative is the better way can seem anticlimactic. After all, Gilkey's biblical theologians emphasized the centrality of narrative didn't they? How does attention to narrative move beyond their inadequate position?

First, my interest is not so much in narrative *per se*. Works in the genre "narrative theology" have proliferated of late. Narrative has not had a necessary connection to history, but has sometimes focused on the quality of narrativity or narrative form instead.[20] My interest is much more in *the* narrative, i.e., the Christian story, than in the form itself. Narratival analysis is useful to a degree, however, in that it helps us see the narratival dimensions of our lives, considered both individually and communally.[21] Our past is essential to who we are and how we see ourselves. With narrative we have a tool for not only understanding who we are and where we have been, but also where we are going. As we place ourselves in a narrative we become players in something larger than ourselves.[22] But if this is how it is for everyone—how is it for the church and those who stand within it? Inasmuch as our priority is the question of doctrine, we must come back to the place of the church in the narrative.

Narrative as a Rejection of Lessing

Centering on narrative is an explicit rejection of the modern position found in the thought of Lessing and his successors. Miroslav Volf claims that since "Christian faith is not a philosophy resting on a principle"—which is where Lessing and the liberals leave it—"but a religion involving a drama (God's complex history with the world he has created), narrative is the most basic way to talk about Christian faith."[23] My claim goes even further: not only is Christian faith "involved with" a drama, but in the church's continuing relationship with God and creation, we continue to live out what can best be described as a narrative. The Christian life does not consist in searching scripture for timeless universal principles to apply to our lives.

The modern era has seen not only the rejection of the relevance of history for Christian faith, but also a profound discomfort with narrative itself. Propositionalists are not sure what to do with it. Surely, they think, its stories can be changed into (or reduced to) true propositions. For conservatives these propositions would be tied to the facticity of the events while for early liberals like Lessing they would be illustrative of universal truths. In my discussion of Gilkey we have already seen how experiential expressivists find universal religious experience in the narratives. The best account of this discomfort and subsequent turn from narrative is described, though sometimes unclearly in detail, in Hans Frei's *The Eclipse of Biblical Narrative*.[24]

Hans Frei: The Bible is Primarily Realistic Narrative

Frei begins his account with the claim that the bible is largely composed of realistic narrative, which for most of Christian history had been read literally and historically.[25] This premodern reading had three key features. First, it was natural to read the texts as talking about actual events. Second, there was a tendency to see an overarching unity in the bible that tied together the diverse stories, usually through typology. Finally, the one world described in these stories was understood to be the same world that current readers inhabited, inclining them to find themselves in the story.[26]

After the Reformation and the turn to individualism and epistemology, such a reading was no longer possible. No longer was the world of the text the world of reference, but as we saw with Lessing, the world of the text was the world of the autonomous agent now reading the text and standing over the text and determining its legitimacy.[27] This modern way not only presupposed a particular reading of the text and a commitment to autonomous individualism, but also a conviction that the world was basically the same now as always: The events we see around us now are essentially the same as those that happened in the distant past. Lessing's temporal ditch is a version of this: my current experience is a reliable guide to understanding the past. This may even be part of what is going on in Schleiermacher's hermeneutics when he claims that interpretation proceeds when the interpreter and the writer become, so to speak, of one mind.[28] Unity of mind in the act of interpretation can be seen as going either direction—coming from the past or being imposed onto the past.[29]

Narrative and the Recovery of Doctrine

In order to overcome the marginalization of doctrine, narrative must be recovered first. This is especially true now that it appears that universal truths are not as readily available as moderns led us to believe. When the narrative (*qua* narrative) is ignored, denied, or at best treated as illustrative of universal truths, the tradition is soon left with increasingly empty concepts. Doctrines detached from historical specificity become rootless and desiccated—dry facts are no more life giving than universal truths. Living in the world depicted by the modern view of narrative is like playing some of the early computer games. That world is a poor replica of reality. Doctrines retain their specificity and fixedness when tied to the narrative. When cut from these moorings—as in modernity—doctrine inevitably will appear arbitrary and heteronomous, and over time will be seen as expendable.

Later in this chapter I will consider the question of the relation between narrative and actual history. As the issue stands right now, all we need is history-*likeness*, a narrative dimension to tie things together. What serves as the bridge between history and narrative within Christianity is eschatology.

ESCHATOLOGY

It is a commonplace that the eschatological milieu of the New Testament was rediscovered in late nineteenth- and early twentieth-century biblical studies, within the circle dominated by an experiential expressivist view of doctrine. Within the circle dominated by a propositionalist view of doctrine, this was also the time when the Scofield Reference Bible was introduced, imparting premillennial dispensationalism, which has become an eschatological scheme popular in American Fundamentalism. The place to begin, then, is with biblical studies.

Christian theology has always valued the bible as an essential source for doctrine and theology. The Protestant Reformation sought to return the church to what it saw as the biblical foundations of the early church. The common assumption was that the first step in theology and doctrinal formulation is to turn to the bible to discover the truth. In the modern era, propositionalists abstracted these truths from the narrative of scripture and took them to be the foundation of the system of Christian doctrine. Experiential expressivists, finding, as they did, the ultimate foundation of doctrine in religious experience, nevertheless, could not, as Christians, turn away from the bible. What they found there, rather than truths, was the crystallization of ancient religious experience, something essential to their own theological enterprise. Biblical studies from the perspective of propositionalism sought to substantiate and clarify the truths and facts found in the bible, while studies done from the perspective of experiential expressivism aimed to clarify and understand the religious experience depicted in the text. Whatever direction we approach the question from, attention to the trajectory of biblical studies is essential.

The Twentieth-Century Rise of Eschatology

Albert Schweitzer is famous for finding in Jesus an apocalyptic prophet who announced the end of the world but turned out, as we all know, to be tragically wrong.[30] The world did not end. The assumption made by Schweitzer was that eschatology (and its wayward cousin apocalyptic) was intending to talk about a literal end of the world. A literal reading of the narratives certainly inclines us toward such a view—and serves as one of the elements in the text that inclines us precisely against such a reading. Dispensationalists, who tended to be propositionalists, and thus wanted to preserve the literal reading of the text, sought strategies to find postponement in Jesus' language since the world did not end "in this generation." In other words, both groups saw the New Testament language as problematic. With an experiential expressivist approach one could bypass embarrassment by simply saying the New Testament was wrong on this issue. Since this option was not open to propositionalists, their primary strategy was to redefine "generation." Instead of referring to a group of people within a certain time span, for example, it was seen as referring to the Jewish people as an ethnic group.

Once eschatology had been "rediscovered," biblical scholars and theologians had to come to terms with it. Rudolph Bultmann, whose work has been so influential in American mainline Christianity, declared eschatology to be another instance of mythology in the bible.[31] It is part and parcel of the three-story universe and the miracles—all elements that modern believers find unbelievable. A good modern, Bultmann read strictly from the present to the past, judging the ancient text by his current culture. Unlike some, Bultmann did not conclude from this that these elements were to be rejected outright. Instead of ignoring or rejecting mythological language, his program called for an interpretation of it—a demythologization. What his approach amounted to was an existentialization of mythology. In essence, his work is another attempt to show that the bible (and the Christianity founded upon it), though it seems foreign to moderns, is really saying something other than it appears to be saying. Where Lessing, Kant, and other eighteenth-century figures found that Christianity was "really about" autonomous moral agents and rational religion, Bultmann found that it was really an ancient depiction of Heideggerian existentialism.

But where is history? Where is the narrative *as* narrative? Are these finally unrelated to eschatology? My argument is exactly the opposite. If we are to understand the role of doctrine in the church, we must regain the narrative. If the narrative is to be regained, we must recover both history and eschatology. Biblical studies more recent than Bultmann's point the way to such a recovery as they offer alternative models for understanding the nature of biblical eschatology.

Since Bultmann, the views on the nature of eschatology have proliferated. N. T. Wright provides a useful summary of the main options:

1. Eschatology as the end of the world, i.e., the end of the space-time universe;
2. Eschatology as the climax of Israel's history, involving the end of the space-time universe;
3. Eschatology as the climax of Israel's history, involving events for which end-of-the-world language is the only set of metaphors adequate to express the significance of what will happen, but resulting in a new and quite different phase *within* space-time history;
4. Eschatology as major events, not specifically climactic within a particular story, for which end-of-the-world language functions as metaphor;
5. Eschatology as 'horizontal' language (i.e., *apparently* denoting movement forwards in time) whose *actual* referent is the possibility of moving 'upwards' spiritually into a new level of existence;
6. Eschatology as critique of the present world order, perhaps with proposals for a new order;
7. Eschatology as critique of the present socio-political scene, perhaps with proposals for adjustments.[32]

According to Wright (1) is the traditional view (and usually what traditional scholars mean by apocalyptic), (2) is the traditional view as modified by Schweitzer, (4) is Marcus Borg's position, (5) is Bultmann's, and John Dominic Crossan holds to a cross between (6) and (7). (3) is Wright's own view and closest to the one I am suggesting. Wright sees C. H. Dodd's position as a variant on (3), though I think the elimination of a future element significantly changes the political dimensions of any doctrine of eschatology drawn from such a position. The key elements of Wright's position include not only a prominent place for historical narrative, but also a reevaluation of apocalyptic. From his espousal of the third definition of eschatology it is not surprising that Wright's position on apocalyptic and its relation to eschatology has shifted from the traditional. Taking his cue primarily from George B. Caird, Wright sees apocalyptic language, whether in scripture or in other writings of the time, as a way to ascribe earthshaking importance to anticipated historical events.[33] Wright says that

> If we imagine the majority of first-century Jews, and early Christians, as people who were confidently expecting the space-time universe to come to a full stop, and who were disappointed, we at once create a distance between them and ourselves far greater than that of mere chronology. We know they were crucially wrong about something they put at the center of their worldview, and must therefore either abandon any attempt to take them seriously or must construct a hermeneutic which will somehow enable us to salvage something from the wreckage.[34]

Taking apocalyptic language literally then, produced an uncharitable interpretation of first-century Judaism. He also does not think it an improvement to take them as Platonists yearning for a realm beyond the physical, as Bultmann would have us believe.[35]

The elements of New Testament eschatology, therefore, center on a particular understanding of history—not the nature of history in general, but of the particular history of the people of God, of Israel. Following Wright, we can see first-century Jews hungering for their God to act and deliver them from exile.[36] When Jesus came preaching the imminent arrival of the Kingdom of God, his words were understood in this context. That he, the son of a carpenter from Nazareth, would be God's chosen agent for bringing about the return from exile seemed far-fetched—and even blasphemous—to many Jews, but they at least understood what he was talking about. What we see in Jesus, then, is God's action in continuity with what God had done in Old Testament times. Just as in the Old Testament, God wanted a people who would be his very own, a people through whom the nations would be reached. Such a hope, far from being peculiar to early Christianity, was clearly in line with Old Testament thinking. The early Christians saw themselves as players in this ongoing narrative of God's action to save his people and redeem all creation.

Seen this way, the link between eschatology and history is clear. Eschatology for the early Christian was not an escape from history, but a particularly momentous happening in history in which they found themselves immersed. The salvation they had experienced was not merely futuristic—the Jesus who had died *had* delivered them from sin, but the fruit of this deliverance was understood to be very much present, with determinative significance for the future. The resurrection of Jesus was a key element in this understanding. First-century Jews looked forward to a resurrection, but it was considered to be an eschatological event, coming later in God's working with the people. Jesus' resurrection, coming when it did, was unexpected, but could be interpreted as God's present vindication of the claims of Jesus and future vindication of those who would follow him.[37]

Eschatology had been set to one side by previous generations not simply due to the foreignness of the biblical worldview and a rejection of narrative.[38] Two other factors were at work, one philosophical and one theological. Both of these, though shaped by modernity, have their roots in much older traditions. The philosophical problem is that eschatology has too much the flavor of teleology, and teleology became decidedly unpopular in the modern era.[39] The church with its appropriation of Greek philosophy (whether Platonism through Augustine and his peers or Aristotelianism through Aquinas) found teleology a useful resource. In some ways, settling for teleology alone seems to be a secular alternative to eschatology. We can speak of each thing having a *telos* apart from any talk about God. What eschatology preserves is not merely the notion of purpose, but also the centrality of *action*, and the action of particular agents in a broader context. As long as the emphasis is on essences (Greek philosophy's strong suit) rather than agents and actions, eschatology is already potentially marginalized.[40] The church would be better off, then, subsuming teleology under eschatology rather than *vice versa*. The modern turn to a closed causal network of atoms, whose movements could be perfectly accounted for through Newtonian science, removed the need for any teleology in nature and hinted in the direction of such a possibility for humans as well. This, it seems to me, is the place to contextualize the modern rejection of miracles. Modernity classed miracles as violations of the laws of nature, and such simply were not allowable. Miracles, or better, direct actions of God, make sense not against the background of a closed continuum of cause and effect, but when God's purposes for and prior action in creation are considered. The modern rejection of such a larger context, which was inescapably eschatological, set the stage for the later rejection of miracles. William Abraham comments along these lines: "Direct actions of God are not bolts from the blue or random events, but are related to a wider conceptual scheme that gives point and intelligibility to their occurrence. As such they provide explanations for events in the world."[41]

The theological reason for the turn away from eschatology also antedates modernity. The decisive factor is that pointed out in chapter three—an inability or unwillingness on the part of the church to differentiate between itself and its host culture—Constantinianism. This sociopolitical commitment meant that eschatology had to be either outside time and space (heaven, hell, purgatory) or completely realized (and thus undifferentiated from socio-political reality), in order to allow the rulers to have their place as *Christian* rulers. Constantinianism, in one form or another, was the dominant perspective in western Christianity from about the fourth century. Although the relationship between church and culture shifted during the Reformation, this shift, in a significant sense, strengthened rather than weakened the bond between church and culture.

A Recovery of Eschatology

If the marginalization of eschatology is due partially to Constantinianism, the resources for a recovery of eschatology might be found in a tradition that has first rejected Constantinianism. The group that fits such a description most closely are the baptists, at least as James W. McClendon, Jr. depicts them. The fundamentally eschatological stance of his conception of the "baptist vision" is exactly what is needed not only for a recovery of eschatology, but also of history, narrative, and finally, of doctrine. It is ironic that a tradition that is known for eschewing explicit doctrinal formulations (in favor of the bible alone) would be the source of salvation for doctrine. That this is not as ironic as it first appears is due to the fact that the doctrine they so often eschew is that of a primarily propositionalist nature, not the sort I am proposing. I will also show that a similar eschatological vision has arisen from time to time in other traditions, including my own Methodist tradition. Such appearances outside the baptist tradition are somewhat muted and very fragile (I will show that Methodism's eschatological heritage did not long survive the fires of modernity), probably because an intentional rejection of Constantinianism tends not to accompany them.[42]

In writing his systematic theology, James McClendon seeks to write from the *baptist* perspective. But what is the baptist perspective? In our own era Southern Baptists dominate the scene, and while their church government and theology of the sacraments are baptistic, the way they have tended to approach politics in America makes them look like they have more Constantinian yearnings than the original baptists. Their soteriology, so often a combination of modern individualism and Calvinism, appears equally at odds with the communal emphasis of the early baptists. McClendon's strategy in this context is to consider the broader baptist tradition.

While he finds several features common to most strains of the baptist tradition, he settles on what he describes as the "baptist vision." Describing what he is looking for in a "vision" he says,

> By a vision I mean the guiding stimulus by which a people ... shape their life and thought as that people.... I mean by it the continually emerging theme and tonic structure of their common life. The vision is thus already present, waiting to be recognized and employed; it must not seem a stranger to those who share in baptist life of to their sympathetic observers.[43]

Notice that his focus is on baptists as a people. In chapter three I argued that what is needed for a recovery of doctrine is a prior recovery of the biblical notion of the church as the people of God, and of this people as a fundamental part of what salvation is all about, to the degree that salvation is inconceivable apart from church. McClendon is heading the same direction.

One of the proposed centers of baptist thought was biblicism. From the beginning baptists have held the bible in high esteem. After committing to looking for a controlling *vision* instead of a set of distinctive beliefs, McClendon returns to the role of scripture, finding there the next element to identify the baptist vision. It is consideration of the role of scripture that first evidences the centrality of eschatology in his reading of the tradition. He claims,

> Scripture in this vision effects a link between the church of the apostles and our own. So the vision can be expressed as a hermeneutical motto, which is shared awareness of *the*

> *present Christian community as the primitive community and the eschatological community.*[44]

The shorthand phrase for this vision, "this is that," is taken from Peter's sermon in Acts 2. The crowds gathered in Jerusalem for Pentecost that year had seen some strange sights, so strange they could not understand them. Preaching to the inquisitive, Peter points them to Joel chapter two saying, in essence, "This (that you see before you) is that (prophesied by Joel)." In this use of Joel's prophecy we see an instance of Caird and Wright's position on apocalyptic language mentioned above. Joel not only prophecies that "I will show wonders in the heaven above and signs in the earth below, blood and fire and billows of smoke. The sun will be turned to darkness and the moon to blood before the coming of the great and glorious day of the Lord," but Peter quotes exactly this section of the prophecy—*even though the text makes no claim that such events were literally happening.* McClendon's recovery of eschatology, though coming from a different place than Caird and Wright, comes to a comparable conclusion.

Scripture then does more than give us the facts, whether in propositional or narratival form. It functions to make the Christian community what it is. McClendon later illustrates how this works in two dimensions.

> A vital feature of the Gospels understood as identity documents: [is that] whereas the identity of Jesus is at once that of the risen Christ present in the reader's church *and* the central figure in the Gospel, the identity of the 'disciples' is by invitation to the readers themselves as well as their originals in the story. *We* are invited to become disciples, and thus to see ourselves figuring in this narrative.[45]

Looking backward then, we can see that the identity of Jesus is something fixed: he is the one who performed the acts and spoke the teachings recorded in the Gospel narrative, the one who out of obedience to the Father died on the cross, and through the Father's power was raised from the dead. But this person so identified is not merely past, he is also present in the community today. Still looking backward, we see a variety of ways of responding to Jesus. The church today has the choice not merely to find itself in these narratives (figuratively) but to live out the same sort of response it finds the disciples making then.

Later in this chapter I will turn to the philosophical work of Alasdair MacIntyre and Hans Georg Gadamer and discuss how their work provides some additional backing for this position. On the face of it, the conviction that the ecclesial community *now* is[46] the same as the community *then*—and in the end—may seem far-fetched. I will suggest that beyond these biblical reasons there are philosophical possibilities for such a position as well.

The baptist vision works through narrative. Through narrative, the people know who they are and where they stand. McClendon asserts that the role of the vision is to "show how a people's identity is construed via narratives that are historically set in another time and place but display redemptive power here and now."[47] My model, which sees Christianity as a dramatic narrative in which the church now lives, is quite close to this position. In the close connection between this model and eschatology we can also see why this is a model for understanding Christianity in particular and not religion in general. It is not merely connection to *a* narrative that makes the church what it is, but continuing participation in precisely the narrative depicted in scripture. Doctrine is the speech act of the church, spoken from within the context of life in this story, *heard* within this same context (though in a different location temporally and possibly spatially), dependent on the fact that the community now is continuous with the community then.

My claim, to reiterate, is that the baptist vision (and I will continue to call it that since that tradition has been most faithful in maintaining it), is necessary for the broader church as well. When it is universalized like this, that is, seen as descriptive of the internal logic of Christianity, a rejection of other models (propositionalism and experiential expressivism) is entailed. The relation to the cultural linguistic model is more complex, perhaps better envisioned as a fuller rendering than a replacement. Once this component has been added to my model, the inadequacy of the cultural linguistic model is seen to lie precisely in its nonrejection (and thus implicit acceptance) of Constantinianism. Whether this political position was imported into that model by way of the modern social scientific analysis Lindbeck relies on, or by way of his ecclesiological tradition, is unimportant.

A further difference is that the use of the baptist vision serves to anchor the Christian tradition in a way not possible in the cultural linguistic. Lindbeck claims that "what is taken to be reality is in large part socially constructed and consequently alters in the course of time."[48] Taken on one level, this is true enough. The Christian claim, articulated in the baptist vision, is that we have not merely the present but also the past, and that the way we have the past is not merely as a present memory of the past but in a real participation in and continuity with it. We have not merely the present (social theory *is* strongest when considering the timeless present), but also history. The reality that is socially constructed is not, for Christians, constructed by just any social group (such as the dominant culture), but by the living society of the followers of Jesus.

If some are afraid that baptist triumphalism will result from my model, I think their fears are misplaced. Echoes of the baptist vision are found in many other traditions—and they ought to be, if I am right that this is a key element in the Christian tradition as a whole. Let us consider a few examples. One unsurprising echo is in the work of Jürgen Moltmann. He says,

> If a single and special phenomenon like the church wants to understand itself in the history of God's dealings with the world, then it has to conceive itself in the movement of this history, for it is itself standing in the midst of that movement, not above it and not at its end.[49]

John Webster proposes a version that, like mine, is contrasted with Lindbeck's cultural linguistic approach. As does Miroslav Volf,[50] Webster finds Lindbeck's focus on Christianity as a semiotic system to be too docetic and in need of some flesh and bones.

> Rather than retaining the identity of Christianity by envisaging is as a tightly structured territory of meaning, it is imperative to locate Christianity's center outside itself, in the history of Jesus Christ. That history, because of its identity with the being and action of God, cannot in principle be assimilated to any one scheme.[51]

Webster's emphasis here is on the nonreducibility of the Christian narrative. This narrative is always more than just the story told, whether we are speaking of the story told by the church today or the story of scripture. The church lives in that ongoing history, not merely in a linguistic structure of meaning derived from it. This is why doctrine can never substitute for the narrative. Conservative theology in the modern period has tried this route, but the real church does not fit in the semiotic box.

John Milbank also echoes the baptist vision, in his own inimitable style. The objective of his *Theology and Social Theory* is to mount a specifically theological challenge to the dominance of modern social theories. In this context, he claims that the church has all too often succumbed to the metanarration of social theory, forgetting its own history and praxis. He says,

> For there to be a salvation with a specifiable Christian content, there must be a directly theological discourse about

the socio-historical.... But just as there must be a gnoseologically primary Christian historical narrative, so also there must be a specifically Christian practice. To be involved in this practice is to entertain the narrative; to entertain the narrative seriously is to continue to enact it.[52]

Christian knowledge and interpretation, whether of life today or life in the scriptural narrative, is primary. The way this happens is not by knowing the facts of scripture but by living in the midst of the same story.

Ronald Thiemann's proposed nonfoundationalist model of revelation is built around a vision akin to that articulated by McClendon. He claims that such a view was present in the Reformers. They taught that

> Scripture, when interpreted in this way [literally, yet extended by the figural], depicts a real world, temporally structured, which encompasses both the times and stories of the text and those of the reader. Since the world depicted by the Bible is the only real world, the reader must fit his or her own experience into scripture's cumulative narrative, thus becoming a 'figure' of the text.[53]

Again, (echoing not only the baptist vision but Lindbeck's intratextuality discussed in chapter three above) we see that the present reader has a place within the Christian narrative as a whole.

Further examples could be given.[54] I have provided this many because it is essential that we not see this as solely a baptist position. It fits the scriptural narrative as read by a number of interpreters from a number of perspectives. It is not universal, of course. If it were, my work here would be unnecessary. After a short discussion of the baptist vision in the Methodist tradition I will reframe my earlier discussion of the modern position on history as the exact opposite of the baptist vision. Instead of "this is that," modernity insists on a "that is this" approach. But first we turn to the Methodists.

As a Methodist appealing to the "baptist" vision the presumption is against me. Recent Methodism, at least in the South, has at least partially defined itself as an alternative to the Baptist (i.e., *Southern* Baptist) church. Methodists may not know what they believe, but they *know* they are not Baptists. Ecumenically we find much more in common with other mainline denominations.

Methodist historian Russell Richey identifies a characteristic of early Methodism that functions in many respects like the baptist vision does in the baptist tradition. Importantly, he also traces how this "Methodist" vision has faded to a close alliance between Methodism and American culture, what I have called (the modern version of) Constantinianism. This alliance has not merely broken the hold of the Methodist vision, but has also led to a secularization of Methodism as an institution.

Richey focuses his attention on the early Methodist Disciplines. Within Methodism, the *Book of Discipline* orders and structures the life of the church. Unlike other traditions, Methodist Disciplines began with a historical section.[55] These historical narratives aimed to set Methodist self-understanding in the context of providence. Richey says that

> The Discipline gathered the entire Methodist movement into Providence, turned mundane into sacred history, [and] conceived of history in redemptive terms. History rendered the work of God.... History said what no other part of the Discipline could quite so directly affirm—God worked through and God *works* through the Methodists.[56]

The early Methodists firmly believed that they were involved in a great adventure that was not merely their own, but God's. John Wesley's fascination with the primitive church fit into this context as well. Though it antedated his leadership of the Methodist revival, it could, perhaps, be seen as a factor shaping his understanding of the providential role of Methodism.[57] Wesley's use of primitive Christianity shows that he thought it relevant for the eighteenth-century church. I do not think, however, that his consciousness of where he stood was as clearly articulated as McClendon's interpretation of the baptist vision. Richey does insist, however, that Methodism's position was different from that common among other Anglicans. He puts it this way: "The Episcopalians prize tradition, but tradition for them does not mean the recent saga of God's work in their midst. Instead it means patristics."[58] One other area of Wesley's ministry in which echoes of the vision can be seen is in the charges of "enthusiasm" leveled against him. Though a large part of this controversy could be considered in terms of individual issues (especially assurance of salvation and perfection), the idea that someone would be able to say with anything approaching confidence that he was currently being used of God was considered very radical in the Church of England then. Especially illuminating on the controversy that arose from this is Wesley's response to Bishop William Warburton.[59] In chapter one I claimed that modernity had turned to Providence to get away from the notion of God's continuing activity in the current age. The Methodist turn to Providence was very different, in that it refused to reduce that Providence to a theoretical backing for Newtonian science. They saw God active in special ways in and through them.

Methodism is now over two hundred and fifty years old and has lost this sense of history. Richey insists that history is still important to Methodists, but they have lost the perspective of their forebears whereby they found themselves in God's story.[60] Few would accuse Methodism today of the "enthusiasm" that brought Wesley into conflict with his superiors in the Church of England. Richey sees two primary reasons for the loss of this vision. First, Methodists were not sufficiently self-conscious of their historical vision. He suggests that

> Had the church been more self-conscious about these historical prefaces, it might have chosen to deal with them in a different way in later years, particularly in the twentieth century. The church . . . has sustained the genre, the historical preface, but lost the sense of it as mediating the work of God.[61]

This lack of self-consciousness made it easier to read the providential claims of the prefaces only in light of Christian *experience*, for Methodism was undeniably experiential, and without adequate connection to the scriptural narrative which they were continuing, effectively severing the tie to the larger history. As American Methodism pursued an educated clergy (which necessarily meant a clergy trained in the culture of the modern academy), personal religious experience became the center of interpretation. The historical view of early Methodism avoided enthusiasm specifically because its view was communal. As the center of Methodist spirituality shifted from the community to the individual, the old reading of the prefaces could only be seen as reckless triumphalism.

The second factor leading to the loss of vision in Methodism was the church's relationship to American culture. Richey comments, "The wedding of denomination to nation, however stimulating it proved to denominational growth, built a fundamental flaw into the church's foundation."[62] As Methodism became unofficial chaplain to America, it lost sight of its identity as part of the transcendent narrative of God's continuing action. Eschatology was naturalized into social progress (as we saw in the account of Knudson's work in chapter one) and Methodism was too easily seen merely as the agent of such progress.

Other than the marginalization of doctrine resulting from this shift in Methodism, the church also evidences a secularization of its institutional structures. This charge cannot be laid only on theological liberals, since signs can be found in the writings of conservative evangelicals as well. Writing in the genre "What's wrong with United Methodism and how to fix it," James Holsinger and Evelyn Laycock write concerning what to do about problem pastors who are hurting churches,

> Competency or lack thereof is not a chargeable offense, or at least it should not be. The call of an individual to the ordained ministry is between that person and God. But *God does not call people to be United Methodist ministers.* That determination is made by the mechanisms that have been established by the church.[63]

Besides the individualism implicit in this understanding of the ministerial calling, this statement shows that God is not expected to be involved in the day-to-day operations of the United Methodist Church. We do not need God for this: that is what the institutional structures mandated by the *Book of Discipline* are for. The vision of a church life centered in the ongoing divine narrative is gone. I believe we also see here evidence of an institutional surrender to Max Weber's theory of institutionalization. We no longer need the original charisma (it is too unpredictable) now that we have a dependable bureaucracy and policies and procedures in place.

It is not the case that all United Methodists have given up on their original vision, a vision so similar to the baptist vision. As might be expected from my discussion in chapter three of their position on the nature of the church, Stanley Hauerwas and William Willimon are suggesting a return to such a vision. Their book *Resident Aliens* is centered on the argument that Christianity makes no sense apart from the church, and that the church is only intelligible when conceived eschatologically. The church places us "within an adventure that is nothing less than God's purpose for the whole world."[64] This position is not derived primarily from their Methodist heritage, however, though it does find support there.[65]

Where the baptist vision, "this is that," confers identity through considering the past—without destroying the pastness of the past—the modern vision, "that is this," does the opposite. Where I stand *now* is the place of judgment, the proper horizon for understanding all texts. This view assumes an underlying universal uniformity in humanity, a miracle-excluding uniformity similar to that David Hume saw in his world. Culture and Christianity are mere epiphenomena. The clearest place to see this is in the monistic systems of the nineteenth century that saw a single line of progress from a single beginning point to a single end point.[66] Terms like "primitive" or "civilized" denoted where a culture stood on this continuum. The strongest influence of this vision was on history and in this way it greatly impacted Christian thought.

What the modern vision amounts to is a thoroughgoing application of Cartesian-style epistemology to history. Julian Hartt sums it up well, "The thing that 'really happened' is something subsumable under categories of explanation taken for granted in the present. Thus the real event is something conceivable in a nexus intelligible to the present state of consciousness."[67] This view has been seen as essential to modern historical studies. Thiselton quotes James Smart as saying that

> It belongs to the essential nature of *historical* interpretation that it widens the distance between the Bible and the modern world. The more thoroughly it accomplishes its task the more completely it removes the Biblical documents into worlds of human existence that very emphatically are not *our* world.[68]

The modern vision impacts more than history: it becomes a key criterion of doctrine as well. Using this principle (though not explicitly), a Methodist theologian is able to reason that since our current experience is that we all sin, we cannot but judge that Jesus too must have sinned. Anything else is unbelievable.[69]

It appears then, that the task of modern historical studies is to rule out the possibility of any version of the baptist vision. Gadamer has detected this stance as well, and finds it poisonous to the work of interpreting texts on their own terms. Discussing the methodology entailed by the modern vision he says,

> for the historian it is a basic principle that tradition is to be interpreted in a sense different than what the texts, of themselves, call for. . . . The historian's interpretation is concerned with something that is not expressed in the text itself and need have nothing to do with the intended meaning of the text.[70]

This is reminiscent of Frei's charge that narrative has been eclipsed in modern reading, first through a reduction of the narrative to ostensive reference, and then, when reference appeared to fail, merely spiritualizing it in some way. John Milbank discusses a similar application of the modern vision to the biblical narratives, though from a different angle.[71]

The difference between the baptist and modern visions is more than a stance toward history. When the baptist speaks of "we," he or she is speaking of the community. Individual believers find their identity in the Christian narrative through their membership in the church. "We" are all different—differently called and differently gifted, yet we find our unity in Christ. Though our personal stories are different (and we come from different communities and different cultures), we find unity as we together become willing actors in the continuing story of Jesus. It is not as if believers first find their identity in Christ and then impart that identity to the church through voluntary association. We have this particular vision because we have been trained within the community to have it. We do not stand alone and isolated, but together in community. When one who lives with the baptist vision (or using my terms, *in* the Christian narrative), the scriptural texts are not merely out there at a distance, they are *ours*, addressed to us.

When the modern says "we," he or she is speaking collectively. "We" are all essentially the same. We moderns approach the past as neutral observers because that is the rational way to do so. All the prejudices of tradition and community have been set side, and we are able to see things as they really are. For the modern, the texts may contain wisdom and truth (and we will recognize it when we see it), but they are not *our* texts. If we may go back to Lessing for a moment, we might say that it is the modern vision that constructs the existential ditch between the "accidental truths of history" and the "necessary truths of reason."

The modern vision affects more than theology and the church. Alasdair MacIntyre, who defends a thoroughly historical view of philosophy, finds a version of it in that field as well. In his *Three Rival Versions of Moral Enquiry* the three versions he compares are the Encyclopaedist (mainline modernity), the Genealogist (the Nietzschean subversion of modernity—which instead of moving beyond modern convictions settles for pessimism regarding their successful application), and Tradition (the Thomistic school of thought). We see "that is this" most clearly in the Encyclopaedist tradition:

> It is the mark of the Encyclopaedist that the present stands in judgment upon the past, assigning to itself a sovereignty which allows it to approve that in the past which can be represented as a precursor of its own standards of judgment.[72]

Though MacIntyre's position, being philosophical rather than theological, does not have the resources to have a "this is that" view, he does seem close, and clearly judges the modern vision inadequate. Another place we see MacIntyre contending against the modern vision is in his critique of what could be called Richard Rorty's metaphilosophy. Rorty reads the history of philosophy as united in seeking to answer a limited set of questions. MacIntyre, on the other hand, claims that though from our perspective the question asked two hundred years ago may appear the same as one asked today, the different historical setting makes it a potentially significantly different question.[73]

PHILOSOPHICAL HELP FOR THE BAPTIST VISION

As people who have been enculturated in modernity the modern vision simply seems obvious to us. That the community now could have any relationship, other than mere succession, to a community of long ago is simply incredible. Alasdair MacIntyre's concept of a tradition and Hans-Georg Gadamer's concept of *Wirkungsgeschichte* provide some space in which we can conceptualize such a connection. I am not suggesting, however, that these two concepts are all that is needed to make the baptist vision work.

The baptist vision cuts against the grain of modernity in at least four important ways. The first is that it is formulated in antithesis to autonomous individualism. "This is that" is a communal vision, not something that can be the property of a lone individual. Second, the present has no privileged status, and the past is seen as more than a mere predecessor of the present. Third, the baptist vision is action oriented, i.e., action is more primary than knowledge. This leads into the fourth feature that most clearly differentiates it from modernity. The baptist vision does not work apart from the action of God. McClendon is not claiming to have studied all communities in their temporal transitions and to have discovered a wonderful mechanism whereby they have diachronic unity. He is proposing the baptist vision not as characteristic of communities in general, but of the *baptist* communities, and I am extending it to *Christian* communities.

The concepts of MacIntyre and Gadamer do not cover this territory. MacIntyre's analysis of traditions, though admittedly done from the matrix of a particular tradition, is nonetheless theorized to be true of all traditions. Modernity and other traditions that fail to recognize that they *are* traditions are necessarily less clear not only about the world but in their own self-understanding than those that have awareness of their tradition-boundedness.[74] Christianity is a tradition-bound discourse, but more must be said. We can recognize *Wirkungsgeschichte* as a factor in the continuity of the Christian tradition, but it is not the only factor. I think neither MacIntyre nor Gadamer would require that all traditions function identically or be isomorphic for their theories to stand.

MacIntyre on Tradition

MacIntyre's mature thinking on the nature of tradition in *Whose Justice? Which Rationality?* shows a continuous development from his 1977 article "Epistemological Crises, Dramatic Narrative and the Philosophy of Science." In *Whose Justice?* he defines a tradition as

> an argument extended through time in which certain fundamental agreements are defined and redefined in terms of two kinds of conflict: those with critics and enemies external to the tradition who reject all or at least key parts of those fundamental agreements, and those internal, interpretive debates through which the meaning and rationale of the fundamental agreements come to be expressed and by whose progress a tradition is constituted.[75]

It is not hard to see ways in which Christianity fits this description of a tradition. Christian doctrine has been formulated in the fires of controversy, sometimes with groups external to the church, but more often as a result of internal conflict. The Arian controversy, for example, is best understood when framed not as Christianity versus a pagan infiltrator, but as an internal debate about the most faithful way to say who Jesus is. Though the roots of the doctrine of the incarnation can be clearly seen even in the scriptures, the formulation that came to be received by the church through the work of Nicea and Constantinople is an articulation from within the context of particular questions raised in particular social settings. Both the sides represented by Arius and by Athanasius used conceptuality drawn from non-Christian traditions. The church decided—not quickly either! —that the Athanasian articulation fit better with the overall Christian tradition and scriptural narratives.[76]

Modernity is uncomfortable with such a coherentist account—it lacks objectivity and the requisite amount of personal detachment necessary of those who seek the truth. For moderns, correct doctrine ought to be readily and easily available just by investigating the data. Traditions are radically anti-Cartesian in this sense. They all have historically contingent starting points. Their construal of the data and the questions to be answered are therefore also always historically contingent.[77] MacIntyre's claim, in line with postmodern philosophy of science, is that apart from a tradition one does not even know what questions to ask or what to count as data.[78]

Through being "indoctrinated" into a tradition, a history of enquiry, one not only learns the heritage of the tradition but also learns how to go on.[79] This is the locus for Christian doctrine. As the church lives the

Christian narrative, doctrine serves to identify our setting—a key element of which is where the church has been before—and what actions are appropriate for the next steps forward. Following MacIntyre's theory of tradition too closely could lead one to an overly intellectualistic conception of Christianity. We have not only the Christian tradition as a tradition of enquiry (actually, a set of traditions of enquiry), but also the church as the people of God who are living the narrative now. To be in the Christian narrative is more than a mental act (or series of mental acts), or a "seeing as." It is an ongoing life—more a "living as" than a "seeing as." The truth the Christian seeks is in the end normed neither by mere correspondence to facts nor coherence among them, but by the person of Jesus who began the tradition, and who, if the tradition is correct, continues to live and act in the midst of the church.

Gadamer and Wirkungsgeschichte

Modernity offers many accounts of how the process of understanding takes place. In chapter one I noted a feature of modern thought that, in Gadamer's view, handicaps it from the beginning of the search for understanding: a rejection of tradition, or as he puts it, prejudice.[80] In opposition to the modern interpretive subject standing in a neutral location Gadamer comments that *"understanding is to be thought of less as a subjective act than as participating in an event of tradition, a process of transmission in which past and present are constantly mediated."*[81] Wirkungsgeschichte refers to this traditionary process, whereby we place ourselves in continuity with what is past, and come to see how where we stand now is an effect of that original event. In a sense, our action of understanding, of merging (perhaps "synchronizing" would be better here) our horizon with the horizon of the original event (or text) seeks out an echo of the original. Gadamer's thought here is complex, and I believe this is a fair extension of his work. We can see similarity here with what MacIntyre claimed about how traditions fit into the process of enquiry: "If we are trying to understand a historical phenomenon from the historical distance that is characteristic of our hermeneutical situation, we are always already affected by history. It determines in advance both what seems to us worth inquiring about and what will appear as an object of investigation...."[82] Where the church stands today in God's story is a function of where the church has gone before. We cannot understand where we now stand (which is one of the chief things doctrine tells us), unless we know where we have stood (here the "we" is historical—

looking backward to the primitive Christian community and every manifestation of the community in between).

Real History?

Through a reappropriation of scriptural eschatology through the baptist vision, we find a way to get across Lessing's existential ditch. Once we see ourselves standing in a community that is not merely what we see before us right now, but is in a real sense the ancient community as well, we are no longer left in the place of the modern who wonders how something ancient can possibly have authority over us in our autonomy. One who lives in a community with this vision knows that he or she is *not* autonomous.

But what about the temporal and metaphysical ditches? The two can be tied together when we ask whether we are dealing with real history in our investigation into the Christian story. Is it necessary that the primitive ecclesial community actually was of a certain nature just as long as we see ourselves in continuity with it? In other words, is what matters imaginative engagement with reality or will engagement with a mere construct suffice? As we find ourselves living in the Christian narrative, does it make any difference whether the events of scripture that constitute the beginning of that narrative—the first few acts of the play—actually happened? If not, the metaphysical ditch is only an apparent problem here, since what we have are narratives that simply illustrate spiritual ideals. The narrative *form* is what counts. Narrative form alone, however, is not enough to bring back doctrine from its marginalization.

Historical Status of the Gospels

We can begin by considering McClendon's admission that the Gospels are not modern biographies, but are "identity documents."[83] They were not written by people adhering to the canons of modern historiography. Yet, McClendon contends, we cannot take them as fictional. This necessity is seen from the perspective McClendon is writing: Christian ethics. As long as ethics is built only on principles (as moderns would have it), history is unneeded. Christian ethics, however, is founded on a person who performed certain deeds. The teaching of Jesus simply cannot be separated from what he did.[84]

The tie between the community now and the community then is not our decision to believe in such a link, but the living and present Jesus. McClendon says that "there must be a vital link between the Christ we know in worship and the Christ who lived and died and rose. The story now and the story then must be linked by the identity of the one risen Christ Jesus."[85] The Christian narrative then, is more than church history. The church believes that the same Jesus identified in the Gospels lives today and is himself an active player in this narrative.

While the Gospels are clearly not in the modern genre of "objective history," and their aims go beyond the desire to report the facts *wie es eigentlich gewesen*, they certainly present themselves as reporting events that actually happened. Julian Hartt notes that

> the Gospel begins and ends with an uncompromising declaration that certain things are facts, that is, that certain things have happened. The Gospel is just as uncompromisingly insistent that anybody who knows these things had better do something about his situation now.[86]

Lessing's temporal ditch causes us to ask the question, "What *really* happened?" Hartt claims this is the wrong question. What we ought to ask is "what has the Lord done?"[87] Holmer has a useful discussion of the grammar of "fact." He says that "'fact' always makes a distinction between what is *not* disputed 'now,' 'here,' 'in this context,' 'under these circumstances,' 'presently,' and what *is* so disputed." A focus on "facts" tends toward skepticism. "With research in every field, the facts do not become plainer, as a superficial use of 'fact' might suggest, but [they] become more difficult to get at, more technical to state, and plainly upset the picture of the 'realm of facts' with which one starts" (*Grammar of Faith*, 103f.). In most areas of life we do not even think to ask after the "facts." As long as Christian life and doctrine is done primarily in an apologetic mode (as modernity has inclined it to do), such a preoccupation seems only natural. In this context Placher's call for "Unapologetic Theology" looks attractive. If we stand nowhere, questions about facticity might make an appropriate starting place, but standing as we are within the Christian narrative *before we even ask any questions*, we must ask questions from that context. This is what Lessing missed.[88]

The most important event according to the New Testament documents is the resurrection of Jesus. Though the idea that a dead man might rise is a scandal to moderns,[89] (to ancients it was *incredible* that a dead man might rise, but the scandal to the ancients was that a *crucified criminal* might be the one to rise), the resurrection is not a dispensable part of Christianity. McClendon says, "the resurrection is central not only for doctrine but also for ethics; it is the *sine qua non* of the Christian life itself."[90] This is not merely a conviction of the baptist tradition. Methodist Albert Outler asserts,

> Christianity, therefore, stands or falls by its claim that its originative Event is historical, that this Event illuminates all other historical events, that this Event is known and 'reproduced' in the ongoing life of an actual community. Undercut any of these and you have shattered the foundations.[91]

The historical question will not be settled by resort to investigation of the facts via historical criticism—that is the wrong starting point. Nor is the Bultmannian turn away from the fickle history produced by such criticism the answer. To recover doctrine, the church needs to first recover the conviction that God acts in history, both in the past and now in the church's midst.

Given the current state of theology, the question of what to do with historical criticism is likely to arise at this point. Since mainline historical criticism has been pursued as an adjunct to the epistemological project, there is a need to find ways to step away from the project before its work can be healthy for the church (and trusted by the church). I am saying neither that epistemology is irrelevant nor that scripture does not give us true knowledge—though those steeped in the epistemological tradition will likely read those as the only options. Richard Rorty has argued that epistemology is fatally flawed and ought to be dropped in favor of "therapy."[92] I do not think his suggestions are tenable. If disciplines of enquiry were hierarchically related to each other as foundationalism requires—or were related this way *because* of epistemology, such a move might make sense. Regardless of the genesis of the centrality of epistemology, it has since established multiple nonhierarchical relations with other disciplines. Though finding nonfoundationalist ways of pursuing epistemology (and I do not see neo-Nietzschean methods as offering anything other than an epistemological *via negativa*)[93] may be exceedingly difficult, there is no reason not to try.

Does this mean that the church should take the perspective, "The Bible says it, we believe it, that settles it"? A popular assumption regarding the purpose of historical criticism is that it is to critique the facticity of the biblical texts. Am I suggesting, then, that no such critique is legitimate? No, to both fears. The notion that the bible is a textbook, a book of true propositions, is just as much a child of modern epistemology as historical criticism is. Turning from a epistemologically driven inerrantism will be just as difficult for parts of the church as turning from a naturalistic historical criticism is for others.

I do believe, however, that Christians must intentionally unlearn the dominant epistemological models before we can fruitfully return to the question of how we know what we know. Because the modern epistemological models are deeply embedded in our culture, so deeply we think they offer the only options, I expect such an unlearning to take at least a generation. This unlearning is not the work of individuals so much as it is of the western Christian tradition as a whole.

As to what the discipline of biblical studies might look like once it has turned from modern epistemology (of both propositionalist and experiential expressive varieties), I am inclined to point to the work of Tom Wright as a step in this direction, but since I am not a specialist in biblical studies, this inclination is uncritical. I *like* the work he is doing. I believe it offers great promise for the church. The question that must be answered, however, is, "How will the church receive his work?" I cannot answer this question as an individual. The church cannot answer it quickly. At the very least, historical criticism that is healthy for the church must be done with a connection that is closer to the church than to naturalism.

The Action of God

Considering the biblical narratives, William Placher highlights the necessary role of the God who acts. "The logic of the stories is that God's action comes first and generates human responses. If I buy into the stories, then I have to buy into that logic."[94] Of course, there is no external and objective compulsion to buy into the stories. Doctrine insofar as it seeks to be *Christian* doctrine, however, requires the church to "buy into" the stories, because the stories are who we are. In his study of the prevenience of God Thiemann brings up a similar point:

> Narrative is useful to nonfoundational theology's assertion of God's prevenience because 1) it provides a coherent theological alternative to those theologies focused on the primacy of philosophical anthropology; 2) it provides a way of construing the canon as a whole which integrates scripture's first-order language and theology's second-order redescription; 3) it focuses attention on the centrality of God's agency within biblical narrative and Christian community.[95]

Apart from the agency of God, the biblical narratives do not make sense. My contention has been that without the action of God the church does not make sense, since the church is now living in the context of God's story, which is not merely a story about God or about people who believe in God, but is the story of God's continuing action to redeem the world. It is not the narrative that saves the Christian: it is God.[96]

Metanarration

The driving force within the church is the desire to be faithful to God through obedience to Jesus' command to make disciples of all nations. The Christian conviction is that the story of God in which we act is a story that includes all people, though not all are willing actors. Christians freely admit that there are other narratives available, some equally as large as Christianity in their compass. When we consider the relations between these competing narratives the question of metanarratives is not far behind. What can be said about a narrative that functions to bring unity to the other narratives?

Lyotard on Modern Metanarrativity

One answer is the one supposedly given by Jean-François Lyotard that metanarratives are themselves a feature of modernity, and to be rejected in postmodernity. Metanarratives, he claims, result from the attempt to use premodern forms of narration to legitimate modern scientific knowledge.[97] He describes this metanarrativity in this way:

> There is universal 'history' of spirit, spirit is 'life,' and 'life' is its own self-presentation and formulation in the ordered knowledge of all its forms contained in the empirical sciences. The encyclopedia of German idealism is the narration of the '(hi)story' of this life-subject. But what it produces is a metanarrative, for the story's narrator must not be a people mired in the particular positivity of its traditional knowledge, nor even scientists taken as a whole.[98]

This version of what a metanarrative amounts to is very different from the conception I am using. Instead of turning to the particularities of traditional (and traditioned) narrative and the contingencies of history, Lyotard has in view a form of metanarration that is the ahistorical universalization of modernity.[99] It is this form of metanarrative that constantly seeks to reduce Christianity to some more basic form, usually in terms of one of the social sciences.[100] The modern invention of "religion" seems to be an early attempt to engage in the kind of metanarrative Lyotard condemns.

Specifically Christian Metanarration

The Christian narrative is a metanarrative in a different sense. Confessedly historically contingent and shamelessly particular, it depends on the activity of agents who cannot be described as faceless and nameless "metasubjects." Narrative (or metanarrative) *form* is not sufficient to account for this.

The call for Christian metanarration comes from several sources. John Milbank asserts that

> the [Christian] metanarrative is *not* just the story of Jesus, it is the continuing story of the church, already realized in a finally exemplary way by Christ, yet still to be realized universally in harmony with Christ, and yet *differently*, by all generations of Christians.[101]

One way to read what happened in modernity, particularly modern theology, is to see it as a preference for creation-discourse over redemption-discourse. With the present activity of God limited to providence (see chapter one)—an extension of creation—universality and a basic continuity could be maintained. The problem with redemption was that it was irremediably particular, a discontinuity in history. It was clearly not universal. Milbank comments:

> The logic of Christianity involves the claim that the 'interruption' of history by Christ and his bride, the church, is the most fundamental of events, interpreting all other events. And it is *most especially* a social event, able to interpret other social formations because it compares them with its own new social practice.[102]

The Christian act of metanarration, then, is finally not a theoretical act but a practical, historical, and social act. It is not the attempt to subsume other theories under the intellectual system of Christian doctrine and theology, but the action of the church to extend the Gospel (the good news of God's redemptive act in Jesus to all people). L. Gregory Jones says that "the biblical narrative seeks to incorporate all people into God's narrative."[103] The Christian narrative, as an extension of the biblical narrative, is first and foremost a *lived story*, and it is this lived story that is seeking out willing actors.

This act of practical metanarration is a primary factor in the development of Christian doctrine. As the church lives the Christian narrative, it continually encounters other people and groups living other narratives (and is itself tempted to live these other stories instead of its own). Since doctrine guides the church in the living of the story, doctrine must be able to account for relations with these competing narratives and their inhabitants. New questions to be answered by doctrine must be asked continually. Some of the questions that originate in foreign narratives not only provoke doctrinal development but also enable the church to see and understand its own narrative better. This is possible because narrative engagement is not done primarily on the theoretical level, but on the interpersonal and intercommunal level. As inhabitants of other narratives not only hear the church talking about its narrative but see and experience the action of God through the church's life, they can come to see the unarticulated background that is the field in which doctrine grows.

SUMMARY

The key to this chapter has been an eschatological view of the church and of history. I have argued that modern dehistoricization is harmful to the church and a main factor behind the marginalization of doctrine. I proposed ways of understanding the nature of the church that avoid this tendency and are in accord with the biblical narratives. When we see the church as engaged in the continued acting out of these narratives, as a continuing agent *with God,* in God's own story, the place of both narrative and history becomes central. James McClendon's conception of the "baptist vision," best maintained by the Baptists, but not foreign to other traditions—including my own United Methodist tradition—was shown to be a particularly appropriate way to see the continuity and unity of this narrative. The church today is not merely the successor of the church then, but is in a sense the same community as the primitive church. In order for this vision to work—and to overcome the modern vision—two things are needful. First, real history must be allowed. The biblical narratives cannot be taken as fictional. Second, the act of metanarration is required, not only to overcome modernity's attempted metanarration of the church, but also to extend God's invitation to others to come join the Christian narrative as willing actors.

In the concluding chapter of this book I will tie together this work on narrative and history with what has gone before. This will be in four parts. First I will summarize the argument that doctrine has been marginalized by modernity. Second, I will suggest some ways in which doctrine relates to, depends upon, and draws from the Christian narrative. Third, having proposed that doctrine is a speech act of the church, I will employ J. L. Austin's notion of happiness to investigate what it might mean to say that doctrine is happy. I will pursue happiness, not because truth is inappropriate, but because truth alone is inadequate as a form of evaluation for doctrine. The notion that doctrine can be evaluated simply as true or false has been one of the contributors to the marginalization of doctrine in the modern age. Finally, I will briefly explore the consequences that adopting my theory will have for the church.

Notes

[1] Nancey Murphy, "Textual Relativism, Philosophy of Language, and the baptist Vision," in *Theology without Foundations*, ed. Stanley Hauerwas, Nancey Murphy, and Mark Nation (Nashville: Abingdon, 1994), 264.

[2] Gotthold Ephraim Lessing, *Lessing's Theological Writings*, A Library of Modern Religious Thought, ed. and trans. Henry Chadwick (Stanford, CA: Stanford University Press, 1956), 51–56. For secondary literature on Lessing see Chadwick's introductory essay in the above; Alister McGrath, *The Genesis of Doctrine: A Study in the Foundations of Doctrinal Criticism* (Oxford: Basil Blackwell, 1990), 140ff., and Alister McGrath, *The Making of Modern German Christology: 1750-1990*, 2nd ed. (Grand Rapids, MI: Zondervan, 1994), 28–33; Colin Brown, *Jesus in European Protestant Thought: 1778-1860* (Grand Rapids, MI: Baker, 1985), 16–29. Brown's treatment is the more substantial. The best analysis of this aspect of Lessing's thought is found in the work of Gordon E. Michalson, Jr., "Faith and History: The Shape of the Problem," *Modern Theology* 1 (July 1985): 277–90; see also Gordon E. Michalson, Jr., *Lessing's "Ugly Ditch": A Study of Theology and History* (University Park: Pennsylvania State University Press, 1985).

[3] Michalson calls these the "temporal," the "metaphysical," and the "existential" ditches. *Lessing's "Ugly Ditch,"* 8.

[4] Anthony Thiselton, *The Two Horizons: New Testament Hermeneutics and Philosophical Description* (Grand Rapids, MI: Eerdmans, 1980), 65.

[5] "For Lessing as for Leibniz, a proposition is necessarily true if its negation is self-contradictory; but if we can, without contradiction, think the negation or denial of a proposition, then it is not necessarily true but is true (if at all) only contingently. . . ." Michalson, *Lessing's "Ugly Ditch,"* 29. Ironically, this view of the nature of religion is itself an "accidental truth of history."

[6] Edward Craig, *The Mind of God and the Works of Man* (Oxford: Clarendon Press, 1987), 39.

[7] Michalson, *Lessing's "Ugly Ditch,"* 39.

[8] "Lessing represents a stage in this development of a new view of the religious self . . . because of his appeal to the inner truth of authentic religion. The metaphor itself signals the modern turn 'inward,' into the recesses of the self, in search of the true basis of religious appropriation. Again the governing principle here—as in the case of the metaphor of 'binding'—is human autonomy and the requirement that authentic religion do justice to the autonomous self. The chief consequence of this principle for the issue of historical revelation constitutes a clear paradigm shift in religious matters: the religious message scores its point because of something that was 'in me' all along and not because of something in an 'outer' message, associated with historical events, that is binding on me in heteronomous ways. The autonomous self gradually becomes the criterion for what can be considered truly revelatory." Michalson, *Lessing's "Ugly Ditch,"* 16.

[9] See Lessing's "Testament of John," *Theological Writings*, 57–61. On the universal availability of real religion, or, as Lessing says, "natural religion," see his "Education of the Human Race," ibid., 82–98, esp. 83. This position ignores the biblical context of the commands to love one another.

[10] John Milbank, *Theology and Social Theory: Beyond Secular Reason* (Oxford: Basil Blackwell, 1990), 53.

[11] "The reductive element in Durkheim's sociology of religion consists rather in the notion that all religion, when clear about itself, would turn out to be the Comtean-Kantian religion of humanity" (Milbank, *Theology and Social Theory*, 65).

[12] Alasdair MacIntyre, *Whose Justice? Which Rationality?* (Notre Dame, IN: Notre Dame University Press, 1988), 335.

[13] One picture of this is in Paul Holmer, *The Grammar of Faith* (San Francisco: Harper and Row, 1978), 41.

[14] John Howard Yoder, *The Politics of Jesus: Vicit Agnus Noster* (Grand Rapids, MI: Eerdmans, 1972), 106f. For the turn back to history see N. T. Wright, *Jesus and the Victory of God*, vol. 2, *Christian Origins and the Question of God* (Minneapolis: Fortress Press, 1996), esp. chs. 1–3.

For a theological reflection on the rejection of facts, see Julian Hartt, *A Christian Critique of Culture: An Essay in Practical Theology* (New York: Harper and Row, 1967), 281f.

[15] Langdon B. Gilkey, "Cosmology, Ontology, and the Travail of Biblical Language," in *God's Activity in the World: The Contemporary Problem*, ed. Owen C. Thomas (Chico, CA: Scholar's Press, 1983), 29–43. The biblical theologians Gilkey studies are Bernard Anderson and G. E. Wright.

[16] Gilkey, "Cosmology," 30.

[17] Ibid., 31.

[18] Ibid., 33.

[19] This is what Ricoeur's position amounts to, according to Anthony Thiselton, *New Horizons in Hermeneutics: The Theory and Practice of Transforming Biblical Reading* (Grand Rapids, MI: Zondervan, 1992), 370.

[20] See chapter one above, and Ronald F. Thiemann, *Revelation and Theology: The Gospel as Narrated Promise* (Notre Dame, IN: University of Notre Dame Press, 1985), 83f.

[21] Alasdair MacIntyre, *After Virtue*, 2nd edition (Notre Dame, IN: University of Notre Dame Press, 1984), 219ff.; Alasdair MacIntyre, *Three Rival Versions of Moral Enquiry: Encyclopaedia, Genealogy, and Tradition*. 1988 Gifford Lectures (Notre Dame, IN: Notre Dame University Press, 1990), 197.

[22] Charles Taylor, *Sources of the Self: The Making of the Modern Identity* (Cambridge, MA: Harvard University Press, 1989), 46f.

[23] Miroslav Volf, "Theology, Meaning and Power" in *The Nature of Confession: Evangelicals and Postliberals in Conversation*, ed. Timothy R. Phillips and Dennis L. Okholm (Downers Grove, IL: InterVarsity Press, 1996), 56.

[24] Hans Frei, *Eclipse of Biblical Narrative: A Study in Eighteenth and Nineteenth Century Hermeneutics*, (New Haven, CT: Yale University Press, 1974).

[25] Ibid., 1.

[26] Ibid., 2–3.

[27] Ibid., 5f., 130.

[28] For a discussion of Schleiermacher's hermeneutics see Frei, *Eclipse*, 290ff.; Thiselton, *New Horizons*, 204–36.

[29] My guess is that neither quite fits Schleiermacher's view, but rather, given his substantive theological position, the historical distance is minimized.

[30] Schweitzer. See Wright, *Jesus and the Victory of God*, 3ff.

[31] Rudolph Bultmann, "New Testament and Mythology," in *Kerygma and Myth:*

The Historical Questions Relating to Doctrine   177

A Theological Debate, ed. Hans Werner Bartsch, rev. ed., Reginald H. Fuller (New York: Harper and Row, 1961), 5.

³²Wright, *Jesus and the Victory of God*, 208.

³³George B. Caird, *The Language and Imagery of the Bible* (Grand Rapids, MI: Eerdmans, 1980), ch. 14. Wright's main discussion of apocalyptic is in *The New Testament and the People of God*, vol. 1, *Christian Origins and the Question of God* (Minneapolis: Fortress Press, 1992), ch. 10.

³⁴Wright, *New Testament and the People of God*, 285.

³⁵Ibid., 286. Considering the various modern approaches, he suggests that their error lies in reading the texts "within a tacitly Deist framework, in which one either believes (a) in an absent god and a closed space-time continuum or (b) in a normally absent God who occasionally intervenes and acts in discontinuity with that space-time continuum." Either sort of view was alien to first-century Jews. Ibid., 298.

³⁶Wright uses the term "exile," suggesting that because of repeated domination by foreign powers, Jews were not liable to have considered the exile to have truly ended. Cf. *Jesus and the Victory of God*, 126ff., 202ff.; *New Testament and the People of God*, 268–71.

³⁷Wright, *New Testament and the People of God*, 332, 399–400; *Jesus and the Victory of God*, 109ff., 127ff.

³⁸For an alternative account of the modern demise of eschatology see Colin E. Gunton, *The One, The Three, and the Many: God, Creation and the Culture of Modernity*, The 1992 Bampton Lectures (Cambridge: Cambridge University Press, 1993), 90–94.

³⁹See MacIntyre, *After Virtue*, 54f., for a discussion of what the loss of teleology meant for morality.

⁴⁰ David J. Bosch, *Transforming Mission: Paradigm Shifts in Theology of Mission*, American Society of Missiology No. 16 (Maryknoll, NY: Orbis, 1997), 196.

⁴¹William J. Abraham, *Divine Revelation and the Limits of Historical Criticism* (Oxford: Oxford University Press, 1982), 111; also 132f. The difference between my position and Abraham's is that my focus is more on eschatology while his is on teleology.

⁴²For a discussion of Wesley's appropriation of early Christianity and his tolerance of Constantinianism in ecclesiology see Luke L. Keefer, "John Wesley: Disciple of Early Christianity," *Wesleyan Theological Journal* 19 (Spring 1984): 23–32.

⁴³James W. McClendon, Jr., *Ethics: Systematic Theology, Volume I* (Nashville: Abingdon, 1986), 27f.

⁴⁴Ibid., 31.

⁴⁵Ibid., 338f.

⁴⁶McClendon says of this identity, "The baptist 'is' in 'this is that' is therefore neither developmental nor successionist, but mystical and immediate." *Ethics*, 33. In an early article Lindbeck argues against such a position in favor of the realistic view of Catholicism. Cf. "A Protestant View of the Ecclesiological Status of the Roman Catholic Church," *Journal of Ecumenical Studies*, 1 (Winter 1964): 249.

⁴⁷McClendon, *Ethics*, 34.

⁴⁸George Lindbeck, *The Nature of Doctrine: Religion and Theology in a Postliberal Age* (Philadelphia: Westminster Press, 1984) , 82. What the baptist vision brings out is that unless we see a parallel between where we stand now—

in the midst of our "stories"—and the scriptural stories, they remain distant from us.

⁴⁹Jürgen Moltmann, *The Church in the Power of the Spirit: A Contribution to Messianic Eschatology*, trans. Margaret Kohl (San Francisco: Harper, 1977), 52. Another current German theologian closely associated with a re-emphasis on eschatology is Wolfhart Pannenberg. Though echoes of the baptist vision are less explicit in his work, some can be found. See his *Theology and the Philosophy of Science*, trans. Francis McDonagh (Philadelphia: Westminster Press, 1976), 338. Moltmann and Pannenberg arrive at this position from a different starting point than McClendon (I have seen some wrongly claim McClendon's work is based on Moltmann's), at least partly through the influence of the Hegelian tradition.

⁵⁰Volf's analysis is in "Theology," in *The Nature of Confession* 45–66.

⁵¹John Webster, "Locality and Catholicity: Reflections on Theology and the Church," *Scottish Journal of Theology* 45:1 (1992): 10.

⁵²Milbank, *Theology and Social Theory*, 249.

⁵³Thiemann, *Revelation and Theology*, 84f. Later in the book (p.143ff.) he demonstrates how the Gospel of Matthew can be read in such a way. His description of the Reformers suggests that they were, perhaps, more committed to individualism than McClendon's baptists. Considering their nonrejection of Constantinianism, such a position would not be surprising.

⁵⁴Two other echoes can be found in Thiselton, *New Horizons*, 598; and in Hartt, *Christian Critique*, 282.

⁵⁵Russell Richey, "History in the Discipline," in *Doctrine and Theology in the United Methodist Church*, ed. Thomas Langford (Nashville: Kingswood Books, 1991), 193. (Henceforth, "History.")

⁵⁶Ibid., 191. Emphasis added. He continues, "History said the first word about Methodism. . . . History declared Methodist meaning and purpose. History functioned appropriately to introduce Methodism's constituting documents. History provided the definition of Methodism" (Ibid., 192).

⁵⁷See Ted A. Campbell, *John Wesley and Christian Antiquity: Religious Vision and Cultural Change* (Nashville: Kingswood, 1991).

⁵⁸Richey, "History," 193.

⁵⁹John Wesley, "A Letter to the Right Reverend Lord Bishop of Gloucester," in *The Appeals to Men of Reason and Religion and Certain Related Open Letters*, vol. 11, *The Works of John Wesley*, ed. Gerald R. Cragg (Nashville: Abingdon, 1989), 459–538.

⁶⁰He says, "In the 1988 Discipline's 'Historical Statement,' (7–15) Methodism's propositions survive . . . only as historical axioms. Methodists continue to turn to their history for self-understanding. They find a narrative from which providence has departed" (Richey, "History as a Bearer of Denominational Identity: Methodism as a Case Study," in *Perspectives on American Methodism: Interpretive Essays*, ed. Russell E. Richey, Kenneth E. Rowe, and Jean Miller Schmidt [Nashville: Kingswood, 1993], 497). (Henceforth, "Identity.")

⁶¹Richey, "History," 196.

⁶²Richey, "Identity," 481. See also Richey, "History," 200, where he points out the strong Americanism side by side with the strong Wesleyanism in recent Disciplines.

⁶³James W. Holsinger, Jr., and Evelyn Laycock, *Awaken the Giant: 28 Prescrip-*

tions for Reviving the United Methodist Church (Nashville: Abingdon, 1989), 37. Emphasis added.

[64]Stanley Hauerwas and William Willimon, *Resident Aliens: Life in the Christian Colony,* (Nashville: Abingdon, 1989), 52.

[65]Hauerwas is a friend and reader of the work of James McClendon and both have been substantially influenced by John Howard Yoder.

[66]For a similar account though in different terms, see Gunton, *The One, The Three, and the Many,* 89.

[67]Hartt, *A Christian Critique,* 278.

[68]Thiselton, *Two Horizons,* 57. The quote is from J. D. Smart, *The Interpretation of Scripture* (London: SCM Press, 1961), 37.

[69]Albert C. Knudson, *The Doctrine of Redemption* (New York: Abingdon-Cokesbury, 1933), 383.

[70]Hans-Georg Gadamer, *Truth and Method,* 2nd, rev. ed., trans. Joel Weinsheimer and Donald G. Marshall (New York: Crossroad, 1989), 336.

[71]Milbank, *Theology and Social Theory,* 121.

[72]MacIntyre, *Three Rival Versions,* 160. Comparing all three he notes, "The Encyclopaedist's narrative reduces the past to a mere prologue to the rational present, while the Genealogist struggles in the construction of his or her narrative against the past, including that of the past which is perceived as hidden within the alleged rationality of the present. The Thomist's narrative, by contrast with both of these, treats the past as neither mere prologue nor as something to be struggled against, but as that from which we have to learn if we are to identify and move towards our telos more adequately" (Ibid., 79).

[73]Alasdair MacIntyre, "Philosophy, the 'Other' Disciplines, and their Histories: A Rejoinder to Richard Rorty," *Soundings* 65 (Summer 1982): 135.

[74]Alasdair MacIntyre, "A Partial Response to My Critics," in *After MacIntyre: Critical Perspectives on the Work of Alasdair MacIntyre,* ed. John Horton and Susan Mendus (Notre Dame, IN: University of Notre Dame Press, 1994), 295. His *Three Rival Versions* is an application of the theory of traditioned rationality to a tradition that recognizes itself as a tradition and to two that strenuously deny such status.

[75]MacIntyre, *Whose Justice?* 12.

[76]On conflict—and Christian unity in spite of conflict—see Stephen Sykes, *The Identity of Christianity: Theologians and the Essence of Christianity from Schleiermacher to Barth,* (Philadelphia: Fortress Press, 1984), 21; McGrath, *The Genesis of Doctrine,* 3. This internal conflict, not merely a product of later development, is present even in the New Testament. James D. G. Dunn, *Unity and Diversity in the New Testament: An Inquiry into the Character of Earliest Christianity,* 2nd ed. (London: SCM Press, 1990), esp. ch. 15.

[77]MacIntyre, *Whose Justice?* 361.

[78]He says that it is "only in the context of a coherent tradition, which supplies a shared conceptual framework, a shared conception of what constitutes a central problem, and a shared view of how data are to be identified that competing theories" can be evaluated.

[79]MacIntyre, *Three Rival Versions,* 201.

[80]Gadamer, *Truth and Method,* 270, 333ff.

[81]Ibid., 290. Emphasis in the original.

[82]Ibid., 299f. Gadamer, *Truth and Method,* 300. For another discussion of

Gadamer's use of *Wirkungsgeschichte* see Thiselton, *New Horizons*, 320–25.

83. McClendon, *Ethics*, 338. He is building on Frei's work here. For recent work on the genre of the Gospels that seeks to class them with Graeco-Roman biography, see Richard A. Burridge, *What are the Gospels? A Comparison with Graeco-Roman Biography* (Cambridge: Cambridge University Press, 1992).

84. McClendon, *Ethics*, 340.

85. Ibid., 332. See also Abraham, *Divine Revelation*, 72f. Leroy T. Howe emphasizes this continuity as well: "Unless the church is to theologize as if the Enlightenment had never dawned at all, she must now affirm that the God who always has been loyal to his chosen people is recognized in history because he makes himself known in *present* power" ("United Methodism in Search of Theology," in *Doctrine and Theology in the United Methodist Church*, ed. Thomas Langford [Nashville: Kingswood Books, 1991], 62).

86. Hartt, *A Christian Critique*, 129. He says later, "The Gospel itself is the criterion of plausibility to which every philosophical prepossession in the church must yield. Jesus Christ contains the definition of historical plausibility; and therefore the church is guilty of a very great error in elevating a common sense or scientific or metaphysical outlook above that definition" (Ibid., 281). This is very far from the modern Cartesian perspective.

87. Ibid., 287. See also William Placher, *Unapologetic Theology: A Christian Voice in a Pluralistic Conversation* (Louisville, KY: Westminster/John Knox Press, 1989), 130, 132, 165; Gadamer, *Truth and Method*, 308f.

88. MacIntyre discusses this from the standpoint of traditions. Cf. *Three Rival Versions*, 151.

89. Hartt, *Christian Critique*, 285.

90. McClendon, *Ethics*, 247.

91. Albert C. Outler, *The Christian Tradition and the Unity We Seek* (New York: Oxford University Press, 1957), 46.

92. Richard Rorty, *Philosophy and the Mirror of Nature* (Princeton, NJ: Princeton University Press, 1979).

93. This is not to deny that the suspicion generated by such modes of thought have been useful to theology. The suspicion that has been harmful is that which claims neutrality and objectivity for itself, that which sees itself as the good hearted friend of the blind. Francis Watson observes: "historical scholarship believes itself to be justified not only in its own right but as a means of exposing and resisting churchly obscurantism in its manifold forms. The results of this scholarship tend to reflect this understanding of its social location. Its chief aim is to establish that Jesus (the historical Jesus, that is, the real Jesus) differed significantly from the images of him set up by the early church and perpetuated ever since; and the relationship between Jesus and the early church is thus the result of a projection or retrojection of the relationship between the scholarly and ecclesial communities back into the past. As Jesus may be distinguished from the early church, so the scholarly community which aims to rediscover and revive him distinguishes itself from the ecclesial community in which he is entombed. The quest of the historical Jesus is, in important respects, the quest of a non- or anti-ecclesial Jesus who will serve the interests of a community which wishes to assert its distinctiveness over against the ecclesial one. Insofar as the products of this mode of scholarship are endorsed by more

'liberal' or 'radical' members of the ecclesial community, the sociological function of such an endorsement is to locate oneself on the frontier at which the church meets the modern, secularized world, thereby setting oneself at a distance from the main body of the ecclesial institution" (*Text, Church, and World: Biblical Interpretation in Theological Perspective* [Grand Rapids, MI: Eerdmans, 1994], 228).

[94] Placher, *Unapologetic Theology*, 134.

[95] Thiemann, *Revelation*, 84.

[96] See Miroslav Volf's discussion of the need to encounter God and not merely 'God' in the midst of a semiotic system; "Theology," in *The Nature of Confession*, 54f.

[97] Jean-François Lyotard, *The Postmodern Condition: A Report on Knowledge*, vol. 10, *Theory and History of Literature*, trans. Geoff Bennington and Brian Massumi (Minneapolis: University of Minnesota Press, 1984), 27ff.

[98] Ibid., 34.

[99] A consideration of Lyotard's examples of such metanarratives shows this to be the case: "dialectics of Spirit, the hermeneutics of meaning, the emancipation of the rational or working subject, or the creation of wealth" (Ibid., xxiii). Writing before the discourse about metanarratives began, Julian Hartt makes essentially the same point about the Christian narrative being a totalizing discourse without reducing persons to abstractions, but including them in their full historical contingency. Cf. *Christian Critique*, 327.

[100] Philip D. Kenneson describes modernity as a time in which "we are encouraged to believe that Christian discourse and practice are best understood and explained by recourse to other more fundamental discourses and practices, such as those of the social sciences" ("The Alleged Incorrigibility of Postliberal Theology: Or, What Babe Ruth and George Lindbeck Have in Common," in *The Nature of Confession: Evangelicals and Postliberals in Conversation*, ed. Timothy R. Phillips and Dennis L. Okholm [Downers Grove, IL: InterVarsity Press, 1996], 102f).

[101] Milbank, *Theology and Social Theory*, 387. Milbank critiques MacIntyre for trying to establish a new form of argumentation to overcome modernity. He insists that instead of seeking to out argue modernity, we must seek to "out narrate" the world. Ibid., 330.

[102] Ibid., 388.

[103] L. Gregory Jones, "Alasdair MacIntyre on Narrative, Community and the Moral Life," *Modern Theology* 4:1 (1987): 67.

Chapter Five

Putting It All Together

OVERVIEW

WE ARE NOW IN A PLACE TO UNDERSTAND SEVERAL OF THE REASONS WHY doctrine has been marginalized in the modern church and to suggest some ways this marginalization might be overcome. In chapter one I discussed the forms this marginalization takes as well as some specifically modern factors in its development. In the course of this investigation, I turned to my own tradition, the United Methodist, and showed some ways this tradition has been influenced by modernity which have, I believe, contributed to the marginalization of doctrine seen within its bounds. I found George Lindbeck's analysis of the nature of religion and doctrine to be helpful, though not thoroughgoing enough in its overcoming of modernity. His study called for the rejection of cognitivist and experiential expressivist conceptualizations of religion in favor of a cultural linguistic approach based on the philosophy of Ludwig Wittgenstein and the anthropology of Clifford Geertz. Accompanying this was a simultaneous rejection of the understanding cognitivism and experiential expressivism had of doctrine, in favor of a regulative theory. Upon evaluation, I found that though Lindbeck overcame the modern commitments to epistemology, procedural rationality, individualism, and rejection of tradition, his cultural linguistic model failed to deal adequately with the modern drive toward dehistoricization. To overcome this final dimension of modern thought, I proposed that Christianity can best be understood as an ongoing dramatic narrative, and that within this context doctrine is a speech act of the church.

In chapter two I began developing my claim that doctrine is the speech act of the church that directs it in its living of the Christian narrative. Building on the work of J. L. Austin, Ludwig Wittgenstein, and Charles Taylor in the philosophy of language, I proposed that such a model of doctrine could resolve the problems of referentiality and performance that are associated with modernity and with incomplete readings of Austin and Wittgenstein. Such a model also provides a way to overcome the centrality of epistemology in modern views of religion. I found in Lindbeck's development of a regulative theory of doctrine an incomplete account of Austin's position that failed to go beyond his identification of the performative as well as a misreading of Wittgenstein's theory of language games that led him to imply that language games are autonomous. The work of both Austin and Wittgenstein allow for strong claims for the referentiality of language while insisting even more strongly that reference is not the primary function of language. With this in view, I claimed that Austin's concept of "happiness" would be the best way to evaluate doctrine. Taylor's work was especially helpful for my claim that doctrine is a corporate speech act. One factor I identified in this corporateness is the necessity for *reception* for doctrine to be doctrine. This formal hearing and receiving of doctrinal formulations has been a feature of the Christian tradition practically since the beginning. In my theory it finds a formal place as the doctrinal equivalent of Austin's concept of "uptake."[1]

Chapter three turned to the consideration of the nature of the speaker of the speech act called doctrine, the church. I suggested that though the place of the church—and doctrines of the church—has been especially marginalized in the modern era, this is not solely due to modern factors, but dates back to the early church and the institutionalization of Constantinianism. The main contribution of modernity has been its thoroughgoing commitment to individualism. Given that commitment, the main understanding of the church available was that it was a voluntary association of like-minded people, and later, like-acting (or like-experiencing) people. From this perspective, the only alternative was an authoritarian church structure, an option not even worth considering for autonomous moral agents. The reductive atomism of modernity functioned to sever the traditional connection between church and salvation. In contrast to this view, I claimed that the bible shows the church to be an integral part of what salvation is about: that in both the Old and New Testaments inclusion in the people of God (Israel, then the Church) is one of God's main objectives in saving people. Salvation, on such a view, includes as a major component, initiation into the ongoing drama of what God is doing, a drama the church lives out together.

Taking up the analysis of Constantinianism, I suggested that this phenomenon is best understood as a view that sees little or no differentiation between the church and its host culture. Such a view, more empirically defensible at some times than others, is no longer an option in the face of our current pluralistic situation (in other words, cultural pluralism is a modern *blessing* to the church). I discussed the various dimensions of the church's relationship to culture in terms of its unity, distinctiveness, and missional nature. When any of these convictions is taken to an extreme the mission of the church is as handicapped as when any are ignored. Closing the chapter with a discussion of apostolicity, I claimed that the church is apostolic to the extent that it takes up the mission of Jesus and his apostles. This mission must take account of both cultural differences and the immersion of the church in history.

History was the central topic in chapter four, though I expanded the discussion to treat related areas such as narrative and eschatology. I identified G. E. Lessing as a paradigmatic example of the modern attitude toward the place of history in religion. Lessing not only saw temporal distance as a problem for a religion based on historical claims—as traditional (orthodox) Christianity was at the time—but also found two other impediments to the orthodox view. The first was a pure form of propositionalism (based on Leibniz and Spinoza) that claimed the essence of religion lay in the rational truths it proclaimed. Not only was there an uncrossable gap between the past and the present, making it so difficult to determine what had actually happened, but there was an even bigger gap between the "necessary truths of reason" and the "accidental truths of history." A final gap arose from Lessing's commitment to the modern view of autonomous individualism. This gap is the gap between the ancient events and where I stand today. How is it possible that events that happened over a thousand years ago can possibly impinge on me today? Moderns simply could not accept such a thing. Even those who wanted to retain the biblical language of a God active in history were unable to cross these ditches.

The so-called metaphysical ditch is the product of the combination of a propositionalist view of doctrine and foundationalist epistemology.

My proposal that doctrine functions to direct us in a Christianity conceived not as a system of rational truths but as a continuing dramatic narrative avoids this ditch. The existential ditch is overcome through participation in the eschatologically constituted people of God. Contrary to Enlightenment thinking, Christians simply are not autonomous individuals. The Christian gains his or her identity through participation in the ongoing Christian story. The logic of Christian eschatology claims that this identity is based on scripturally narrated events in which God was acting. The temporal ditch between the current believer and these ancient events is bridged by the continuing presence of God in the drama and in worship, and by the gifts of the Spirit within the church.

The final step, to be taken in this chapter, will be to tie these elements together. The first way I will bring them together is in a consideration of how the marginalization of doctrine has happened and how it can be overcome in terms of the three dimensions I investigated in chapter one: substance, conceptualization, and performance. Secondly, and itself simultaneously an instance of this reconceptualization and a framework for doctrinal performance, will come an analysis of doctrine as a speech act. In chapter two I claimed that it is better to ask whether doctrine is happy rather than whether it is true. My objective here is neither to find a subjectivist account of doctrine (as "happy" may lead some to believe), nor to insulate doctrine from a relation to the world and consequent claims to truth. Rather, happiness is Austin's term for evaluating speech acts. Though this will be overly simple, I will show what it takes for doctrine to be happy in such a scheme. My discussion will be overly simple in that I will not attend to the ways various forms of doctrine differ in their structure and possibilities for happiness. Neither will I develop an account of the effects of the textual form the bulk of doctrine comes in and how this form affects its function as a *speech* act. Understanding doctrine as a speech act of the church has important implications for denominational differences and ecumenism. Finally, I will briefly discuss the consequences my model will have for theology and the church.

UNDERSTANDING AND OVERCOMING DOCTRINAL MARGINALIZATION

In chapter one I identified three dimensions in which doctrine can be said to be marginalized. The first dimension, substance, is that which propositionalists see most easily. The marginalization of doctrinal substance is what conservatives see in the liberal approach to doctrine. Doctrinal substance is marginalized when particular doctrines that are considered essential to the faith or the healthy life of the church are no longer taught. The second dimension, conceptualization, is most easily seen by experiential expressivists. When attacked for ignoring doctrine, liberals accuse conservatives of misunderstanding the nature of doctrine. In their reaction against propositionalism their strength is in claiming what doctrine is *not*. Performance, the third dimension, is highlighted by both Lindbeck's cultural linguistic approach and my own. The consideration of this third dimension flows out of the work of reconceptualization described in the previous chapters. The modern church has suffered the most from the lack of performance of doctrine. Why has the church had a problem with performance? Performance has failed because modernity allowed only certain conceptions of doctrine (propositionalism and experiential expressivism) that did not allow for a performative dimension. Without a reconceptualization of the nature of doctrine, any mere recovery of doctrinal substance will be ineffective, and apart from the church's performance of this doctrine, reconceptualization will be a mere academic exercise.

Doctrinal Substance

A cognitivist view finds religion to be constituted by having a certain set of beliefs. Marginalization of doctrine according to this way of thinking amounts to the church no longer retaining some of these essential doctrines. Considering the United Methodist Church, such a claim on the surface seems untenable. Since 1808 the church (through its predecessor denominations) has had a constitutional rule that General Conference (the legislative body of the church) "shall not revoke, alter, or change our Articles of Religion or establish any new standards or rules of doctrine contrary to our present existing and established standards of doctrine."[2] Because of this, the official doctrine of the United Methodist Church has continued unchanged for almost two centuries. Some have claimed that the 1972 Theological Statement, with its enshrinement of the Wesleyan Quadrilateral, did add new doctrine to the church. The Judicial Council of the United Methodist Church considered this charge when the statement was first approved by General Conference. In the Council's judgment the statement did not constitute new doctrine. The primary factor they considered in reaching this decision was General Conference's understanding that the statement did not constitute new doctrine.[3] When ordained, pastors are required to affirm their acceptance of United Methodist doctrine, so these doctrines (and their importance) are implicitly affirmed every year at Annual Conference. A cognitivist then, might judge that doctrine has not been marginalized in the United Methodist Church since the official doctrinal substance is the same now as it always has been.

To make the case, then, that doctrine has been marginalized in the United Methodist church, another account of the nature of religion and the role of doctrine must be developed. That such a case is worth pursuing seems indicated by the features of Methodist life—both theological and practical—mentioned in chapter one. Methodism once was characterized by vigorous defense of what were perceived to be its doctrinal distinctives. Of course the curious thing about this is that one of the most central doctrinal distinctives of early Methodism was the centrality of holiness and Christian Perfection, doctrines not included in the Articles of Religion. This seems to be evidence for a broader construal of the First Restrictive Rule where it says that "our present existing and established standards of doctrine" shall not be altered. Wesley's Sermons and *Explanatory Notes on the New Testament*, traditionally included (though not without contest) as doctrinal standards, do contain these distinctive Methodist doctrines.[4] Notwithstanding official statements, United Methodism is frequently characterized, at least on the popular level, as a church one can be a member of and believe whatever one wants.

There are two dynamics at work here, neither of which a strictly cognitivist view of doctrine can account for. First, though the doctrines are still "believed," they have been reinterpreted. Cognitivism can recognize this reinterpretation as such, but has difficulty describing what is going on. It becomes all too easy to accuse those who reinterpret doctrine of "not really believing" what they say they believe. The best account cognitivist propositionalism can provide is a differentiation of form and content, suggesting that the reinterpreters have kept the form of the doctrine while (illegitimately) bringing in foreign content. Usually maintaining a more epistemologically based theory of language, they lack some of the resources Lindbeck's similar differentiation makes possible. Though both make a distinction between form and content, they do not mean the same things by these terms. Lindbeck's distinction between form and content is made to facilitate doctrinal change in the midst of continuing faithfulness. The form of the doctrine changes, but the substance does not. The problem I am describing is the reverse of this: the doctrinal form remains the same while the content (or so it seems) changes.

A better account of the marginalization of doctrinal *substance* would take advantage of the postmodern awareness of the social dimension of doctrine. This is the second dynamic, and for a cognitivist to recognize it he or she must modify the cognitivist view toward a more social epistemology. Lindbeck's cultural linguistic model of religion, however, has the best account of this dimension. Doctrinal substance has been marginalized not simply because it has been reinterpreted, but because it has ceased to be operative in the formation of the ecclesial community. Particular doctrines, though officially among the beliefs of United Methodism, no longer function to shape the community.

This adaptation in the direction of sociality also helps us understand the phenomenon of reinterpretation. Given the modern view of universal rationality, reinterpretation seems only explainable as a case of individual (or group) willfulness. When the reality of community is figured in, the significance of this community in shaping how we understand things (including our beliefs) becomes evident. At least since the early twentieth century, Methodist theology has evidenced a commitment to be modern and to speak to modern people. This is not merely the case of Methodists being attracted to modernity or feeling the need to proclaim the Gospel to moderns, as important as these motivations are. Rather, the more important dimension is that Methodists themselves have been uncritically enculturated into modernity. Modern positions on issues, including those affecting doctrinal issues, seem not only obvious, but Christian. This is the weakness introduced into the system by Methodism's failure to reject Constantinianism. When modernity believes one thing, and Christian doctrine teaches another, something must give, or a dichotomy must be maintained between religious beliefs and "secular" beliefs. Since our primary enculturation has been enculturation into modernity, it is most commonly doctrine that gives, and this in one of two ways. The first is the way we have already mentioned: reinterpretation. Traditional doctrines are reinterpreted so that they can be affirmed along with specifically modern affirmations: whatever the traditional doctrine *appears* to be saying, it is really saying something a modern could affirm (and come to believe on purely universal grounds). This is the way taken by Knudson and Bultmann.[5] If the reinterpretation of doctrine in the first generation leads to a separation from the Christian narrative, it is likely that in the succeeding generations the Christian community will no longer find those reinterpreted doctrines operational. An example of this is the rationalistic reinterpretation of the doctrine of the Trinity, which has led to Unitarianism. The second way is to leave the church, either for another that contains doctrine acceptable to modernity or for no church at all.

So far my account seems especially hard on moderns and overly complacent about the role of enculturation of nonmoderns. In chapter three I claimed that one reason doctrine has been marginalized is because the church has failed in its work of enculturating believers into the ecclesial community. I will discuss this in greater detail below. Let it suffice now to observe that a cognitive propositionalist view of doctrine made it too easy to see enculturation as a process of transferring information (beliefs) from one mind (the mature believer) to another (the new convert), making the reinterpretation option almost inevitable.

We also cannot assume that doctrinal reinterpretation is always equivalent to the marginalization of doctrinal substance. Inasmuch as language and the communities in which we seek to practice and communicate doctrine change, our conceptualization of doctrine and the language we use to express it must change as well. What the church needs is an account of doctrine that will allow for change of this kind without compromising the essentials of the faith. This book is but the first part of such an account.

Modernity has brought about a reduction in substantive doctrine in another way: through its ethics of belief. Modern individualism and epistemology work together to give us a model that claims that authority has no place in the formation of a person's beliefs. A person begins as a blank slate (as far as beliefs go) and whatever beliefs seem rational and supported by evidence are to be accepted; those that do not are to be rejected. The idea that doctrine could be communally authoritative is rejected as infringing on personal autonomy.

The will, according to this picture, has nothing to do with faith. Either one believes or one does not. Of course an opposite conclusion from the premise of the dichotomy of will and knowledge has also been drawn in modern theology. Existentialist theology sees belief as having nothing (or at best very little) to do with real Christianity, while a choice of the will makes all the difference. Both of these depend on something like Kant's distinction between the phenomenal and the noumenal worlds: the difference comes in where they locate that which is religiously significant.

In the modern period certain classes of doctrine have been the hardest hit. Those that refer to historical events, particularly purported events that appear miraculous to moderns, have been the first to go. It has been easier to speak of the "rise of Easter faith" than of "the resurrection of Jesus." Anyone can find evidence in the texts that the early church believed in Jesus' resurrection. Modernity does not challenge the observation that the early community believed in the resurrection—simply that such belief is now a live option for modern people. Along with this reticence to speak of the resurrection have come major shifts in Christology, with the humanity of Christ usually in the forefront. A separation is made between the Jesus of history and the Christ of faith, effectively severing the historical continuity of Christianity, while seeking to maintain its ideological continuity.

The Conceptualization of Doctrine and Religion

In my discussion of the substantive marginalization of doctrine above, I have already touched on the role of the conceptualization of doctrine. Seeing doctrine as an adjunct of epistemology has not been a helpful move for the church's appropriation and use of doctrine. The experiential expressivist strategy that sees religion as flowing from experience and doctrine as a symbolization of that experience has not been able to escape the shadow of epistemology either.

Experiential expressivism claims that religion is based on experience and that doctrine symbolizes that experience. Lindbeck argues to the contrary, that experience flows from religion and is shaped by doctrine.[6] This can be seen as a social form of Kantianism: instead of religion being an expression of the individual, it is an expression of society or culture. Though Lindbeck can be read this way, I do not think such a reading is true to his objectives. To avoid this possible lack of clarity, we must acknowledge that there is a dialectical relationship between experience and Christianity (and doctrine). It is necessary, in this process, to deprivatize experience. Experience is not something that takes place inside of me; rather, it finds its ultimate intelligibility in social and historical relations and events. The church, therefore, is simultaneously shaping and being shaped by doctrine.

My model of Christianity, which likens it to a dramatic narrative, overcomes the defects of the modern views. Most importantly, it emphasizes the particularity of Christianity, in both its historical and communal dimensions. Christianity can then be treated on its own terms and not simply subsumed under the category "religion." Given this model it is also possible to make sense of the traditional understanding of doctrine as *action* and not simply information. Finally, my model allows for the centrality of eschatology and a nonreductive account of the Kingdom of God.

Doctrinal Performance

The performance of doctrine in modernity has been crippled by cognitivist and expressivist views of doctrine that cannot conceive of the performative role of doctrine. Even in churches that have preserved their entire doctrinal heritage, doctrine has been marginalized because their ecclesiology has become functionally individualist and their eschatology solely realized or futurist.

The performance of doctrine, as Lindbeck rightly claims, is more than the building of a religious noetic system, and more than the symbolization of inner experience. I go beyond Lindbeck to claim that it is also more than the regulation of Christian discourse. Doctrine identifies the characters of the drama: Jesus, God, sinners, saints, church, world, principalities and powers, etc. Doctrine identifies the stage and setting of the drama. Doctrine lays out the plot line—what has happened, what is happening, and where the plot is going. Finally, the performance of doctrine enables the church to see where it stands in the drama and to know what actions come next.

Seen this way, doctrine is essentially an articulated understanding of our life in the Christian narrative. There is always infinitely more to articulate—and such articulation is a means to the end of living the drama, not an end in itself.[7] As time passes some articulations will no longer be needed and will be dropped due to nonuse. The church needs to keep in mind two questions as these changes take place. First, Are these doctrines becoming unintelligible because of our progress (temporally speaking) in the story, or because we have found our center outside the ecclesial community? This is a hard question to deal with insofar as it requires the church to be humble and self-critical. Second, How close to the center of the narrative—how essential to the logic (or grammar) of the story—are these doctrines? Those that are closer to the center will not be easily given up.

In her work *Theology in the Age of Scientific Reasoning*,[8] Nancey Murphy discusses the methodology of Imre Lakatos and concludes that it is the best for understanding what science is about and therefore the best for helping understand theology. According to Lakatos, science is made up of a series of successive (and competing) research programs. These research programs have a hard core that represents the central idea or concept of the program. Sometimes this hard core can only be stated in vague terms. The negative heuristic is the plan that defends the hard core, seeking to turn away all attempts at falsification. This could be looked at as the defense. The offensive part of the research program is the positive heuristic. The positive heuristic seeks to build up a "protective belt" of auxiliary hypotheses that surround (speaking in spatial terms) the hard core, protecting, explaining and extending it. The positive heuristic also seeks to attack the auxiliary hypotheses of research programs that it finds in conflict with itself. Research programs can be fractally related to each other: the hard core of one may function as an auxiliary hypothesis of another. Some doctrines, on my account, function as a Lakatosian hard core, while others relate to these as auxiliary hypotheses.

God's plan is that the church be a peculiar people representing God to the nations. The "point" of the drama is to glorify God by obeying Jesus' Great Commission—to make disciples of all nations (or, using other terminology, to bring other people into a place where they become willing actors and teammates in the drama). This requires the church to reach out constantly and encounter outsiders, seeking to draw them into the story. To do this requires continual doctrinal refinement as engagement with new cultures and communities raises new questions and causes us to articulate aspects of the narrative (and its characters, etc.) that we have not previously considered.

The Happiness of Doctrine

Simply framing doctrine as a speech act of the church is a reconceptualization of the role of doctrine. My model combines this with a reconceptualization of the nature of Christianity, seeing it not as a science (a system of true propositions), an aesthetic experience, or even a cultural linguistic system, but as a dramatic narrative whose first few acts are narrated in scripture and whose current act the church lives today. The first move breaks out of the straight jacket imposed by foundationalist epistemology while the second overcomes radical individualism and dehistoricization. These reconceptualizations will not simply overcome modernity and its commitments, but are also truer to the Christian tradition and to what we read in scripture.

One of the great breakthroughs of J. L. Austin's philosophy of language is his account of the various ways speech acts can go wrong. As long as language was conceived within the bounds of foundationalist epistemology the best evaluative terms one had were variations on "true," "false," or "meaningless." Expressive language could be "authentic" or "inauthentic," depending on whether it accurately expressed the inner experience of the autonomous self. As far as I know, Austin never explicitly confronted individualism, but his analysis of speech acts effectively removes us from the thought world that sees the self simply as a describer of "objective" reality, a reality from which that self is essentially detached.

My analysis is modeled on Austin's in *How to Do Things With Words*,[9] and on James W. McClendon and James Smith's use of Austin in their *Convictions*.[10] I will also consider John Searle's development of Austin's work in his *Speech Acts* as well as his differentiation of different kinds of speech act in *Expression and Meaning*.[11] The complexity of the case of doctrine goes beyond any of the samples I have seen, in that doctrine, like its anglicized concept, teaching, is a compound action composed of a multitude of speech acts. I intend to show, nonetheless, that this form of analysis is relevant. As the conditions of happy doctrine are laid out, some of the reasons for the lack of doctrinal happiness in the modern context will become apparent.

The first challenge my proposal faces is doctrine's level of complexity in comparison with simple speech acts. Most of the analysis in Austin and Searle, as well as McClendon and Smith, focuses on single sentences. Even when doctrine is considered solely in the form of its constitutive sentences, complexity remains. If doctrine were to be considered on this level alone, there would be no reason to think there is a single category *doctrine* made up of the various sentences claimed to be such.

Complex Speech Acts

We need to find a way to understand sets of sentences or a text, not merely a single sentence, as a speech act. It is not hard to see that any text is *about* something. There is (usually) some subject matter or content about which it speaks as well as some particular way it deals with this content. Given that a text composed of a network of utterances is more complex than a single utterance, is there a way in which speech act theory can still work for texts, or in particular, doctrinal texts? In other words, is it possible to speak not only of doctrine*s* as speech acts, but of *doctrine* itself as a speech act?

In textual interpretation the hermeneutical circle is used in two senses. The first is that the dialectical relationship between the part and the whole is a major factor in understanding the text. A sentence is understood in the context of the paragraph, the paragraph in light of the chapter, and the chapter in light of the whole—while at the same time the whole can itself only be understood through its constituent parts. The second way of expressing the hermeneutical circle is a more recent development that considers a similar dialectical relationship between the text and the reader, between the speaker and the hearer. The interpreter working within this second scheme aims for a "fusion of horizons"—the reader's and the text's.[12] What if we take the first usage of the hermeneutical circle (part to whole) and use it to consider the nature of the text as a speech act? Just as no individual utterance can be understood apart from its context and no context, no whole can be understood apart from its parts, so no individual speech act can be completely characterized in abstraction from the larger conversation of which it is a part.

In "The Logical Status of Fictional Discourse,"[13] Searle gives two examples of paragraphs that look like assertions, one taken from a newspaper story, the other from a work of fiction. The illocutions in both appear to be literal. So how can fiction be distinguished from nonfiction? Searle rejects the answer that writers of fiction are "not performing the illocutionary act of making an assertion but the illocutionary act of telling a story or writing a novel."[14] The problem with this position, according to Searle, is that it means that fiction contains a different kind of illocutionary act from nonfiction and leads to the absurd claim that "words do not have their normal meanings in works of fiction."[15] Searle's usually careful writing is a bit loose here. He fails to see the distinction between writing sentences in a novel and writing a novel. Searle ignores the possibility that there can be more than one level of illocutionary force, one that applies to the microcosm of the utterance at hand, the other to the macrocosm of the whole text. Surely there is a difference between speaking of the fictionalist engaging in a different illocutionary act (singular) than the nonfictionalist and speaking of a fictionalist using different types of illocutionary acts (plural). Searle's solution is to claim that what the fictionalist is doing is pretending to make assertions (or other illocutionary acts). This appears too reductive a strategy, reducing a work to a combination of pretended illocutions. Searle improves his position by going on to speak of the "illocutionary intentions" of the author, but it is unclear whether he is considering these intentions in relation to the work as a whole or to the illocutions that compose it.

It would be much clearer to speak of the entire work exhibiting illocutionary force (though to avoid confusion it may be helpful to find a word other than "illocutionary" to use when speaking on the textual level) while also containing illocutionary acts. On the "macro" level of the text, the question of direction of fit becomes more complex. As we see in fiction, there are multiple worlds that a text can appear to fit. In this case we can characterize nonfictional texts as seeking to fit the real world and fictional texts as creating and then fitting an imagined world. There is a limit both to the exactness of the fit in nonfictional texts (no text is an exact and perfect reproduction of the real world with no element of the creative) and the extent of pretense in the fictional work (we are familiar with green folk from Mars, populations who communicate through telepathy rather than speech; in some cases pretense equals creation: we cannot have a pretended color or shape).

Doctrine, then, would fit midway between nonfiction and fiction in terms of how each relates to the world. It is midway in the sense that doctrine aims both to depict accurately the features of the Christian narrative and at the same time to project the hearer (the church) imaginatively into the narrative that is not yet entirely "real," because although God's purposes for creation are stated in the narrative, the exact outworking of these purposes remains unclear. In this light, the analysis of doctrine as speech act that follows will necessarily be somewhat loose. The conditions for the happiness of a broad category like doctrine are analogous to, rather than simply the same as, the happiness of individual speech acts.

One other analogy that may be used to support my claim that both doctrines and doctrine can be interpreted as speech acts comes from the philosophy of science. I suggested above that some doctrines relate to other doctrines similarly to the way a Lakatosian hard core relates to auxiliary hypotheses in a scientific research program. When scientific theories are conceived this way it is possible to see one research program as itself part of a broader research program, thus serving as an auxiliary hypothesis in that larger context. We can speak of research programs on both levels. My suggestion is that the relation between speech acts and texts is similar, with *speech act* being the broader category. For example, church doctrine includes teaching about the person of Christ, while the teaching about the person of Christ itself contains a number of auxiliary doctrines.

Moving beyond the issue of complexity, how do we decide whether the speech act of doctrine is happy or not? McClendon and Smith identify a number of conditions any speech act must satisfy in order to be happy. These conditions, the details of which vary from one kind of speech act to another, include preconditions of the speech act, the primary conditions, the representative conditions (Searle's term is propositional), and the affective or psychological conditions. In what follows I suggest some conditions for the happiness of the doctrinal speech act.

Preconditions:
1. The church exists as the people of God, empowered and united by the Holy Spirit.
2. Doctrine is spoken from the context of the Christian community and requires that the hearer be situated in a particular relationship not only to this community but also to the Christian narrative.
3. The speaker and the hearer must share a common language, both literally and culturally so that the hearer can hear the doctrinal utterance with minimal distortion.
4. The church understands itself to be unified diachronically.

The most basic precondition for doctrine is the existence of the church which is the speaking agent of doctrine. McClendon and Smith illustrate the role of the preconditions by looking at football: "The *preconditions* are related to the speech act in somewhat the way in which, in football, the requirement that the players and the officials shall be on the field and functioning is related to making a move in the game (slanting off tackle [for example])."[16] The church is the arena in which doctrine's intelligibility is found. Just as "slanting off tackle" makes no sense apart from the institution of football, *doctrine* makes no sense apart from the institution of the church. Doctrine also presupposes that the church is more than a voluntary association, but is best understood as God's own people, united by the Spirit. Against propositionalism, doctrine's intelligibility is not found in the systematicity of its (true) statements against the background of other true statements. Against the experiential expressivist, the intelligibility of doctrine is not found in its being understood as the explication of some sort of experience common to all humanity.

In addition to the necessary social particularity of the church, there is the relation to a particular enacted narrative. While the kind of intelligibility associated with the former might be described as linguistic, the relation to the narrative may be termed logical. Apart from the ongoing history of God's work with humanity through the people called church, doctrine has no point. This is where approaches generated by the sociology of knowledge fall short. What we see in doctrine is not merely the noetic structure of the Christian community, the way this particular group of people sees reality—although a view of reality is certainly implied in doctrine—but more importantly the place this people has in universal history. In other words, doctrine is nonneutral in two ways: it originates from the context of a particular people and from the context of a particular strand of history.

Because of this double particularity happy doctrine requires a determinate positioning vis-à-vis both the community and the narrative, that is, both the synchronic and diachronic dimensions. The normal hearer of doctrine, paradoxically, is the church itself. I have suggested the usefulness of fractal imagery at several points, and this is yet another place it can be applied. "Church" exists on many levels. We can speak of congregations, denominations, the sum of all Christians within particular geographical boundaries, or the church universal. When the church speaks doctrine, the tendency is for this speech to be directed from the broader church to the more particular and local manifestation.

As the church lives the drama in relationship with God and the world, new questions (and then answers) arise. Through a testing process these questions and answers are received (heard) by the church as authoritatively relating details of the narrative: where the church now stands, who the actors are and how their relationships are to be understood, and what actions are appropriate at this stage of the play. Doctrine thus regulates the life of the church—its proclamation, evangelistic ministry, worship, education, social work, etc.—by contextualizing each within the narrative as a whole. Individuals hear doctrine through these particular uses of it. In contrast to both cognitivism and experiential expressivism, doctrine is the property of the church and not individuals.

In order for doctrine to even happen, the church must maintain its discipling of its members into a cohesive community that stands (at least to some degree) apart from the world. The sociology of knowledge is correct to the degree that enculturation is a prime factor in the process of understanding. When the church's primary enculturation is in terms of its host culture, whether that be modern American culture, modern Serbian culture, or ancient Roman culture, doctrine becomes hard to hear.

Almost since the beginning, the church has been multilingual. It is possible that Jesus himself was multilingual. Nazareth and Capernaum both had Gentile communities in close proximity and it is possible that he knew some Greek and Latin in addition to Aramaic and Hebrew. Though the church originated as a primarily Aramaic speaking community, by the end of the first century Greek had been established as the dominant language of the church.[17] Later Latin became the dominant language of the church in the West, maintaining this position for more than a millennium. The use of a common language enabled the church to share doctrine over a wide area. With the coming of the Reformation and the rise of the vernaculars, Latin remained the essential language for doctrinal work for a time, but gradually came to be replaced by the languages of the local churches. The church now lives as a multilingual community where no single language predominates. Because even churches that speak different languages are participants in the same drama, they have an obligation to seek mutual understanding, an act that will frequently require the willingness and ability to translate one church's speech into the language of another. Because of this, the requirement that a common language be used is not as important as in other types of speech act. The narrative itself is based on action and not words, it serves as an extralinguistic point of unity, bringing clarity to doctrinal utterance.

A final precondition of the speech act of doctrine is that the church see itself as a diachronic unity. Though I believe the best way to conceive of this unity (as I explained in chapter four) is in terms of eschatology and something like McClendon's baptist vision, the church must have some way of seeing itself as the same institution as that founded by Jesus and led by the apostles. This is an aspect of doctrine that makes it fundamentally different from other kinds of speech acts: it takes time, sometimes a long time, for an utterance to become doctrine. The Nicene Creed, first formulated in 325, was restated at Constantinople in 381. At which point did it become doctrine? I think the best way to explain it is that although it was a candidate for doctrinal status following Nicea, it was only after Constantinople that it was effectively received as doctrine. For this reception to take place, the church in 381 needed to see itself in unity with the church in 325. Many churches today continue to express their own unity with Nicea and Constantinople by use of the Nicene Creed in worship.

Primary Conditions:
1. The church performs a doctrinal act in the common language.
2. The church intends its action to be heard as guidance in the living of the Christian drama.
3. The church intends its act to be addressed to believers as a whole or to a subset of the church.
4. By means of doctrine the church differentiates itself from other communities.
5. The church intends its act to be taken as authoritative, not merely as opinion.
6. The doctrinal speech act is uttered to achieve the health of both the church and its constituent parts.

7. Linguistic conventions exist which enable the church to be understood as speaking and which can effectively shape the life and actions of the community.

It is the primary conditions that make an utterance *doctrine*. When Searle created his taxonomy of speech acts, the first item he picked out as differentiating one kind of speech act from another is what he calls the *illocutionary point*. This is the description of what the speech act is trying to do, its purpose or point.[18] Not everything the church does is doctrine: not even every speech act of the church is doctrine. Doctrine's main point is to guide the church in the living of the Christian narrative.[19] The intended audience of doctrine, therefore, is not humanity in general, but the church itself. In its role as guide, it could be likened to an itinerary. When one travels, the itinerary identifies the routes to take, the sights to see, the people to meet, and where to stay.

Apart from doctrine the church would not know how to perform the drama. The tasks the church performs regularly in the living of the drama: worship, witness, proclamation, discipleship, and service find their theoretical coherence and rationale in doctrine. Doctrine identifies the players in the drama. Doctrine tells us the nature and mission of the church and what it means to be a member. Doctrine tells the church what the world is and how to relate to it in all its multiplicity and rebellion against God. Doctrine tells the church about God—Father, Son and Holy Spirit—because God is not merely the object of our worship and devotion, but is also a continuing agent—the most important one, in fact—in the drama. If the church does not know who God is, what God's character and purposes are, the church cannot do its part in the story. The church also must know what God (and the other actors) have done up until now. Otherwise, the church could not know where it now stands in the narrative.

Within the church there are subsets of people that have special tasks that are addressed by doctrine. The most commonly mentioned group (especially in the United Methodist Church) is the ordained ministry. Doctrine assigns to pastors as members of a category, particular tasks, including administering the sacraments, *leading* the church in ministry, worship and evangelism, and preaching the Gospel.

Doctrine also serves to identify the church, to differentiate it from other social groups.[20] Propositionalism sees this differentiation lying in the things doctrine proposes for belief. Community A has set X of beliefs while community B has belief set Y. In light of the model of the church I proposed in chapter three, this explanation is insufficient.

Doctrine *can* be described as beliefs, but it is not merely the having of this set of beliefs that makes the community different. Rather, the community is differentiated as doctrine shapes the community. Proper performance of doctrine makes the community different. This is the community that follows Jesus, who was God incarnate. This is the community that loves in the same way Jesus did. This is the people who are joyfully expecting to spend eternity with the God who has saved them. This is the community that bases its doctrine on the canonical books of the Old and New Testaments. None of these is simply a belief, though all entail certain beliefs.

Lindbeck's understanding that doctrine is regulative is essentially correct. Doctrine is only doctrine when it is treated—and allowed to function—as authoritative. He is also correct when he notes that the chief problem moderns have with doctrine is not so much what it says, but its very nature as authoritative.[21] The difference between our accounts does not lie in the issue of authority but in the images we use to understand Christianity (culture/language or dramatic narrative) and subsequently in the way doctrine functions authoritatively. This difference is not merely cosmetic, but reaches to the core of my proposal.

Within modern moral thought the position that evaluative discourse could be derived from descriptive discourse has been called the naturalistic fallacy. If this is indeed a fallacy, then there is to be no connection suggested between "is" statements and "ought" statements. Doctrine functions, according to Lindbeck, more like "ought" statements than like "is" statements, since it directs the Christian community in the living of the Christian drama (or, for Lindbeck, regulates the discourse of the Christian community). It seems strange, however, to exclude "is" statements from Christian doctrinal thinking, given the number of doctrinal statements that look descriptive. Speech acts are too complex to have *either* a word to world *or* a world to word direction of fit. Because doctrine looks at what was, what is, and what is promised, it seeks to shape the world accordingly. In my discussion of this in chapter two I point out Lindbeck's counterintuitive claim that doctrine is solely regulative, artificially (it appears to me) rephrasing or reinterpreting "is" statements as if they were really "ought" statements. Modern epistemology's disembodied conception of knowledge has given us a poor account of human action (though its poor account of divine action is more often noted). What my account attempts to do is get beyond the divide between knowledge and action since doctrine is intimately related to both. Lindbeck's claim that doctrines are rules—and rules only—when combined with his pessimism about the referentiality of doctrine, makes it too easy to read him as not getting beyond the division between knowledge and action, where in my thinking these two must be connected.

I will say more about the referentiality of doctrine in the next section (on the representative conditions for doctrine as a speech act), but it is necessary at this point to say that doctrine's authority does not lie only in its forward look—in commanding a particular course of action—but also in its backward look—in describing the actors and their actions, the setting and plot line thus far, and in telling the church where it now stands. Insofar as it has this descriptive dimension, my model is similar to propositionalism. The difference lies in the nature of the descriptions and the use to which they are put. Epistemology plays the key role in propositionalism: the descriptions doctrine gives provide the noetic structure of the believer. In my model epistemology is replaced by action. Knowledge clearly has a role in any conception of action, but it is a subservient role.

Doctrine does not only guide the church in the living of the Christian narrative, but it also is necessary for the health of the church. The best way to put this is to say that a church that is faithfully acting out its role in God's story is a healthy church. This faithful acting has the external dimension of the varied relationships with the world and its peoples, as well as the internal dimension of the formation of disciples and relationships that exhibit the character of Jesus. A consequence of this is that a church in which doctrine has been marginalized (or distorted) will fail to be a healthy church, just as a human trying to breathe on Mars would fail to be a healthy human (though the failure in this latter case is much more quickly evident and permanent).

The final primary condition for doctrine is the formal one that linguistic conventions exist for the expression of doctrine. The most recognized conventions for these are textual forms, either lists of articles such as the Anglican or Methodist Articles, or confessions like the Westminster Confession and the ancient creeds. In these forms doctrine has been widely received and recognized as official. Other forms, however, while not explicitly recognized as doctrine, have functioned as doctrine. Within the Methodist tradition (and I suspect within others as well) one of the major loci of doctrine has been hymnody. Methodists speak of "their" hymns. From the beginning these were heavily influenced by the Wesleys. Charles Wesley's composition of almost ten thousand hymns combined with his brother

John's publishing of his work (as well as the translation and inclusion of many hymns from the German church) produced a body of doctrine that shaped many generations of Methodists. Consider the following hymn, written by Charles immediately after his conversion.

> And can it be, that I should gain
> An interest in the Savior's blood?
> Died he for me who caused his pain?
> For me? Who him to death pursued?
> Amazing Love! How can it be
> That thou, my God, shouldst die for me?
>
> 'Tis myst'ry all: th'Immortal dies!
> Who can explore his strange design?
> In vain the first-born seraph tries
> To sound the depths of love divine.
> 'Tis mercy all! Let earth adore!
> Let angel minds inquire no more.
>
> He left his Father's throne above
> (So free so infinite his grace!),
> Emptied himself of all but love,
> And bled for Adam's helpless race.
> 'Tis mercy all, immense and free,
> For, O my God, it found out me!
>
> Long my imprisoned spirit lay,
> Fast bound in sin and nature's night.
> Thine eye diffused a quickening ray;
> I woke; the dungeon flamed with light.
> My chains fell off, my heart was free,
> I rose, went forth, and followed thee.
>
> No condemnation now I dread,
> Jesus, and all in him, is mine.
> Alive in him, my living head,
> And clothed with righteousness divine,
> Bold I approach th'Eternal throne,
> And claim the crown through Christ my own.[22]

In writing this hymn Wesley used his knowledge of Christian theology and doctrine to shape the telling of his experience using language derived from those sources. Later generations of Methodists have not only found this hymn an apt expression of their own conversions,[23] but have found (or could find with investigation) that their experience has been shaped by this hymn.

I suspect that the fact so many Methodists have encountered doctrine through hymnody lies behind some of the marginalization of doctrine we see in the denomination today. This is not because hymns have some intrinsic defect that makes them ineffective vehicles for the transmission of doctrine. Far from it! I would judge them to be among the most effective forms. What has happened is that the rise of a Methodism doctrinally determined by hymnody took place at the same time experiential expressivism arose as an understanding of religion. The use of hymnody was at home in the romantic setting in which experiential expressivism rose, and thus was too easily interpreted as merely an example of expression. Through experiential expressivism, the hymns came to be understood as mere expression and the speech acts within the hymn were, to a great degree, treated as of minor importance in comparison to the overall tone of the hymn.[24]

Generalizing from the way the function of hymns has paralleled shifts in the conceptualization of doctrine, we might suppose that the influence works both ways. That is, it is not simply the case that the conceptualization shapes the use of the form, but that the form shapes the conceptualization. Just as doctrine in poetic form (in an age of romanticism) lends itself to an experiential expressivist view, doctrine in a more highly structured form (such as the Articles of Religion) might lend itself to a propositionalist view. However much we go in this direction, however, we cannot make the mistake of seeing a simple equation here. Both forms of doctrinal expression antedate the rise of these modern conceptualizations of doctrine and will likely survive long after both are footnotes in theology textbooks. What is significant is that we cannot ignore form as a factor in doctrinal conceptualization. It is also essential for the church to attend to the forms in which it propounds doctrine and to consider whether the form can now convey what the church seeks to convey.[25]

Representative Conditions:
1. In performing doctrine the church describes the characters, plot and setting of the Christian narrative.
2. The Christian drama must be the actual arena of God's action with the world through God's people.

The representative conditions are those that describe the speech act's connection with the world. There is great variety in the ways speech acts connect with the world. Under the dominance of epistemology this relation was pretty much limited to the descriptive: speech acts either *described* the world, were personal expressions, or were meaningless, with these latter two possibilities being ways of nonrelation with the world. Austin and those who have developed his theory have shown clearly that such an account is far too simplistic.

McClendon and Smith consider the speech act of requesting.[26] Beth says, "Please pass the bread." Clearly Beth has described neither the bread nor the table. Those who insist on the descriptive function of language might want to interpret Beth's utterance as a description of her desire for bread. What "Please pass the bread" means, then, is "I want bread." This kind of reductionism not only ignores the differences between a wide variety of things one could say about wanting bread, but it also assumes that individualism is the norm. "I want bread" is something a person can say when alone. "Please pass the bread" *requires* other people—a determinate social setting—in order to make sense.

"Please pass the bread," therefore, is not a descriptive act—either of the bread or of Beth's desires. If it is to be intelligible or happy, however, it does require a representative or descriptive dimension. If there is no bread available for passing, or if Beth already has the bread, the utterance fails to work. Requests are to be understood, therefore, as social acts within the world. Doctrine is to be understood in this context as well.

This is also the place to discuss Searle's concept of "direction of fit." He observes that "some illocutions have as part of their illocutionary point to get the words . . . to match the world, others to get the world to match the words."[27] While requests and commands aim to make the world "fit" the words—the point of "Take out the garbage!" is not to say the garbage *has* been taken out, but to *get* it taken out—assertions and descriptions aim to make the words "fit" the world.

The primary point of doctrine can be described as aiming to get the world to fit the words. In "doctrining" the church gives direction for the living of the narrative and does not simply describe the living of the narrative. Doctrine fails to fit Searle's categories in two important ways, however. First, one of the chief ways doctrine gives direction is through description—through making its words fit the world God has made and acted in—so that the church can know where it stands and where it is going. This is the main place where the textual complexity of doctrine (as opposed to particular doctrines) shows itself. Some doctrines, those dealing with Christology, for example, perform their objective through identifying Jesus Christ. Though this act of identification is not simple description (it aims to have the church recognize and respond to Jesus, not just know the facts about him), if what it says about Jesus is untrue, it will be judged unhappy. Other doctrines, especially those termed "practical," will not have such a prominent role for the representative dimension, but primarily seek a "world to word" fit. Even these, however, have some connection with the world. Consider the Christian doctrine of love. This teaching, often summarized as "Love one another," is more faithful to scripture when summarized as "Love one another in the same way Jesus loved." "Love" is too culturally variable to maintain much meaning without further specification, and in Christianity it is the "in the same way Jesus loved" that provided the needed specificity. This specification not merely ties the command to the historical Jesus, but to the narrative that describe his acts as love. Doctrines are interrelated. This practical doctrine of love depends on doctrinal descriptions of the person of Christ that make sense of how his seemingly masochistic action in willingly going to the cross can be taken as love and not merely delusion, foolishness, or plain bad luck.

Is the tie to the narrative enough to satisfy this condition? Consider another command, "Do not allow your imagination to control your actions the same way Tom Sawyer did." A person who heard this command need only know how powerful Tom's imagination was and what sorrow it led to in the end of *Huckleberry Finn* in order for the command to be intelligible. The fact that the story is fictional affects the happiness of the command not at all. Perhaps all doctrine needs is the *story* of Jesus, without any requirement that the story be factual.

There are several differences between the two cases. First, there has been no community developed out of the narrative of *Huckleberry Finn* in any way similar to the development of the church out of the scriptural narrative. Second, the command about imagination, though a particularly apt lesson to learn from Tom's actions and easily understood by those who know Twain's work, is not drawn from the logic of the work in the same way that the love command is drawn from the logic of the biblical narrative. Finally, there is no system of teaching based on *Huckleberry Finn* in the same way there is in relation to the bible. This may seem like a truism, but what this difference notes is the difference between a command treated in isolation from a way of life, and one intimately connected with a way of life—with other directives, characters, the plot, etc. Though it is theoretically possible that even the expanded form of the love command could be used as an isolated moral prescription as if Jesus and his love were merely illustrative elements drawn from a nice story, the church has in fact used it as part of its overall teaching, and it is within *this* field of use that the meaning of the doctrine is to be discerned.

Happy doctrine does not depend only on the happiness of the representative conditions of particular doctrines. This is the second feature of doctrine that does not fit Searle's analysis. Since doctrine's illocutionary point is to direct the church in living the ongoing Christian drama, there must be such a drama for doctrine as a whole to be happy. There must be a world describable as "creation," and an ongoing action of God for which "redemption" is the apt description. If there is no ongoing action of God, no called-out community named "church," doctrine will necessarily be unhappy. It is possible, then, for *a* doctrine (taken in isolation *from doctrine*) to be happy in its representative dimension, and for doctrine still to be unhappy. Other theories of doctrine, i.e., the propositionalist, expressivist, and even the regulative, do not have this requirement.[28]

Affective or Psychological Conditions:
1. The church intends the hearer to be a participant in the narrative.
2. The hearer has, at some point, become a willing participant in the drama.
3. The hearer receives the doctrine as the voice of the church.
4. The hearer hears the doctrine as guidance in living the Christian narrative.
5. The hearer discerns, by means of the doctrinal utterance, where he or she stands in the narrative as well as what the next step in the drama should be.

Through doctrine, the church intends the hearer to be a participant in the continuing narrative. Inasmuch as doctrine is spoken to all Christians, it is implied that all Christians are to be actors in God's story. Given this understanding of doctrine, there is no place for the "normal" Christian who is only a passive receiver of grace and no more, just as there is no place for the church that exists solely for the benefit of its own members. A strong missionary and evangelistic impetus is built into this model of doctrine. On the other side, the speaking church is not permitted to judge its members by worldly standards—by their sinful past, their physical limitations or lack of abilities. Through the Spirit all are called and gifted and have a role to play in the drama.

Though the church is the agent of the speech act of doctrine, the hearer also has a role to play. Jesus taught that people must come to him in faith. This act of faith is not merely a belief that Jesus will solve my problems with sin and death, but is also a taking up of my cross and following him. This crucified life (which can be generalized as "loving as Jesus did") is a life of obedience to God in the story of redemption.

The third affective condition for happy doctrine is that it be heard as the voice of church. This is where the doctrine of reception comes into play. Churches do many things: evangelize their communities, make disciples, feed the hungry, visit the sick, build new buildings, maintain old buildings, etc. Only some of these actions are direct consequences of doctrine. The decision of a church to build a "family life center" may be based on doctrinal convictions and duly voted on by the entire membership, but the decision to build such a building is not what I mean by "hearing the voice of the church." In some dimensions doctrine has a universality to it that applies to all churches everywhere and at all times. This universality is based on those features of the drama that are constants, most importantly the character and actions of God as narrated in Scripture. Local needs will, however, determine the form and conceptualization of these doctrines. Doctrine, unlike buildings, is viewed as the possession of the whole church and not merely of local churches. Theological statements that have not yet been broadly received may function as doctrine in local settings, but have not yet reached the status of *Christian* doctrine. I will say more about this later in the chapter where I deal with the consequences my theory has for ecumenism.

As a fourth affective condition, doctrine must be heard as guidance for the Christian narrative. This is perhaps the hardest condition—and the most questionable. My theory is not the dominant one in the church. Many segments of the church explicitly maintain propositionalist or expressivist understandings of the function of doctrine. My contention, however, is that the church's practice is generally better than its theory. As long as theory dominates over practice in this area, doctrine *qua* doctrine will be marginalized. The church's practice is likely to be better in this respect the more faithful it is in discipleship—in enculturating its members into the Christian way of life.

The fifth affective condition may be better described as the perlocutionary result of happy doctrine. The speech act of persuasion can be persuasion even if no one is persuaded, but it certainly has missed its point. Likewise with doctrine. If doctrine is successful in every other dimension of happiness, yet the church in actuality fails to be guided in its life and action, doctrine has missed its objective.

Overview of the Conditions for Doctrinal Felicity

The conditions I have presented for the happiness of doctrine have a necessary amount of inexactness to them. Doctrine is a complex speech act composed of many speech acts and presented in a diversity of forms. The conditions for the happiness of doctrine as a whole are different from the conditions of happiness for particular doctrines, though in this latter case different doctrines would have different conditions since they would have different illocutionary points. In another work, it would be useful for me to investigate particular doctrines to see how their conditions of happiness related to the conditions of the happiness of doctrine as a whole. One way this further study might proceed is as an investigation of the structure of doctrine using the analogy of Lakatosian philosophy of science. My suggestion is that though different types of doctrine have different illocutionary points, each of these points is to be contextualized by the illocutionary point of *doctrine*, to the direction of the church in living the story, that is.

THE CONSEQUENCES OF MY MODEL

Does adopting my model make any difference? Most obviously my position entails a rejection of models of the faith that center on knowledge. Being a Christian is significantly more than knowing things, whether the things known be statements drawn from theology or truths about ourselves, our right standing with God through faith in Christ, for example. Since the Christian life is not about knowledge, my model will have consequences for the way we handle the bible and will shape the way we think about how one becomes a Christian. Just as obviously, accepting my model entails a conviction that Christianity is not something we do alone. Church is more than a voluntary association of Christians who organize around an agreed upon mission. This "not alone" refers not merely to the solitary Christian, but also to the solitary congregation and denomination. If the Christian claim that Jesus is Lord—and active in history here and now—is correct, then his story is something in which we are all invited to be actors.

In what follows, I will very briefly consider the implications my model has for these areas. I will begin by addressing the role of the bible. If the bible is to be treated neither as the storehouse of propositions to be mined, nor as a guidebook to ancient religious experience to be accessed via the methods of historical criticism, what ought we to do with it? Answering this question has important implications for our life as Christians as well as the way we operate as a church. Second, I will consider the impact my model will have on the theology and practice of evangelism. If my model is correct, then an initial assessment would lead us to conclude that many current models of evangelism are missing important features of the gospel. Finally, I will discuss the consequences my model has for the relations between churches, whether that ecumenism be local, national, or global.

What About the Bible?

The bible contributes to doctrine in two ways. Formally, the overall narrative of scripture contributes the controlling image I have suggested. Scripture tells a story beginning with creation and ending with a new heavens and a new earth. The obvious objection to this is that scripture contains more than narrative. Law, wisdom, poetry, and instruction make up major sections of the bible. The best way to make sense of these other genres, I believe, is to see them from within the overarching narrative. Consider the Ten Commandments. In modern America these are usually abstracted from their context and put forth as universal rules for morality. Claims are even made that these commandments can be posted in government buildings and courthouses without infringing the separation of church and state. Exodus 20 sets the context quite differently, however. The focus there is not first of all on the commands, but on the one who commands. "I am the LORD your God who brought you out of Egypt, out of the land of slavery." These commands are not (at least at this stage) directed at all of humanity. They are aimed directly at Israel, and set firmly within the narrative of God's actions of deliverance. These commands do not come as rules that all rational people should submit to, but as guidance from a God the people of Israel have come to know through their own experience.

Consider also the Psalms. Though many Psalms only have a minimal narrative connection, the background of several is God's action in the past (with Israel, with creation, with the psalmist) or God's promises for the future. Some Psalms cry out to a particular God for deliverance, One who has a reputation for delivering his people. Other psalms sing praise to the redeemer God.

The weakest part of my case here is the wisdom literature like that found in Proverbs. These nuggets of wisdom have much in common with other cultures (of the Ancient Near East and beyond), and are apparently innocent of any narratival connection. Clearly many of these texts at most rely on a creation, but specify little in the way of

God's continuing action. Living wisely is simply living in accordance with the way the world works.

If a group of people had banded together with the intention of creating a religion, and in the process of their work had lighted upon the book of Proverbs, they would surely be justified in taking it as abstracted wisdom that could be practiced in almost any context—without reference to a God who is still involved in the world. But that is not where we now stand. The Christian church deals today not with sixty-six haphazardly selected books from antiquity but with the canon of scripture. Because the overarching form of this literature is narrative, the wisdom literature is best understood as teaching what is wise in light of God's character and action, even when that context is not explicit.

Scripture's contribution to doctrine is more than formal. The idea is not merely that because scripture is narratival that we ought to see ourselves in a narrative. Rather, when we attend to the content of scripture we read of constant invitations to join what God is up to. It is possible that even given the narrative structure of scripture, a sort of timeless wisdom could predominate. But the word of scripture is not, "do this and avoid that and you will be happy and successful." Rather, the premise is that God is up to something. The one who hears God's word is invited to become part of the action. Reading scripture shows us what this action has been in the past, what kinds of things this God might be up to, how God operates, how people have worked with God in the past and hints for the future.

One resource that has been much used in churches of many denominations in the past several years looks at the bible from this perspective. *Experiencing God: Knowing and Doing the Will of God* by Henry Blackaby begins with the premise that God is always at work all around us. Through this work God pursues a love relationship with all people. One dimension of this love relationship is God's invitation for people to join in this mission.[29] Given the continuing action of God to bring all people into a love relationship, the point of bible study is not simply, "What *does* it mean?" (with pietism), or, "What *did* it mean?" (with historical criticism), but, "What do we do?" It is fair to Blackaby's work to emphasize this "we." Discerning the current work of God and our role in that work is dependent on the Holy Spirit, who speaks through the bible, prayer, circumstances, and the church. The way Blackaby frames this discussion shows some bias toward the individual, but the logic of his position is very much oriented toward the whole church. Though Blackaby seems unaware of McClendon's portrayal of the baptist vision, his work certainly exemplifies it. Adoption of the understanding of doctrine in this book would lead to churches pursuing an approach like Blackaby's. The key contrast is likely to be found in his highly congregationalist ecclesiology, which differs from my emphasis on the whole church over a much larger time frame.

Reading the bible, finally, whether for guidance or for doctrinal development, is something we do together. When we read we are not simply reading the text as it now stands, as if it were timelessly addressed to us. Because we—both we the church and we who as individuals trust in Christ—are who we are through the historical mediation of those who went before us (whether we turn to Hebrews 11 or Gadamer's concept of *Wirkungsgeschichte*), we read not only the text before us, but also the text as heard by the original community and the embodiments of that community that lie between us. This reading is hard work. It will take time. If Blackaby's approach is weak, such weakness lies in oversimplifying this history. Yes, the Christian (and the church) does not simply "do what we've always done." But at no point do we know nothing. Doctrine tells us how to go on—yet we do not constantly start with a *tabula rasa*. Most of what the church (and believers) today needs to know is already known from the past, because as each new believer is added to the body he or she joins a community that already engages with the story.

What the church of the past does not know is our cultural world. Though we have innumerable models before us of how (and how not) to live out the narrative in changing cultural situations, the calling to adapt faithfully is always before us. Thus we read not only the scripture, but also our culture in light of scripture and in accordance with the direction we receive from doctrine. Reading is not one thing and doing another. I reject the dichotomy between epistemology and ethics (and I am taking ethics in the broad sense, not narrowly as does modern decisionism), so while I admit a logical distinction between gaining information, developing doctrine, etc., and using that knowledge, obeying God, etc., the former does not take priority over the latter but can itself be understood as a subset of the latter.

Doctrine and Evangelism

It is common to find evangelism centered on the cross of Christ. There is much biblical support for the position that in his death on the cross, Jesus bore the sins of the world, attaining salvation for all who come to trust in him. Given this conception of the work of Christ, evangelism amounts to producing in people an understanding of this work and leading them to a place of trust in Christ. It is not my intention to dispute this, but rather to contextualize it.

Willowcreek Community Church in South Barrington, Illinois (just outside Chicago) has a solid reputation as an evangelistic church. The leaders of the church aim to have all their members mobilized as part of their evangelistic ministry. Reaching people for Christ is so important to them that as a church they have invested heavily in helping other congregations become effective in evangelism. Church leaders from around the world, and from a wide variety of denominations come to their annual evangelism conferences and use their training materials.[30]

The Willowcreek conception of the evangelistic process is available in a number of versions; the most nuanced I know of is found in Mark Mittelberg's *Building a Contagious Church*. In its simplest form, their model sees evangelism as leading a sinner across the chasm of sin (which separates them from God) via the bridge of the cross of Christ. The problem to be overcome is sin; the *only* solution is the cross. The strength of this model is that it views evangelism as a process. They do not expect that the sinner will make a move across the bridge of Christ through one encounter with the evangelist. Rather, coming to Christ is a journey. In his most recent work, Mittelberg discusses a number of other obstacles, greatly enhancing the model's fit with actual situations. I want to highlight the second major hindrance he identifies.

Once upon a time in America, Christianity so imbued our culture that churches could depend on the people they evangelized being fairly close to the chasm of sin. Mittelberg says that being in such proximity means that they tended to have "at least some understanding that they were sinners who had rebelled against God and needed his forgiveness. They had memories, even if distant and fading, of Sunday school classes, Bible stories, and lessons about Jesus dying on the cross."[31] As long as the audience had this stock of images and teaching to rely on, the evangelist had something to appeal to. Simple preaching of the gospel—meaning something like: (a) You're a sinner; (b) Jesus died for your sins; (c) You can be forgiven if you turn to Christ today—would likely result in a positive response. But times have changed. Mittelberg continues:

> The problem is that people in our culture have *moved*. They no longer live close to chasm where they can look over the edge and see the depth of their sins. They don't realize how far away God is or where the bridge can be found. . . . The

term we use to describe this is *secularization*. People in our culture have gradually taken steps away from Christian beliefs, values, and morals.[32]

What this change points up is that now there is an additional chasm that must be bridged, the "cultural chasm."

We have seen that the sin chasm was bridged by the cross of Christ. What bridges the cultural chasm? Mittelberg points to the church. Because it has been called to bring people to Christ, the church has a responsibility to help people overcome the culture chasm through diminishing the features of church culture that make it difficult for the sinner to hear the message. To see what this diminishment looks like, one only has to look at the weekend seeker services at Willowcreek where this conviction is embodied. When they attend one of these services seekers will hear music in a style probably indistinguishable from what they listen to on the radio. They will see a drama performed that highlights various questions common to both Christians and seekers, setting the stage for the message. Weekend messages at Willowcreek are created with the seeker in mind—and not just any seeker, but the kinds of seekers that live in their immediate area. The objective is to help the seeker see the relevance of the faith, the reliability of scripture, and the availability of Christ. No biblical or theological knowledge is assumed. Willowcreek has received much criticism for "watering down the gospel" in pursuing this strategy, but I think such criticism is misplaced. If the entire ministry of Willowcreek is considered, I do not think a strong case can be made against their practice.

The first thing to notice is that Willowcreek's concept of evangelism seems to be dependent on modern epistemology. The route to salvation lies in knowledge: knowledge of our sin, knowledge of Christ's saving power, knowledge, finally, that we have been forgiven and accepted through faith. The church's crossing of the culture chasm is an exercise in clarifying the transmission of information. I do not want to suggest that knowledge is unimportant—a quick perusal of I John would disabuse one of that notion. Rather, what seems to be happening is that evangelizing has become primarily the impartation of information—about ourselves, our sin, and about Christ.

What about Jesus? We know from the Willowcreek model that Jesus bridges the chasm of sin through his death on the cross. How does Jesus relate to the culture chasm? To answer this we need a little historical perspective. What Mittelberg describes as the culture chasm is the result of the demise of Christendom, a period in our history where a basic continuity between church and the broader culture was assumed. When many non-Christians look at the church today they see an institution that appears firmly planted in the culture of the American past. This kind of church, it is said, gives people the idea that Christianity is out of date, a cardinal sin for moderns. The culture chasm, however, is not new, or unique to the demise of Christendom. The first-century church saw such a chasm as well, though instead of being characterized as pertaining to date, it pertained to ethnicity. Since Jesus and the first Christians were Jews, it was easy to see Christianity as something for Jews only. The first evangelists had to bridge the gap between Jewish culture and Gentile culture (both of which were far from monolithic) to draw people into the faith.

At first glance, we see nothing odd here. Then a question comes to mind. Why did God, the creator of the universe, start an organization (the church) aimed at bringing salvation to the whole world begin with such a large culture chasm? Jesus, whom the church confesses to be God incarnate, came to live as a Jew—a member of a particular culture, and a marginalized one ruled by a world power at that. If Jesus had come as a Roman the culture chasm would remain, but the truth about him could have been more readily communicated to more people (and we could have had Christendom much sooner).

The difference is that the best way to describe what Jesus did is to say that in Jesus God became incarnate to fulfill his promises to Israel, or to use my terminology from above, to play the climactic role in the narrative begun in creation and continued through the history of God's dealings with Israel. The first bridging of the culture gap, then, was the incarnation when Jesus himself bridged the gap between God and Jewish culture.

Traditional incarnation language has looked more to metaphysics than to culture. When it is said that in Jesus God became human, the church developed doctrine that addressed the two natures of Christ, coming to the conclusion that Jesus was fully human and fully divine. James McClendon has suggested as a supplement to that understanding of the incarnation a model he calls "two narratives" Christology. He avers that in Jesus the story of God and the story of Israel (and by extension, the story of humanity) intersect.[33] I do not want to explore this in detail, but merely want to show that more than one dimension of incarnational thinking is available. When we recognize that the Son was incarnate not merely as a human but as a first-century Jewish human, we are able to gain a resource to help us see how the work of Christ overcomes the so-called culture chasm—as well as the sin chasm.

I need to make one more detour before bringing this section to a close. The traditional model of evangelism is oriented toward working from plight to solution. The plight of humanity is sin, the solution is the cross of Christ. Since this way of thinking is reliant on Paul, particularly his presentation in Romans, it may be worthwhile to consider some recent scholarship on Paul's own approach to this question. E. P. Sanders, most famously, has suggested that instead of arguing from plight to solution, Paul's practice was to work the other way around. He would begin with a declaration of what God had done in Christ and then work from that to the plight, showing how that solution connects with the current reality of his audience.[34] If the solution, the work of God in Christ, *which includes the incarnation, life, ministry, death, and resurrection of Jesus*, stands in continuity with the whole story of God and Israel (beginning with Abraham) and not just the sacrificial system, the plight can be seen to be not primarily sin (which separates people from God), but the separation from God itself. Working "backwards" from the solution and finding this lack of a harmonious relationship with God as the first stage of the plight allows us to see the problem—which *is* a sin problem—as much broader than the problem of the sin of individuals. As a sinner I am separated from God not just by my sin (which *could* do the job on its own) but by the fact that I live in the midst of a world and a culture distorted and broken by sin. In living out his part of the story, Jesus did what was necessary to bring sinners into eternal life—an eternal relationship with God—thus overcoming all the brokenness of sin.

Where does this leave the practice of evangelism? Jesus bridges not merely the sin chasm but also the culture chasm—and any other chasm that separates people from God. The evangelist's message, therefore, is not just about a few hours of Jesus' life on a Friday—or a few days stretching from the crucifixion through the resurrection. A happy doctrine of the incarnation requires the church to receive that teaching in such a way that they not merely lead people to believe that Jesus is fully human and fully divine, but that the church itself lives in the same story Jesus did (and does!), a kind of living that will bring outsiders into the body and take them along to its final conclusion. Further, not only is Jesus involved in bridging both the sin and culture chasms, but so is the church. In other words, the church is called not merely to incarnate the gospel in whatever culture it finds itself (paralleling Jesus' act of incarnation), but also to suffer for sinners (paralleling Jesus' suffering on the cross).[35] The invitation to come to Christ, therefore, is not merely an invitation to receive forgiveness of sins but to become a willing participant in this very story.

If my arguments in this section are correct, doctrine is not something we hold at a distance from the practice of evangelism, but is intimately connected to it. The church must attend to the God who acted in Christ two thousand years ago and who continues to act to this very day. The church must discern what God is up to in this age, because evangelism is not just the church's transmission of information, but is the invitation to join the story of the ever living God. Following the direction provided by doctrine is clearly essential to this whole process.

Relations Between Churches

In John 17:21 an explicit connection is made between the unity of believers (today we can say *churches*) and the world coming to believe in Jesus. The main question I want to address now is about the relationship between Christian doctrine and the doctrine of particular ecclesial communities. We speak not only of Methodist doctrine, Roman Catholic doctrine and Baptist doctrine, but also of Christian doctrine. It seems only natural for members of a given community to equate their community's doctrine with Christian doctrine under normal circumstances, but when they are intentionally relating to other communities, they can intentionally identify their own doctrine as one expression (though usually the fullest) of Christian doctrine.

This question gets at the issue of Christian unity, an issue central to Lindbeck's investigation of doctrine. I want to suggest that the various ecclesial communities find their unity in the common life (though not identical location) and purpose they have in the Christian narrative.[36] Understood this way, efforts at doctrinal reconciliation and unity are not primarily aimed at saying the same words, but at shared apprehension of the narrative combined with a common understanding of what is to be done now in order to be faithful to God.

Seen this way, Christian unity has three aspects. First, churches have unity in their connection to Jesus and the action of the God that generated the tradition. It is not merely that these events are claimed by the church today, but in a real sense the church today is claimed by these events: today's church is what it is only because of these events. This instantiation of *Wirkungsgeschichte* is very different from the kind of illustrative use made of history and literature in other situations.

Second, the various communities are prospectively united in the future fulfillment of God's purposes. When the end comes, all God's people will be one. Finally, the churches now have unity through their common action of obedience and love in the one drama. The churches cannot rest on this as a merely theoretical unity, however, but must (through obedience!) constantly seek fuller common understanding of the narrative they live and of the actions currently called for by their place in that story.

The other side of ecumenism is the doctrinal differentiation of ecclesial communities. The most popular current ways of differentiating groups are sociological and by so-called doctrinal distinctives. In light of my theory, the key to this differentiation (while allowing for social factors) is the reception of doctrine. What have been known as doctrinal distinctives are the doctrinal developments within a particular community that have not yet been received by the broader church. Two jobs remain for the church. First, against the backdrop of modernity the church must recover the sense of history that will allow both its relation to the drama to be recognized and diachronic reception to take place. Second, each ecclesial community has a continuing responsibility to interact with other church communities and to find ways to receive them.

Conclusion

Any time we are faced with the proposal of a third option in an environment dominated by two longstanding positions, it is easy to assume that the new position is a synthesis or an attempt to "split the difference" between the dominant positions. In this case propositionalism and experiential expressivism, or, more popularly (and simplistically) conservatism and liberalism, are the dominant positions. One is assumed to be either conservative *or* liberal. If these are the only two options, if the conceptual space is best mapped on a single one dimensional line, my position would likely be taken as conservative by liberals (since I adhere to traditional doctrinal substance) and as liberal by conservatives (since I reject foundationalist epistemology, even as it pertains to the issue of biblical authority). My position is not, first of all, that conservatism and liberalism are wrong, but rather that mapping the Christian conceptual world in such a way is tied to particularly modern convictions, convictions that I believe are at worst destructive to the church, and at best unhealthy for its obedience to God.

So how should the conceptual space by mapped? I do not know yet. Like the early explorers and map-makers of five hundred years ago, we live in an age of marking new territory. Much of what we know of the postmodern world we know only through its contrast with modernity. Many look at the primitive maps that have been made and see only the monsters. They counsel that we should stay in safe modern waters. If God was a modern God and the people we are called to reach were modern people, staying put would make sense. But our God, the God who created the universe, claimed Israel as his very own, became incarnate in Jesus—who lived, died, and rose—is both eternal and intimately related with every age. God is not afraid of postmodernity. As for modern people—without question they still populate our neighborhoods. But they do so in the same way that we still hear of people who live like they did in the 1950's—or 1980's. Our call is to make disciples of people wherever they are, even if there be monsters nearby.

At least for the contemporary American church this postmodern map will require us to step away from an identification of the American way as the Christian way. Whether "the American way" means conservative traditionalism or liberal activism, it still fails to match the biblical vision of what Christianity is about. At the same time we are distancing ourselves from our culture, we must also remain close to our culture. Anthropologists tell us culture is made up of artifacts, rituals, customs, and institutions—and so it is. But without people there would be no culture. If we are to reach this and coming generations with the gospel, we must allow doctrine to connect us to the story of God and direct us as we live out the faith.

Notes

[1] See also David J. Bryant, "Christian Identity and Historical Change: Postliberals and Historicity," *Journal of Religion* 73 (Jan. 1993): 41.
[2] *The Book of Discipline of the United Methodist Church* (Nashville: The United Methodist Publishing House, 1996), 26.
[3] Judicial Council Decision 358. <http://www.umc.org/judicial/300/358.html>
[4] See the discussion in Richard P. Heitzenrater, "At Full Liberty: Doctrinal Standards in Early American Methodism," and Thomas C. Oden, "What Are 'Established Standards of Doctrine'? A Response to Richard Heitzenrater," both in *Doctrine and Theology in the United Methodist Church*, ed. Thomas Langford (Nashville: Kingswood Books, 1991), 109–24, 125–42.
[5] Both of these, incidentally, were schooled in German neo-Kantianism.
[6] George Lindbeck, *The Nature of Doctrine: Religion and Theology in a Postliberal Age* (Philadelphia: Westminster Press, 1984), 36ff.
[7] Paul Holmer puts it this way in speaking of theology: "If theology is grammar, then there is the task, always pertinent, of learning to extend the rules, the order, the morphology, of Godliness over the ever-changing circumstances" (*The Grammar of Faith* [San Francisco: Harper and Row, 1978], 23). See also Alasdair MacIntyre, *Whose Justice? Which Rationality?* (Notre Dame, IN: Notre Dame University Press, 1988), 7f.
[8] Nancey Murphy, *Theology in the Age of Scientific Reasoning* (Ithaca, NY: Cornell University Press, 1990).

[9] J. L. Austin, *How to Do Things With Words* (Cambridge, MA: Harvard University Press, 1975).

[10] James W. McClendon, Jr. and James M. Smith. *Convictions: Defusing Religious Relativism*, rev. ed. (Valley Forge, PA: Trinity Press International, 1994).

[11] John R. Searle, *Speech Acts: An Essay in the Philosophy of Language* (Cambridge: Cambridge University Press, 1969); John R. Searle, "A Taxonomy of Illocutionary Acts," in *Expression and Meaning: Studies in the Theory of Speech Acts* (Cambridge: Cambridge University Press, 1979), 1–29.

[12] Hans-Georg Gadamer, *Truth and Method*, 2nd, rev. ed., trans. Joel Weinsheimer and Donald G. Marshall (New York: Crossroad, 1989), 306.

[13] In *Expression and Meaning*, 58-75.

[14] Searle, "Fictional Discourse," 63.

[15] Ibid., 64.

[16] McClendon and Smith, *Convictions*, 57.

[17] This is a retrospective judgment. Though other languages were significantly represented in the church, all the documents that were to form the New Testament canon appear to have been composed in Greek for Greek speaking audiences.

[18] Searle, "Taxonomy," 2-3. See also his discussion in *Speech Acts*, 60, 66–68.

[19] Thomas Langford says that "For Wesley, doctrines are not ends in themselves but are guidelines which help us know how to tell the story of God's grace rightly and to live it with integrity" ("The United Methodist Quadrilateral: A Theological Task," in *Doctrine and Theology in the United Methodist Church*, ed. Thomas Langford [Nashville: Kingswood Books, 1991], 239).

[20] Michael Root, "Identity and Difference: The Ecumenical Problem," in *Theology and Dialogue: Essays in Conversation with George Lindbeck*, ed. Bruce D. Marshall (Notre Dame, IN: University of Notre Dame Press, 1990), 167.

[21] Lindbeck, *Nature of Doctrine*, 77.

[22] Charles Wesley, traditional title "And Can It Be?" *A Collection of Hymns for the People Called Methodists*, vol. 7, *The Works of John Wesley*, ed. Franz Hildebrant and Oliver A. Beckerlegge (Nashville: Abingdon, 1983), 322f.

[23] We can say that the Methodist tradition "received" this hymn, appropriating it not merely as something from Charles Wesley, but as its very own discourse. See the discussion of reception in chapter two.

[24] The way in which hymns function as speech acts while containing within them speech acts is a subject for future writing.

[25] This is a place where the church needs gifted communicators. I do not mean simply preachers, teachers, and writers, but people who are creative in various media who can find new ways of putting forth doctrine without these new forms simply being received as an individual's creativity.

[26] This illustration is found in *Convictions*, 56ff.

[27] Searle, "Taxonomy," 3.

[28] Lindbeck's regulative approach seems to be framed solely in terms of "world to word" direction of fit—doctrine does not refer, it simply shapes the community. The necessary world connection for such a scheme would be the actuality of the ecclesial community: if there is no community to be shaped, then doctrine is unhappy.

[29] Henry T. Blackaby and Claude V. King, *Experiencing God: How to Live the Full Adventure of Knowing and Doing the Will of God* (Nashville: Broadman and Holman, 1994).

³⁰As a pastor I have great respect for their ministry and have used their materials on many occasions.

³¹Mark Mittelberg, *Building a Contagious Church: Revolutionizing the Way We View and Do Evangelism* (Grand Rapids, MI: Zondervan, 2000), 40.

³²Ibid., 41.

³³James W. McClendon, Jr., *Doctrine: Systematic Theology*, Vol. 2 (Nashville: Abingdon, 1994), 263ff.

³⁴E. P. Sanders, *Paul and Palestinian Judaism: A Comparison of Patterns of Religion* (Minneapolis: Fortress Press, 1977), 442ff.

³⁵This is not as far-fetched as it may at first appear. My case here makes good sense of the parallels between Paul's description of Jesus in Philippians 2:5–11 and of himself in 3:4ff. As to the church joining in the suffering of Christ, consider 3:10 (and its parallel in Colossians 1:24).

³⁶See the discussion of the early church in N. T. Wright, *The New Testament and the People of God*, vol. 1, *Christian Origins and the Question of God* (Minneapolis: Fortress Press, 1992), 456. One advantage of this approach is that it allows us to make sense not only of large-scale ecumenism, such as what we see in the National Council of Churches and the World Council of Churches, but also of local ecumenism.

Bibliography

Abraham, William J. *Canon and Criterion in Christian Theology: From the Fathers to Feminism.* Oxford: Clarendon Press, 1998.

———."Confessing Christ: A Quest for Renewal in Contemporary Christianity." *Interpretation* 51:2 (April 1997): 117–29.

———. *Divine Revelation and the Limits of Historical Criticism.* Oxford: Oxford University Press, 1982.

———. "How to Dismantle the Wesleyan Quadrilateral: A Study in the Thought of Albert C. Knudson," *Wesleyan Theological Journal* 20 (Spring 1985): 34–44.

———. "Response [to H. Ray Dunning]: The Perils of a Wesleyan Systematic Theologian." *Wesleyan Theological Journal* 17 (Spring 1982): 23–29.

———. *Waking from Doctrinal Amnesia.* Nashville: Abingdon, 1996.

Austin, J. L. *How to Do Things With Words.* Cambridge, MA: Harvard University Press, 1975.

———. *Philosophical Papers*, 3rd ed. Ed. J. O. Urmson and G. J. Warnock. Oxford: Oxford University Press, 1979.

Barrett, Lee C. "Theology as Grammar: Regulative Principles or Paradigms and Practices." *Modern Theology* 4 (Jan. 1988): 155–72.

Barth, Karl. *Protestant Theology in the Nineteenth Century: Its Background and History.* Trans. B. Cozens and J. Bowden. Valley Forge, PA: Judson Press, 1973.

Behrens, Georg. "Schleiermacher *contra* Lindbeck on the Status of Doctrinal Sentences." *Religious Studies* 30 (Dec. 1994): 399–417.

Blackaby, Henry T. and Claude V. King. *Experiencing God: How to Live the Full Adventure of Knowing and Doing the Will of God*. Nashville: Broadman and Holman, 1994.

Bliss, Frederick M. *Understanding Reception: A Backdrop to Its Ecumenical Use*. Marquette Studies in Theology. Marquette, WI: Marquette University Press, 1993.

Bloor, David. *Knowledge and Social Imagery*. London: Routledge and Kegan Paul, 1976.

The Book of Discipline of the United Methodist Church. Nashville: The United Methodist Publishing House, 1980.

The Book of Discipline of the United Methodist Church. Nashville: The United Methodist Publishing House, 1996.

Bosch, David J. *Transforming Mission: Paradigm Shifts in Theology of Mission*. American Society of Missiology No. 16. Maryknoll, NY: Orbis, 1997.

Borradori, Giovanna. "Interview with MacIntyre." In *The American Philosopher: Conversations with Quine, Davidson, Putnam, Nozick, Danto, Rorty, Cavell, MacIntyre and Kuhn*. Trans. Rosanna Crocitto. Chicago: University of Chicago Press, 1994.

Brown, Colin. *Jesus in European Protestant Thought: 1778-1860*. Grand Rapids, MI: Baker, 1985.

Bryant, David J. "Christian Identity and Historical Change: Postliberal and Historicity." *Journal of Religion* 73 (Jan. 1993): 31–41.

Bultmann, Rudolph. "New Testament and Mythology." In *Kerygma and Myth: A Theological Debate*. Ed. Hans Werner Bartsch. Trans. Reginald H. Fuller. New York: Harper and Row, 1961.

Burridge, Richard A. *What are the Gospels? A Comparison with Graeco-Roman Biography*. Cambridge: Cambridge University Press, 1992.

Caird, George B. *The Language and Imagery of the Bible*. Grand Rapids, MI: Eerdmans, 1980.

Campbell, Ted. "Christian Tradition, John Wesley, and Evangelicalism." *Anglican Theological Review* 74 (Winter 1992): 54–67.

_____. *John Wesley and Christian Antiquity: Religious Vision and Cultural Change*. Nashville: Kingswood, 1991.

_____. "The 'Wesleyan Quadrilateral': The Story of a Modern Methodist Myth." In *Doctrine and Theology in the United Methodist Church*. Ed. Thomas Langford. Nashville: Kingswood Books, 1991.

Catechism of the Catholic Church. Nahwah, NJ: Paulist Press, 1994.

Cavanaugh, William T. "'A Fire Strong Enough to Consume the House': The Wars of Religion and the Rise of the State." *Modern Theology* 11 (Oct. 1995): 397–420.

Charry, Ellen. *By the Renewing of Your Minds: The Pastoral Function of Christian Doctrine*. Oxford: Oxford University Press, 1997.

_____. "Reviving Theology in a Time of Change." In *The Future of Theology: Essays in Honor of Jürgen Moltmann*. Ed. Miroslav Volf, Carmen Krieg, and Thomas Kucharz. Grand Rapids, MI: Eerdmans, 1996.

Chiles, Robert E. *Theological Transitions in American Methodism: 1790–1935*. Lanham, MD: University Press of America, 1983.

Christian, William. *Meaning and Truth in Religion*. Princeton, NJ: Princeton University Press, 1964.

Clapp, Rodney. *Peculiar People: The Church as Culture in a Post-Christian Society*. Downers Grove, IL: InterVarsity Press, 1996.

Cobb, John B., Jr. "Is Theological Pluralism Dead in the UMC?" *The Christian Century* 105 (April 6, 1988): 343–47.

_____. "Only One Thing!" *Circuit Rider* 14 (April 1990): 6–7.

A Collection of Hymns for the People Called Methodists. Vol. 7, *The Works of John Wesley*. Ed. Franz Hildebrant and Oliver A. Beckerlegge. Nashville: Abingdon, 1983.

Coppedge, Allan. "John Wesley and the Issue of Authority in Theological Pluralism." *Wesleyan Theological Journal* 19 (Fall 1984): 62–76.

Craig, Edward. *The Mind of God and the Works of Man*. Oxford: Clarendon Press, 1987.

Cyprian. "Epistle LXI: To Pomponius, Concerning Some Virgins." In *The Ante-Nicene Fathers: Translations of the Writings of the Fathers down to A.D. 325*. Ed. Alexander Roberts and James Donaldson. American Reprint of the Edinburgh ed., vol. 5, *Hippolytus, Cyprian, Caius, Novation*. New York: Charles Scribners' Sons, 1926.

_____. "Epistle LXXII: To Jubaianus: Concerning the Baptism of Some Heretics." In *The Ante-Nicene Fathers: Translations of the Writings of the Fathers down to A.D. 325*. Ed. Alexander Roberts and James Donaldson. American Reprint of the Edinburgh ed., vol. 5, *Hippolytus, Cyprian, Caius, Novation*. New York: Charles Scribners' Sons, 1926.

Davidson, Donald. "On the Very Idea of a Conceptual Scheme." In *Inquiries into Truth and Interpretation*. Oxford: Clarendon Press, 1984.

Davies, Rupert E. *Methodists and Unity*. London: A. R. Mowbray, 1962.

_____. "What Methodist Theology Has to Learn from Ecumenical Theology." In *Our Common History as Christians: Essays in Honor of Albert C. Outler*. Ed. John Deschner, Leroy T. Howe, and Klaus Penzel. New York: Oxford University Press, 1975.

_____, ed. *The Works of John Wesley*. Vol. 9, *The Methodist Societies: History, Nature and Design*. Nashville: Abingdon, 1989.

Deats, Paul and Carol Robb, eds. *The Boston Personalist Tradition in Philosophy, Social Ethics and Theology*. Macon, GA: Mercer University Press, 1986.

Dulles, Avery. *Models of the Church*. Garden City, NY: Image Books, 1974.

Dunn, James D. G. *Unity and Diversity in the New Testament: An Inquiry into the Character of Earliest Christianity*, 2nd ed. London: SCM Press, 1990.

Dunning, H. Ray. "Systematic Theology in a Wesleyan Mode." *Wesleyan Theological Journal* 17 (Spring 1982): 15–22.

Evans, Donald D. *The Logic of Self-Involvement: A Philosophical Study of Everyday Language with Special Reference to the Christian Use of Language about God as Creator*. New York: Herder and Herder, 1969.

Fish, Stanley. *Is There a Text in This Class? The Authority of Interpretive Communities*. Cambridge, MA: Harvard University Press, 1980.

Freeman, Curtis W. "Toward a *Sensus Fidelium* for an Evangelical Church: Postconservatives and Postliberals on Reading Scripture." In *The Nature of Confession: Evangelicals and Postliberals in Conversation*. Ed. Timothy R. Phillips and Dennis L. Okholm. Downers Grove, IL: InterVarsity Press, 1996.

Frei, Hans. *Eclipse of Biblical Narrative: A Study in Eighteenth and Nineteenth Century Hermeneutics*. New Haven, CT: Yale University Press, 1974.

_____. *Types of Christian Theology*. Ed. George Hunsinger and William C. Placher. New Haven, CT: Yale University Press, 1992.

Gadamer, Hans-Georg. *Truth and Method*, 2nd, rev. ed. Trans. Joel Weinsheimer and Donald G. Marshall. New York: Crossroad, 1989.

Gilkey, Langdon B. "Cosmology, Ontology, and the Travail of Biblical Language." In *God's Activity in the World: The Contemporary Problem*. Ed. Owen C. Thomas. Chico, CA: Scholar's Press, 1983.

Gunter, W. Stephen. *Resurrection Knowledge: Recovering the Gospel for a Postmodern Church*. Nashville: Abingdon, 1999.

Gunter, W. Stephen, Scott J. Jones, Ted A. Campbell, Rebekah L. Miles, and Randy Maddox. *Wesley and the Quadrilateral: Renewing the Conversation*. Nashville: Abingdon, 1997.

Gunton, Colin E. *The One, The Three, and the Many: God, Creation and the Culture of Modernity*. The 1992 Bampton Lectures. Cambridge: Cambridge University Press, 1993.

Harrison, Peter. *'Religion' and the Religions in the English Enlightenment*. Cambridge: Cambridge University Press, 1990.

Hartt, Julian N. *A Christian Critique of Culture: An Essay in Practical Theology*. New York: Harper and Row, 1967.

Hauerwas, Stanley. *After Christendom: How the Church is to Behave if Freedom, Justice, and a Christian Nation are Bad Ideas*. Nashville: Abingdon, 1991.

_____. "No Enemy, No Christianity: Theology and Preaching Between Worlds." In *The Future of Theology: Essays in Honor of Jürgen Moltmann*. Ed. Miroslav Volf, Carmen Krieg, and Thomas Kucharz. Grand Rapids, MI: Eerdmans, 1996.

Hauerwas, Stanley and William Willimon. *Resident Aliens: Life in the Christian Colony*. Nashville: Abingdon, 1989.
Heitzenrater, Richard P. "At Full Liberty: Doctrinal Standards in Early American Methodism." In *Doctrine and Theology in the United Methodist Church*. Ed. Thomas Langford. Nashville: Kingswood Books, 1991.
Holmer, Paul. *The Grammar of Faith*. San Francisco: Harper and Row, 1978.
Holsinger, James W., Jr., and Evelyn Laycock. *Awaken the Giant: 28 Prescriptions for Reviving the United Methodist Church*. Nashville: Abingdon, 1989.
Howe, Leroy T. "United Methodism in Search of Theology." In *Doctrine and Theology in the United Methodist Church*. Ed. Thomas Langford. Nashville: Kingswood Books, 1991.
Hunsberger, George R. and Craig Van Gelder, eds. *The Church Between Gospel and Culture: The Emerging Mission in North America*. Grand Rapids, MI: Eerdmans, 1996.
Hunsinger, George. "What Can Evangelicals and Postliberals Learn from Each Other?: The Carl Henry–Hans Frei Exchange Reconsidered." In *The Nature of Confession: Evangelicals and Postliberals in Conversation*. Ed. Timothy R. Phillips and Dennis L. Okholm. Downers Grove, IL: InterVarsity Press, 1996.
Jones, Curtis. "Personalism as Christian Philosophy." Th.D. diss., Union Theological Seminary, 1944.
Jones, L. Gregory. "Alasdair MacIntyre on Narrative, Community, and the Moral Life." *Modern Theology*, 4 (1987): 53–69.
_____."Toward a Recovery of Theological Discourse in United Methodism." *Quarterly Review* (Summer 1989): 16–34.
Jones, L. Gregory and Michael G. Cartwright. "Vital Congregations: Toward a Wesleyan Vision for the United Methodist Church's Identity and Mission." In *The Mission of the Church in Methodist Perspective: The World is my Parish*. Ed. Alan G. Padgett. Studies in the History of Missions 10. Lewiston, NY: Edwin Mellen Press, 1992.
Keefer, Luke L. "John Wesley: Disciple of Early Christianity." *Wesleyan Theological Journal* 19 (Spring 1984): 23–32.
Kenneson, Philip D. "The Alleged Incorrigibility of Postliberal Theology: Or, What Babe Ruth and George Lindbeck Have in Common." In *The Nature of Confession: Evangelicals and Postliberals in Conversation*. Ed. Timothy R. Phillips and Dennis L. Okholm. Downers Grove, IL: InterVarsity Press, 1996.
_____. *Beyond Sectarianism: Re-Imagining Church and World*. Christian Mission and Modern Culture. Harrisburg, PA: Trinity Press International, 1999.
Kerr, Fergus. "Idealism and Realism: An Old Controversy Dissolved." In *Christ, Ethics and Tragedy: Essays in Honour of Donald McKinnon*. Ed. Kenneth Surin. Cambridge: Cambridge University Press, 1989.

_____. *Theology After Wittgenstein.* Oxford: Basil Blackwell, 1986.

Kinnamon, Michael. *Truth and Community: Diversity and its Limits in the Ecumenical Movement.* Geneva and Grand Rapids, MI: WCC and Eerdmans, 1988.

Knight, Henry H. III and Don E. Saliers. *The Conversation Matters: Why United Methodists Should Talk with One Another.* Nashville: Abingdon, 1999.

Knudson, Albert C. *The Doctrine of God.* New York: Abingdon-Cokesbury, 1930.

_____. *The Doctrine of Redemption.* New York: Abingdon-Cokesbury, 1933.

_____. "The Evolution of Modern Bible Study." *Methodist Review* 93 (November 1911): 899–910.

_____. "A Personalistic Approach to Theology." In *Contemporary American Theology: Theological Autobiographies.* Ed. Vergilius Ferm. New York: Round Table Press, 1932.

_____. *The Philosophy of Personalism.* Boston: Boston University Press, 1927.

_____. *Present Tendencies in Religious Thought.* New York: Abingdon, 1924.

_____. *The Principles of Christian Ethics.* New York: Abingdon-Cokesbury, 1943.

_____. "Religious Apriorism." In *Studies in Philosophy and Theology: By Former Students of Borden Parker Bowne.* Ed. E. C. Wilm. New York: Abingdon, 1922.

_____. *Validity of Religious Experience.* New York: Abingdon-Cokesbury, 1937.

Kraft, Charles H. *Christianity in Culture: A Study in Dynamic Biblical Theologizing in Cross-Cultural Perspective.* Maryknoll, NY: Orbis, 1984.

Langford, Thomas A. "Doctrinal Affirmation and Theological Exploration." In *Doctrine and Theology in the United Methodist Church.* Ed. Thomas Langford. Nashville: Kingswood Books, 1991.

_____, ed. *Doctrine and Theology in the United Methodist Church.* Nashville: Kingswood Books, 1991.

_____. "The United Methodist Quadrilateral: A Theological Task." In *Doctrine and Theology in the United Methodist Church.* Ed. Thomas Langford. Nashville: Kingswood Books, 1991.

Lash, Nicholas. "When Did Theologians Lose Interest in God?" In *Theology and Dialogue: Essays in Conversation with George Lindbeck.* Ed. Bruce D. Marshall. Notre Dame, IN: University of Notre Dame Press, 1990.

Lessing, Gotthold Ephraim. *Lessing's Theological Writings.* Ed. and trans. Henry Chadwick. Stanford, CA: Stanford University Press, 1956.

Lindbeck, George. "Barth and Textuality," *Theology Today* 43 (1986): 361–76.

_____. "The Church's Mission to a Postmodern Culture." In *Postmodern*

Theology: Christian Faith in a Pluralist World. Ed. Frederick B. Burnham. San Francisco: Harper, 1989.

_____. *The Nature of Doctrine: Religion and Theology in a Postliberal Age*. Philadelphia: Westminster Press, 1984.

_____. "A Panel Discussion: Lindbeck, Hunsinger, McGrath and Fackre." In *The Nature of Confession: Evangelicals and Postliberals in Conversation*. Ed. Timothy R. Phillips and Dennis L. Okholm (Downers Grove, IL: InterVarsity Press, 1996), 246–53.

_____. "A Protestant View of the Ecclesiological Status of the Roman Catholic Church." *Journal of Ecumenical* Studies 1 (Winter 1964): 243–70.

Luidens, Donald A., Dean R. Hoge and Benton Johnson. "The Emergence of Lay Liberalism." *Theology Today* 51 (July 1994): 249–55.

_____.*Vanishing Boundaries: The Religion of Mainline Protestant Baby Boomers*. Louisville KY: Westminster/John Knox, 1994.

Lyotard, Jean-François. *The Postmodern Condition: A Report on Knowledge*. Vol. 10, *Theory and History of Literature*. Trans. Geoff Bennington and Brian Massumi. Minneapolis: University of Minnesota Press, 1984.

Machen, J. Gresham. *Christianity and Liberalism*. Grand Rapids, MI: Eerdmans, 1923.

MacIntyre, Alasdair. *After Virtue: A Study in Moral Theory*. 2nd ed. Notre Dame, IN: University of Notre Dame Press, 1984.

_____. "Epistemological Crises, Dramatic Narrative and the Philosophy of Science." *The Monist* 61 (1977), 453–72.

_____. "The Intelligibility of Action." In *Rationality, Relativism and the Human Sciences*. Ed. J. Margolis, M. Krausz, and R. M. Burian. Studies in the Greater Philadelphia Philosophy Consortium. Dordrecht: Martinus Nijhoff, 1986.

_____. "An Interview with Alasdair MacIntyre." *Cogito* 5 (Summer 1991): 67–73.

_____. "A Partial Response to My Critics." In *After MacIntyre: Critical Perspectives on the Work of Alasdair MacIntyre*. Ed. John Horton and Susan Mendus. Notre Dame, IN: University of Notre Dame Press, 1994.

_____. "Philosophy, the 'Other' Disciplines, and their Histories: A Rejoinder to Richard Rorty." *Soundings* 65 (Summer 1982): 127–45.

_____. *Three Rival Versions of Moral Enquiry: Encyclopaedia, Genealogy, and Tradition*. 1988 Gifford Lectures. Notre Dame, IN: Notre Dame University Press, 1990.

_____. *Whose Justice? Which Rationality?* Notre Dame, IN: Notre Dame University Press, 1988.

MacIntyre, Alasdair and Paul Ricoeur. *The Religious Significance of Atheism*. New York: Columbia University Press, 1969.

Matthews, Rex Dale. "'Religion and Reason Joined': A Study in the Theology of John Wesley." Th.D. diss., Andover-Harvard, 1986.

McClendon, James W., Jr. *Doctrine: Systematic Theology Volume II*. Nashville: Abingdon, 1994.

———. *Ethics: Systematic Theology Volume I*. Nashville: Abingdon, 1986.

McClendon, James W., Jr. and James M. Smith. *Convictions: Defusing Religious Relativism*. Rev. ed. Valley Forge, PA: Trinity Press International, 1994.

McCutcheon, William John. "Theology of the Methodist Episcopal Church During the Interwar Period (1919–1939)." Ph.D. diss., Yale, 1960.

McGrath, Alister. *The Genesis of Doctrine: A Study in the Foundations of Doctrinal Criticism*. Oxford: Basil Blackwell, 1990.

———. *The Making of Modern German Christology: 1750–1990*. 2nd ed. Grand Rapids, MI: Zondervan, 1994.

———. *The Renewal of Anglicanism*. Harrisburg, PA: Morehouse Publishing, 1993.

Mead, Loren B. *The Once and Future Church: Reinventing the Congregation for a New Mission Frontier*. Washington, DC: Alban Institute, 1991.

Meeks, M. Douglas, ed. *The Future of the Methodist Theological Traditions*. Nashville: Abingdon, 1985.

———. *What Should Methodists Teach? Wesleyan Tradition and Modern Diversity*. Nashville: Kingswood Books, 1990.

Michalson, Gordon E., Jr. "Faith and History: The Shape of the Problem." *Modern Theology* 1 (July 1985): 277–90.

———. *Lessing's "Ugly Ditch": A Study of Theology and History*. University Park, PA: Pennsylvania State University Press, 1985.

———. "The Response to Lindbeck." *Modern Theology* 4 (Jan. 1988): 107–20.

Milbank, John. "An Essay Against Secular Order." *Journal of Religious Ethics*. 15 (1987): 199–224.

———. *Theology and Social Theory: Beyond Secular Reason*. Oxford: Basil Blackwell, 1990.

Mittelberg, Mark. *Building a Contagious Church: Revolutionizing the Way We View and Do Evangelism*. Grand Rapids, MI: Zondervan, 2000

Moltmann, Jürgen. *The Church in the Power of the Spirit: A Contribution to Messianic Eschatology*. Trans. Margaret Kohl. San Francisco: Harper, 1977.

Murphy, Nancey. *Anglo-American Postmodernity: Philosophical Perspectives on Science, Religion, and Ethics*. Boulder, CO: Westview Press, 1997.

———. *Beyond Liberalism and Fundamentalism: How Modern and Postmodern Philosophy Set the Theological Agenda*. Valley Forge, PA: Trinity Press International, 1996.

———. "Textual Relativism, Philosophy of Language, and the baptist

Vision." In *Theology Without Foundations*. Ed. Stanley Hauerwas, Nancey Murphy, and Mark Nation. Nashville: Abingdon, 1994.

_____. *Theology in the Age of Scientific Reasoning*. Ithaca, NY: Cornell University Press, 1990.

Murphy, Nancey and James W. McClendon, Jr. "Distinguishing Modern and Postmodern Theologies." *Modern Theology* 5 (April 1989): 191–214.

Nagel, Thomas. *The View from Nowhere*. Oxford: Oxford University Press, 1986.

Nelson, J. Robert. *One Lord, One Church*. London: United Society for Christian Literature, Lutterworth Press, 1958.

The New Catholic Encyclopedia. New York: McGraw-Hill, 1967. S.v. "Marks of the Church," v. 9 (Ma-Mor), 240–41; "Unity of the Church," v. 14 (Tha-Zwi), 450–51; "Catholicity," v. 3 (Can-Col), 339–40; "Apostolicity," v. 1 (A-Azt), 699–700; by Gustave Thils.

Nichols, Aidan. *The Panther and the Hind: A Theological History of Anglicanism* Edinburgh: T and T Clark, 1993.

Niebuhr, H. Richard. *Christ and Culture*. New York: Harper and Row, 1951.

Oberman, Heiko Augustinus. *A Harvest of Medieval Theology: Gabriel Biel and Late Medieval Nominalism*. Rev. ed. Grand Rapids, MI: Eerdmans, 1967.

Oden, Thomas C. *After Modernity . . . What? Agenda for Theology*. Grand Rapids, MI: Academie/Zondervan, 1990.

_____. *Doctrinal Standards in the Wesleyan Tradition*. Grand Rapids, MI: Francis Asbury Press, 1988.

_____. "What Are 'Established Standards of Doctrine'? A Response to Richard Heitzenrater." In *Doctrine and Theology in the United Methodist Church*. Ed. Thomas Langford. Nashville: Kingswood Books, 1991.

Ogden, Schubert. "Doctrinal Standards in the United Methodist Church." In *Doctrine and Theology in the United Methodist Church*. Ed. Thomas Langford. Nashville: Kingswood Books, 1991.

O'Neill, Colman. "The Rule Theory of Doctrine and Propositional Truth." *The Thomist* 49 (July 1985): 417–42.

Osborn, Robert T. "From Theology to Religion." *Modern Theology* 8 (January 1992): 75–88.

Outler, Albert C. *The Christian Tradition and the Unity We Seek*. New York: Oxford University Press, 1957.

_____. *That the World May Believe: A Study of Christian Unity and What it Means for Methodists*. New York: Joint Commission on Education and Cultivation, Board of Missions of the Methodist Church, 1966.

_____. "The Wesleyan Quadrilateral in John Wesley." *Wesleyan Theological Journal* 20 (Spring 1985): 7–18.

_____. *The Wesleyan Theological Heritage: Essays of Albert C. Outler*. Ed.

Thomas C. Oden and Leicester R. Longden. Grand Rapids, MI: Zondervan, 1991.

Pannenberg, Wolfhart. *Theology and the Philosophy of Science.* Trans. Francis McDonagh. Philadelphia: Westminster Press, 1976.

Phillips, D. Z. "Lindbeck's Audience." *Modern Theology* 4 (January 1988): 133–54.

_____. *Wittgenstein and Religion.* Swansea Studies in Religion. New York: St. Martin's Press, 1993.

Phillips, Timothy R. and Dennis L. Okholm, eds. *The Nature of Confession: Evangelicals and Postliberals in Conversation.* Downers Grove, IL: InterVarsity Press, 1996.

Placher, William. "Paul Ricoeur and Postliberal Theology: A Conflict of Interpretations?" *Modern Theology* 4:1 (1987): 35–52.

_____. *Unapologetic Theology: A Christian Voice in a Pluralistic Conversation.* Louisville, KY: Westminster/John Knox Press, 1989.

Reardon, Bernard M. G. *Religion in the Age of Romanticism: Studies in Early Nineteenth Century Thought.* Cambridge: Cambridge University Press, 1985.

Richardson, Kurt Anders. "The Contemporary Renewal of Trinitarian Theology: Possibilities of Convergence in the Doctrine of God." In *The Nature of Confession: Evangelicals and Postliberals in Conversation.* Ed. Timothy R. Phillips and Dennis L. Okholm. Downers Grove, IL: InterVarsity Press, 1996.

Richey, Russell E. "History as a Bearer of Denominational Identity: Methodism as a Case Study." In *Perspectives on American Methodism: Interpretive Essays.* Ed. Russell E. Richey, Kenneth E. Rowe, and Jean Miller Schmidt. Nashville: Kingswood Books, 1993.

_____. "History in the Discipline." In *Doctrine and Theology in the United Methodist Church.* Ed. Thomas Langford. Nashville: Kingswood Books, 1991.

Rodger, P. C., and Lukas Vischer, eds. *The Fourth World Conference on Faith and Order: Montreal 1963.* New York: Association Press, 1964.

Root, Michael. "Identity and Difference: The Ecumenical Problem." In *Theology and Dialogue: Essays in Conversation with George Lindbeck.* Ed. Bruce D. Marshall. Notre Dame, IN: University of Notre Dame Press, 1990.

Rorty, Richard. *Philosophy and the Mirror of Nature.* Princeton, NJ: Princeton University Press, 1979.

Rusch, William. *Reception: An Ecumenical Opportunity.* Philadelphia: Fortress Press, 1988.

Sanders, E. P. *Paul and Palestinian Judaism: A Comparison of Patterns of Religion.* Minneapolis: Fortress Press, 1977.

Saussure, Ferdinand de. *Course in General Linguistics.* Ed. Charles Bally and Albert Sechehaye. Trans. Wade Baskin. New York: McGraw-Hill, 1959.

Schleiermacher, Friedrich. *The Christian Faith*. Trans. H. R. MacKintosh and J. S. Stewart. Edinburgh: T. and T. Clark, 1928.

———. *On the Glaubenslehre: Two Letters to Lücke*. Trans. Francis Fiorenza and James Duke. Chico, CA: Scholars Press, 1981.

Schneewind, J. B. "MacIntyre and the Indispensability of Tradition." *Philosophy and Phenomenological Research* 51 (March 1991): 165–68.

Searle, John R. *Expression and Meaning: Studies in the Theory of Speech Acts*. Cambridge: Cambridge University Press, 1979.

———. *Speech Acts: An Essay in the Philosophy of Language*. Cambridge: Cambridge University Press, 1969.

Sjogren, Bob. *Unveiled at Last*. Seattle: YWAM Publishing, 1992.

Smart, J. D. *The Interpretation of Scripture*. London: SCM Press, 1961.

Smith, Wilfred Cantwell. *The Meaning and End of Religion: A New Approach to the Religious Traditions of Mankind*. New York: Macmillan, 1962.

Spong, John Shelby. *Rescuing the Bible from Fundamentalism*. San Francisco: HarperCollins, 1991.

Stout, Jeffrey. *Flight from Authority: Religion, Morality, and the Quest for Autonomy*. Notre Dame, IN: University of Notre Dame Press, 1981.

Sykes, Stephen. "The Genius of Anglicanism." In *The English Religious Tradition and the Genius of Anglicanism*. Ed. Geoffrey Rowell. Nashville: Abingdon, 1992.

———. *The Identity of Christianity: Theologians and the Essence of Christianity from Schleiermacher to Barth*. Philadelphia: Fortress Press, 1984.

Taylor, Charles. "Comparison, History, Truth." In *Myth and Philosophy*. Ed. Frank Reynolds and David Tracy. Albany: SUNY Press, 1990.

———. "Explanation and Practical Reason." In *The Quality of Life*. Ed. Martha Nussbaum and Amartya Sen. Oxford: Clarendon Press, 1993.

———. "Justice After Virtue." In *After MacIntyre: Critical Perspectives on the Work of Alasdair MacIntyre*. Ed. John Horton and Susan Mendus. Notre Dame, IN: University of Notre Dame Press, 1994.

———. "Overcoming Epistemology." In *After Philosophy: End or Transformation?* Ed. Kenneth Baynes, James Bohman, and Thomas McCarthy. Cambridge, MA: MIT Press, 1987.

———. *Philosophical Papers*, v. 1. Cambridge: Cambridge University Press, 1985.

———. "Philosophy and its History." In *Philosophy in History: Essays on the Historiography of Philosophy*. Ed. Richard Rorty, J. B. Schneewind, and Quentin Skinner. Cambridge: Cambridge University Press, 1984.

———. "Rorty in the Epistemological Tradition." In *Reading Rorty: Critical Responses to Philosophy and the Mirror of Nature*. Ed. Alan Malachowski. Oxford: Basil Blackwell, 1990.

———. *Sources of the Self: The Making of the Modern Identity.* Cambridge, MA: Harvard University Press, 1989.

———. "To Follow a Rule." In *Rules and Conventions: Literature, Philosophy, Social Theory.* Ed. Mette Hjort. Baltimore, MD: Johns Hopkins University Press, 1992.

Thielicke, Helmut. *The Relation of Theology to Modern Thought Forms.* Vol. 1, *The Evangelical Faith.* Trans. and ed. Geoffrey W. Bromiley. Grand Rapids, MI: Eerdmans, 1974.

Thiemann, Ronald F. "Revelation and Imaginative Construction." *Journal of Religion* 61 (July 1981): 242–63.

———. *Revelation and Theology: The Gospel as Narrated Promise.* Notre Dame, IN: University of Notre Dame Press, 1985.

Thiselton, Anthony. *New Horizons in Hermeneutics: The Theory and Practice of Transforming Biblical Reading.* Grand Rapids, MI: Zondervan, 1992.

———. *The Two Horizons: New Testament Hermeneutics and Philosophical Description.* Grand Rapids, MI: Eerdmans, 1980.

Thorsen, Donald A. D. *The Wesleyan Quadrilateral: Scripture, Tradition, Reason and Experience as a Model of Evangelical Theology.* Grand Rapids, MI: Zondervan, 1990.

Tilley, Terrence. "Incommensurability, Intratextuality and Fideism." *Modern Theology* 5 (Jan. 1989): 87–111.

Toulmin, Stephen E. *Cosmopolis: The Hidden Agenda of Modernity.* New York: The Free Press, 1990.

———. *Uses of Argument.* Cambridge: Cambridge University Press, 1958.

Tracy, David. "Lindbeck's New Program for Theology: A Reflection." *The Thomist* 49 (July 1985): 460–72.

Tracy, Thomas F. "Enacting History: Ogden and Kaufman on God's Mighty Acts." *Journal of Religion* 64 (Jan. 1984): 20–36.

Volf, Miroslav. "Theology, Meaning and Power." In *The Future of Theology: Essays in Honor of Jürgen Moltmann.* Ed. Miroslav Volf, Carmen Krieg, and Thomas Kucharz. Grand Rapids, MI: Eerdmans, 1996.

———. "Theology, Meaning and Power." In *The Nature of Confession: Evangelicals and Postliberals in Conversation* Ed. Timothy R. Phillips and Dennis L. Okholm. Downers Grove, IL: InterVarsity Press, 1996. [This is a different version of the essay above.]

Wainwright, Geoffrey. *Doxology: The Praise of God in Worship, Doctrine, and Life.* New York: Oxford University Press, 1980.

———. *The Ecumenical Moment : Crisis and Opportunity for the Church.* Grand Rapids, MI: Eerdmans, 1983.

Walls, Andrew F. "The Gospel as the Prisoner and Liberator of Culture." *Missionalia* 10:3 (1982): 93–105.

Walls, Jerry. *The Problem of Pluralism: Recovering United Methodist Identity.* Wilmore, KY: Good News Books, 1986.
Watson, Francis. *Text, Church and World: Biblical Interpretation in Theological Perspective.* Grand Rapids, MI: Eerdmans, 1994.
Webster, John. "Locality and Catholicity: Reflections on Theology and the Church." *Scottish Journal of Theology* 45:1 (1992): 1–17.
──────. "A Letter to the Right Reverend Lord Bishop of Gloucester." In *The Appeals to men of Reason and Religion and Certain Related Open Letters.* Vol. 2, *The Works of John Wesley.* Ed. Gerald R. Cragg. Nashville: Abingdon, 1989.
──────. "The Character of a Methodist." In *The Works of John Wesley.* Vol. 9, *The Methodist Societies: History, Nature and Design.* Ed. Rupert E. Davies. Nashville: Abingdon, 1989.
Westphal, C. "The Marks of the Church." *Anglican Theological Review* 42 (April 1960): 91–100.
Williams, Rowan. "Trinity and Revelation." *Modern Theology* 2:3 (1986): 197–212.
Wittgenstein, Ludwig. "Lectures on Religious Belief." In *Lectures and Conversations on Aesthetics, Psychology and Religion.* Ed. Cyril Barrett. Oxford: Basil Blackwell, 1966.
──────. *On Certainty.* Ed. G.E.M. Anscombe and G. H. von Wright. Trans. G. H. von Wright and Denis Paul. New York: Harper and Row, 1969.
──────. *Philosophical Investigations,* 3rd ed. Trans. G.E.M. Anscombe. New York: Macmillan, 1958.
Wolterstorff, Nicholas. *Divine Discourse: Philosophical Reflections on the Claim that God Speaks.* New York: Cambridge University Press, 1995.
──────. *Reason Within the Bounds of Religion,* 2nd rev. ed. Grand Rapids, MI: Eerdmans, 1984.
Wright, N. T. "How Can the Bible Be Authoritative?" *Vox Evangelica* 21 (1991): 7–32.
──────. *Jesus and the Victory of God.* Vol. 2, *Christian Origins and the Question of God.* Minneapolis: Fortress Press, 1996.
──────. *The New Testament and the People of God.* Vol. 1, *Christian Origins and the Question of God.* Minneapolis: Fortress Press, 1992.
Yoder, John Howard. "The Constantinian Sources of Western Social Ethics." In *The Priestly Kingdom: Social Ethics as Gospel.* Notre Dame, IN: University of Notre Dame Press, 1984.
──────. "The Otherness of the Church." In *The Royal Priesthood: Essays Ecclesiological and Ecumenical.* Ed. Michael Cartwright. Grand Rapids, MI: Eerdmans, 1994.
──────. "A People in the World." In *The Royal Priesthood: Essays Ecclesiologi-*

cal and Ecumenical. Ed. Michael Cartwright. Grand Rapids, MI: Eerdmans, 1994.

_____. *The Politics of Jesus: Vicit Agnus Noster*. Grand Rapids, MI: Eerdmans, 1972.

Yoder, John Howard, Glenn Stassen, and D. M. Yeager. *Authentic Transformation: A New Vision of Christ and Culture*. Nashville: Abingdon, 1996.

Zuurdeeg, Willem. *An Analytical Philosophy of Religion*. New York: Abingdon, 1958.

Index

Abraham, William J., 1, 2, 13, 44n50, 100n54, 177n41
Austin, J. L., xi, 29, 38, 51, 57ff., 65, 75, 81, 89, 96n2, 101n79, 184, 193f.
Baptist Vision, 116, 154ff., 162f., 165, 169f., 177n46, 177n48, 199, 212
Barth, Karl, 10, 29, 82, 101n86, 117, 134n22
Berger, Peter, 29
Blackaby, Henry, x, 211f.
Bloor, David, 98n35
Borg, Marcus, 152
Bosch, David J., 43n47, 46n74
Bowne, Borden Parker, 43n43
Bultmann, Rudolph, 5, 93, 150ff., 189
Burridge, Richard, 180n83
Caird, George B., 152, 156
Cartwright, Michael, 136n62
Charry, Ellen, 14, 44n53
Christendom, 35, 43n41, 214
Clapp, Rodney, 2, 122
Comte, Auguste, 144

Constantinianism, 4, 37, 54, 122, 125, 129f., 130, 135n45, 154ff., 161, 177n42, 185, 189
Crossan, John Dominic, 152
Culture, 4, 6ff., 37, 41n17, 50n132, 121ff., 130, 133n12, 161, 213f.
Cyprian, 30, 109
Davidson, Donald, 134n29
Dehistoricization, xi, 13, 20ff., 33, 36, 47n81, 48n95., 72, 95, 140f., 144, 151
Descartes, Rene, 12ff., 28, 62
Dodd, C. H., 152
Durkheim, Emile, 29, 46n77, 176n11
Ecclesiology, 6, 18, 29f., 37ff., 54, 76, ch 3., 140, 155, 164, 166, 197f., 209
Ecumenism, 22, 32, 40, 217f.
Epistemology, ix, x, xi, 13ff., 18f., 24ff., 36f., 55, 60, 68, 70, 77, 116, 143, 163, 170f., 193, 202, 214
Eschatology, 11, 22, 39, 141, 149ff., 161f., 168, 177n38
Evangelism, xii, 45, 212ff.

Evans, Donald, 97n15
Experiential Expressivism, 23, 26ff., 36f., 48n104, 54f., 81, 146, 150, 187, 191
Fish, Stanley, 118f.
Foundationalism, viii, ix, 13, 19, 24, 27, 62, 80, 96n9, 114, 117, 170
Freeman, Curtis, 136n59
Frei, Hans, 33, 47n88, 148, 163
Gadamer, Hans-Georg, 18, 69, 163, 165, 167, 212
Geertz, Clifford, 29
Gilkey, Langdon, 21f., 35, 146
Gunter, W. Stephen, 96n7
Gunton, Colin, 43n47, 112, 177n38
Happiness (of a Speech Act), 58, 60f., 95, 193ff., 207f.
Hartt, Julian, 163, 169, 180n86
Hauerwas, Stanley, xi, 8, 46n72, 104n121, 107, 110, 116, 121f., 162
Harrison, Peter, 21, 35, 46n78, 49n128
Heitzenrater, Richard P., 219n4
History, 19ff., 34ff., 47n88, 47n91, 52, 88, 92, 115f., 123, 140, 142ff., 151, 158, 163f., 168ff., 180n85, 190
Holmer, Paul, 1, 131, 169, 219n7
Holsinger, James, 162
Howe, Leroy T., 180n85
Hume, David, 25, 29, 96n9, 162
Hylomorphism, 90ff., 117, 188
Individualism, xi, 13, 18, 28ff., 36, 46n74, 55, 68, 70, 74, 77, 107ff., 112f.f., 126, 130, 162
Interpretive Community, 79, 87, 107, 113ff., 141f., 170, 198, 206
Intratextuality, 116, 134n20, 159
James, William, 14
Jones, L. Gregory, 132n7, 136n62, 173
Kant, Immanuel, 25, 27ff., 67
Kenneson, Philip, 46n78, 181n100
Kerr, Fergus, 98n32
Knudson, Albert C., 9ff., 14, 18f., 22, 28, 42n37, 43n42, 43n43, 44n56, 189
Kraft, Charles, 125ff., 136n49
Lakatos, Imre, 192f., 196
Laycock, Evelyn, 162
Lessing, G.E., 19f., 47n88, 141ff., 151, 164, 169, 175n5, 175n8, 185

Lindbeck, George, x, xi, 3, 5, 8, 18, 22ff., 40n7, 48n97, 48n98, 48n104, 49n112, 51, 54, 67, 77ff., 99n53, 101n86, 102n96, 116f., 121f., 131, 133n9, 142, 157ff., 177n46, 187ff., 201, 217
Lotze, Rudolf Hermann– 43n43
Lyotard, Jean-François, 53, 172, 180n99
Machen, J. Gresham, 41n10
MacIntyre, Alasdair, 5, 8, 10, 42n23, 43n46, 45n60, 48n97, 82, 113f., 120, 144, 164ff., 181n101
Marx, Karl, 29
McClendon, James Wm., 12f., 31, 38, 59ff., 75, 96n3., 97n20, 120, 154ff., 165, 168f., 177n46, 194, 196, 199, 205, 215
McCutcheon, William John, 9
McGrath, Alister, 49n110, 99n52
Mead, Loren B., 135n38
Metanarrative, 53, 172ff., 180n99
Michalson, Gordon, 40n7, 143, 175n3, 175n5, 175n8
Milbank, John, 8, 101n86, 102n90, 158, 163, 173, 176n11, 181n101
Mittelberg, Mark, 213f.
Moltmann, Jürgen, 129, 132n7, 158, 178n49
Murphy, Nancey, 6, 12f., 141, 192
Narrative, 21, 33f., 47n89, 69, 71, 73, 75, 82f., 87, 89, 93f., 100n54, 104n108, 108, 116ff., 124f., 128f., 140, 146ff., 167ff., 179n72., 189, 192, 200, 206ff.
Newton, Isaac, 20
Nichols, Aidan, 41n9
Niebuhr, H. Richard, 121f., 126, 135n36, 136n49
Oden, Thomas C., 41n11, 134n26
Ogden, Schubert, 2, 111
Osborn, Robert, 19, 35
Outler, Albert, 16, 136n46, 170
Phillips, D. Z., 41n7
Placher, William, 41n20, 169, 171
Procedural Rationality, 15ff., 36, 44n58
Propositionalism, 23ff., 36f., 49n114, 50n132, 54, 82ff., 88, 150, 187ff.
Realism, 65f., 84, 98n32, 104n110, 113f.

Reception, 62, 75ff., 100n64, 125, 184, 208, 220n23
Reductionism, 13, 18, 36, 176n11
Reference, 13, 34, 58, 67, 78ff., 100n72, 102n90, 201, 204ff.
Religion, xi, 20, 23ff., 28, 30, 35ff., 47n78, 49n128, 54, 82, 111, 142, 144, 146, 157, 191
Richardson, Kurt A., 5
Richey, Russell, 159f.
Robinson, John, 5
Rorty, Richard, 164
Rusch, William, 75, 100n64
Salvation, 109ff., 130
Sanders, E.P., 216
Saussure, Ferdinand de, 136n47
Schleiermacher, Friedrich, 9, 19, 27, 33, 47n84, 69, 98n35, 143, 149
Schweitzer, Albert, 150, 152
Science, 9f., 21, 24, 26, 133n16, 142, 153, 160, 192f.
Scripture, viii, ix, 22, 33f., 38, 44n56, 52, 75f., 94, 118, 146, 155f., 170f., 210ff.
Searle, John, 59, 97n14, 194ff., 200, 205, 207
Secularization, 145, 160, 213f.
Smart, James, 163
Smith, James, 13, 38, 59ff., 75, 97n20, 120, 194, 196, 205
Spong, John Shelby, 5
Stout, Jeffrey, 43n47
Sykes, Stephen, 41n9, 44n52, 179n76
Thielicke, Helmut, 43n47
Taylor, Charles, x, 7, 15, 20, 51, 67ff., 81, 89, 115, 133n16, 184

Thiemann, Ronald, 33, 47n89, 76, 83, 159, 171, 178n53
Thiselton, Anthony, 96n12, 142, 163
Thorsen, Don, 4
Tilley, Terrence, 95
Tillich, Paul, 5
Toulmin, Stephen, 43n47, 114
Tracy, David, 41n7
Tradition, 18, 29, 165f.
Troeltsch, Ernst, 14, 28
Truth, 34, 38, 58, 60f., 72, 81, 88f., 103n98, 104n109, 142, 193, 195
Vaihinger, Hans, 67
Van Buren, Paul, 5
Volf, Miroslav, 102n90, 117, 121, 147, 158, 181n96
Walls, Andrew, 127ff.
Watson, Francis, 96n4, 180n93
Weber, Max, 162
Webster, John, 134n24, 158
Wesley, Charles, 86, 202f.
Wesley, John, 4, 16f., 86, 160f., 177n42, 202f., 220n19
Wesleyan Quadrilateral, 15ff., 32, 45n63, 45n66, 187
Winch, Peter, 29
Wirkungsgeschichte, 167f., 212, 217
Wittgenstein, Ludwig, xi, 29, 36, 51, 62ff., 73, 79, 82, 95, 96n2, 98n29, 98n32, 101n88, 102n96, 184
Wolterstorff, Nicholas, 76, 97n15
Wright, N. T. (Tom), 52, 96n3, 136n51, 151f., 156, 171, 177n36, 221n36
Yoder, John Howard, 122, 135n40, 145

www.ingramcontent.com/pod-product-compliance
Lightning Source LLC
Chambersburg PA
CBHW030341240426
43661CB00052B/1701